D1604160

The 21st-Century Black Librarian in America

Issues and Challenges

Edited by
Andrew P. Jackson (Sekou Molefi Baako)
Julius C. Jefferson Jr.
Akilah S. Nosakhere

THE SCARECROW PRESS, INC.
Lanham • Toronto • Plymouth, UK
2012

Published by Scarecrow Press, Inc.
A wholly owned subsidiary of The Rowman & Littlefield Publishing Group, Inc.
4501 Forbes Boulevard, Suite 200, Lanham, Maryland 20706
http://www.scarecrowpress.com

10 Thornbury Road, Plymouth PL6 7PP, United Kingdom

British Library Cataloguing in Publication Information Available

Library of Congress Cataloging-in-Publication Data

The 21st-century black librarian in America : issues and challenges / edited by Andrew P. Jackson, Julius C. Jefferson Jr., Akilah S. Nosakhere.
p. cm.
Includes bibliographical references and index.
ISBN 978-0-8108-8245-4 — ISBN 978-0-8108-8246-1 (ebook)
1. African American librarians. 2. African Americans and libraries.
I. Jackson, Andrew P., editor of compilation. II. Jefferson, Julius, Jr., 1968– editor of compilation. III. Nosakhere, Akilah, 1956– editor of compilation. IV. Title: Twenty-first century Black librarian in America.
Z682.4.A37A13 2012
020.89960732 23

2011042051

™ The paper used in this publication meets the minimum requirements of American National Standard for Information Sciences—Permanence of Paper for Printed Library Materials, ANSI/NISO Z39.48-1992.

Printed in the United States of America

Dedicated to

Dr. E. J. Josey at ALA Mid-Winter Meeting,
Denver, Colorado, January 2009.
Photo by Pam Goodes

Dr. E. J. Josey
January 20, 1924–July 3, 2009
Activist Librarian
Educator
Scholar
Humanitarian

Contents

Selected Bibliography of Works by Dr. E. J. Josey

Andrew P. Jackson (Sekou Molefi Baako)

Of the many strengths of E. J. Josey's legacy for us, one of the most valuable is the strong body of work by and about black librarianship for us to read, learn, refer to, and pass on to new generations of librarians in the profession. Fortunately, many of his works are still available for purchase and are in both academic and public library collections. Although there are more inclusive bibliographies of his books, essays, speeches, and articles available in print and online, I felt it valuable to include these titles as they relate directly to this new edition of *The Black Librarian in America.* Every time I refer to one of these works for my own research or teaching, I learn something new. We owe E. J. a great deal of gratitude for leaving us these valuable life lessons in print. I also added Ismail Abdullahi's biography of E. J.'s life as an activist librarian.

Handbook of Black Librarianship, 2nd ed. Edited with Marva L. DeLoach. Scarecrow Press, 2000.

The Black Librarian in America Revisited. Scarecrow Press, 1994.

Politics and the Support of Libraries, with Dr. Kenneth Shearer. Neal-Schuman Press, 1990.

Libraries, Coalitions and the Public Good. Neal-Schuman Press, 1987.

Ethnic Collections. Edited with Marva L. DeLoach, Neal-Schuman Press, 1983.

Libraries, in the Political Process. Oryx Press, 1980.

The Information Society: Issues and Answers. Oryx Press, 1978.

Handbook of Black Librarianship. Edited with Ann Allen Shockley, Libraries Unlimited, 1977.

Opportunities for Minorities in Librarianship. With Kenneth Peeples, Jr. Scarecrow Press, 1977.

A Century of Service: Librarianship in the United States and Canada. Edited with Sidney Jackson and Elinor Herling. American Library Association, 1976.
New Dimension for Academic Library Service. Scarecrow Press, 1975.
What Black Librarians Are Saying. Scarecrow Press, 1970.
The Black Librarian in America. Scarecrow Press, 1970.
E.J. Josey: An Activist Librarian. By Ismail Abdullahi. Scarecrow Press, 1992.

A Tribute to Dr. E. J. Josey

As we pay tribute to the productive life of Dr. E. J. Josey, I charge the Black Caucus of the American Library Association (BCALA) (and other caucuses) leadership and individual members to remember that his dedication was not just to BCALA, but to librarianship universally, with particular attention to:

1. *The quality of our education and training.* (He would encourage prioritizing collaborations with other caucuses, Association for Library for Information and Science Education [ALISE], the American Library Association [ALA] Office for Diversity, and ALA divisions.)
2. *Our significant support and mentoring of each other, especially those new to the profession, no matter their ethnicity.* (He would advise prioritizing initiatives on recruitment and mentoring, partnering with others for broader benefit.)
3. *Familiarizing members on global issues of importance to library professionals*, often (but not only) addressed through ALA initiatives, honoring his presidency of the largest library association in the world! (He would suggest highlighting, educating, encouraging individual participation by members on these issues, and BCALA and like organizations taking public positions, as was done in his era.)

Dr. Josey was an academic as well as a pragmatist who valued education and information and expected no less from those he mentored. We can each honor him by following the noble model he (and others in his generation) left to us, following in those giant footprints!

What will our next steps be? How will they impact future generations?

—Satia Marshall Orange
Retired Director, Office for Library Outreach Services,
American Library Association
ALA Spectrum Doctoral Fellowship

Goodbye, E. J.

Thank you for your many years of vision and leadership. Your efforts and the decisions you made through the years have impacted all of librarianship. We have many memories of a changing profession. We shall also remember the standards in which you believed as we continue to offer a perspective that serves the entire profession. The Caucus stands firmly today as a visible contributing part of the American Library Association.

You have built and left a legacy.

Thank you, E. J. We shall miss you.

—Effie Lee Morris
Grand Dame of Children's Librarianship
Founding Member, Black Caucus of the American Library Association

The information industry has the technology to control information, but its price tag on information distribution and its profit goal create a bias in what information is made available and how it is dispensed. Only the nonprofit organization, the library, dedicated to a total community service goal with trained experts, librarians, running the operation can provide the full scope of information for the total population in a fair and objective manner.

—E. J. Josey, Inaugural Address American Library Association, June 1984

Preface

The Need for Continued Activism in Black Librarianship

The opening words to Bernard J. Keller's poem "Harvard 8/9/85" begins: "If you cannot be the best for yourself, do it for those who were denied an opportunity to be the best."[1] Those who attended the Dr. Martin Luther King, Jr., American Library Association (ALA) Mid-Winter Celebration in the early Monday morning hours heard this poem as a tribute to the spirits of those whose names may not be remembered, but who were none the less warriors not to be forgotten. The thoughts in Keller's poem have stayed with me since I first read it at a Brooklyn high school. Since then thousands have heard this poem. Our historical past is too important for us to forget how we got here and where we are going.

One interpretation of the African Adinkra symbol Sankofa means "we must return and claim our past in order to move toward our future."[2] This is a constant reminder of the journey we have traveled, obstacles overcome, and work that still needs to be done in this world and in librarianship. In 1992, when I attended the first National Conference of African American Librarians (NCAAL) in Columbus, Ohio, my eyes were opened to the mission and purpose of the Black Caucus of the American Library Association (BCALA). I met caucus officers and board members and seized the opportunity to observe numerous black librarians at one time. Reading the history of this pioneering organization in the conference program and listening to speakers and panelists gave me a new perspective on our profession. As a result, I was moved to become a part of this movement—the movement of black librarians in America.

As I had not yet attended graduate school or become familiar with the history of librarianship, I was unaware of the struggles for access to library services, jobs, or opportunities. I was unaware of the African "keepers of the scroll" in ancient Africa or early black librarians in America. I was riveted by Itibari M.

Zulu's conference paper presentation, "The Ancient Kemetic Roots of Library and Information Science."[3] When I entered my library graduate program in 1993, this history was omitted from the introductory course in a similar way that chapters of pre-American black history are missing from traditional history courses and textbooks. This sparked an interest in the African roots of library science and caused me to ponder about where we fit in the history of libraries here in America. These memorable experiences convinced me it was not adequate to just have membership in the Black Caucus without being active, learning its history, and remaining committed to the vision and legacy paved by Dr. E. J. Josey and others. The 21st-century *Black Librarian in America* was inspired by that first library conference and activist librarians, especially E. J. Josey.

The struggle for equality in librarianship is no different from and, if anything, parallels the struggles for civil and human rights in America. By reading the first two volumes of *The Black Librarian in America*, two editions of *The Handbook of Black Librarianship*, conference proceedings of earlier NCAALs, and other works and essays by E. J. Josey, *Educating Black Librarians* (1991) by Benjamin F. Speller, Jr., Donnarae MacCAnn's *Social Responsibility in Librarianship Essays on Equality* (1989), John Mark Tucker's *Untold Stories Civil Rights, Libraries, and Black Librarianship* (1998), *In Our Own Words* (1996) by Teresa Y. Neely and Khafre K. Abif, and Binnie Tate Wilkin's *African American Librarians in the Far West Pioneers and Trailblazers* (2006), or works by other authors in this profession, we are introduced to and reminded of who these black librarians are and how they contributed to the development and participated in the evolution of libraries. Despite being ignored, dismissed, denied jobs and promotions, discriminated against in the workplace, and denied entry into libraries, hotels, and restaurants, black men and women librarian ancestors and living elders broke down barriers, kicked in doors, sat in, prayed in, and withstood insults. Black librarians attended conferences and meetings, participated in council sessions and roundtables at ALA annual conferences and mid-winter meetings to move forward an agenda of change and resistance, with or without the cooperation of the status quo. I encourage young librarians to read the books, essays, and papers to understand the significance of their sacrifices and accomplishments in spite of the odds. Because of those black librarians of yesterday, black librarians today stand tall.

Pioneers and trailblazers such as Daniel Alexander Payne Murray (1852–1925), Edward Christopher Williams (1871–1929), and Thomas Fountain Blue (1866–1935) through Virginia Lacy Jones (1912–1984), E. J. Josey (1924–2009), Effie Lee Morris (1921–2009), and others have taught us lessons of strength, leaving a blueprint of revolution on how to make changes within organizations and the profession, inside or outside the system, and how to make the necessary preparations behind closed doors when necessary. As Frederick Douglass once said, ". . . Without struggle, there is no progress. Power concedes nothing without a demand, it never did and it never will . . ."[4]

All is not well in librarianship. Despite all that has been accomplished and all that black librarians have overcome, there is still work to be done, glass ceilings to be shattered, closed doors to be opened. As with any movement, after major progress has been made, there comes a period of adjustment, growth, and a shift of power, and then complacency, so it is now the time to go back and renew that energy. It is not the time for black librarians to get comfortable or shift the agenda now that new players are at the table. Progress can only be sustained with commitment, involvement, and mentoring of the next generations of librarians of all cultures and interests. As we have learned, the struggle for equity and equality is no longer a black versus white struggle; it is a multiethnic, multicultural, multidimensional, multi-issue struggle in the second decade of the 21st century. As with the Civil Rights Movement, progress can be made when we work together with colleagues of like minds, other organizations, and other ethnic groups. Power to the people!

Sadly, we are witnessing the transition of elder librarians and retirement of the generation that entered the profession as a result of battles won and obstacles overturned in the 1950s and 1960s, a time when black librarians were looked up to as mentors and followed as trailblazers. Today's call for action is for young and new black librarians to stand tall and firm on the shoulders of our ancestors, to benefit from their nurturing and work. It is your time to keep on pushing, to make a difference and address the challenges in the 21st century. Activism is as necessary today as it was during the civil rights era. But, as it was back in the day, some people are still afraid of revolution, afraid to stand, fight, or belong to an organization with "black" in its name. And yes, some do not see themselves as "black librarians" or "activist librarians," only librarians who happen to be black and in many cases do not see the need for activism. No need to join the Black Caucus, no need to attend a NCAAL, or a Joint Conference of Librarians of Color (JCLC). Some feel that, in the 21st century, membership in an American Library Association, a roundtable, or a professional organization of their choice is sufficient. Is it? Are the issues of black librarians so high on their agenda that we no longer need our own organizations to address issues affecting our community? As with our founders, I don't think that will ever be the case.

This is still America, and there will always be racism, classism, and other -isms that separate and withhold access and services. It is the American way! Just as there is still a need for the National Association for the Advancement of Colored People (NAACP) or black chapters of other professional organizations and black Greek organizations, BCALA serves that same purpose. Involvement of black librarians within ALA and its respective roundtables, committees, and professional organizations is warranted and necessary. We can only hope that in the future racism will cease to exist in America. However, until that day, the need for BCALA, the NAACP, and other like organizations is necessary.

Our responsibility to ancestor warriors and elders has not yet been fulfilled. The work of the first generation of black librarians was not completed with the advent of BCALA in 1970. As E. J. Josey and Marva L. DeLoach wrote in their introduction to the second edition of *The Handbook of Black Librarianship*: "As one reviews the history of African Americans, it becomes quite obvious that black Americans have had a long and distinguished history in American librarianship,"[5] and the profession's focus on cultural diversity should not cloud the need to address issues that affect black librarians, libraries that focus on public and academic Africana collections across the diaspora. As Dr. Josey wrote in his introduction to *The Black Librarian in America: Revisited*: "[T]he country, including all of its institutions and libraries, have given mainly lip service to the concept [of cultural diversity]. They have not implemented the concept so that there would be change in our society. In spite of cultural diversity, African Americans in general, and African American librarians in particular, would contend that until the United States comes fully to grips with its most historic, endemic, and pervasive problem—the problem of racism—it will be incapable of fashioning a real cultural diversity climate throughout the land."[6]

As Bernard J. Keller stated: ". . . If you cannot fight the fight for yourself do it for those who fought the wars but were without weapons. If you cannot dream the dream for yourself do it for those who could dream but could never make their dreams come true. If you cannot love you for yourself do it for those who loved you even as they stepped off the slave ships into a new world where they were not considered men or women. If you cannot be proud for yourself do it for those who used pride to sustain themselves even when they were sentenced to ride in the back of the bus or braved the wild dogs and fire hoses in order to cast a vote for a candidate of their choice. Do it for yourself if you can, but whenever you cannot do it for yourself, do it for them."[7]

—Andrew P. Jackson (Sekou Molefi Baako)

NOTES

1. Bernard J. Keller, "Harvard 8/9/85." *Essence Magazine* 19 (7), 1987.
2. Degruy J. Leary, *Post Traumatic Slave Syndrome: America's Legacy of Enduring Injury and Healing*. Milwaukie, OR: Uptone Press, 2005.
3. Itibari M. Zulu, First National Conference of African American Librarians (Columbus, OH: 1992). *Culture Keepers: Enlightening and Empowering Our Communities*: Newark, NJ: Black Caucus of the American Library Association, 1992.
4. Frederick Douglass. "The Significance of Emancipation in the West Indies." Speech, Canadaigua, New York, August 2, 1857.
5. E. J. Josey and M. L. DeLoach, *The Handbook of Black Librarianship*, 2nd ed. Metuchen, NJ: Scarecrow Press, 2000.
6. E. J. Josey, *The Black Librarian in America Revisited*. Metuchen, NJ: Scarecrow Press, 1994.
7. Keller, "Harvard 8/9/85."

Acknowledgments

First, I thank Our Creator for giving us all things great and small, for my life and my family. A very special thank you to Dr. E. J. Josey, my mentor and friend, for his guidance and encouragement throughout my career; thank you to E. J. and the ancestors who gave us the Black Caucus of the American Library Association, the platform for my growth, activism, and passion for black librarianship. Thank you to Martin Dillon, Andrew Yoder, and the Scarecrow Press family for accepting our proposal to produce this edition of *The Black Librarian in America.* A special thanks to Akilah S. Nosakhere and Julius C. Jefferson, Jr., for accepting the challenge to coedit this work with me and for their cooperative spirit and teamwork as we made this journey together. A special thanks to all those who addressed some of the many challenges black librarians face in the 21st century in their essays that appear in this book. A very special thank you to Pam Goodes for the wonderful photograph of E. J. on the dedication page: this book would not have been complete without this photo. Finally, thank you to all who will read this book in hopes it will have the lasting power and historic relevance of the first two editions. To *empyrean*, for your inspiration and love.

—Andrew P. Jackson (Sekou Molefi Baako)

I thank Andrew and Akilah for their commitment, determination, vision, and support. It was truly a pleasure to work with you both. I would also like to thank my friend and mentor E. P. Boyd.

—Julius C. Jefferson, Jr.

It has been a pleasure working on this project with Andrew P. Jackson and Julius C. Jefferson, Jr., to produce this new edition of Dr. Josey's series, *The Black Librarian in America*. It has been an enlightening experience full of professional challenge and growth. Thanks for allowing me to work on this project with you.

I also thank my former supervisor, mentor and friend, Mrs. Lucelia Flood Partridge for suggesting that I go see Dr. Lorene Brown, dean of the Atlanta University School of Library and Information Studies, about applying for library school back in 1986. That day changed my life and I thank you for it.

—Akilah Shukura Nosakhere

Introduction

Akilah Shukura Nosakhere

It was 1970, a mere six years since the passage of the PL 88-352, commonly known as the U.S. Civil Rights Act of 1964, that E. J. Josey, librarian and community activist, published the first edition of The Black Librarian in America. In this groundbreaking publication of 11 essays by black librarians, Josey sought to focus attention on the incongruities within librarianship and challenge the national organization, the American Library Association (ALA), to do more to include black librarians into the organization and increase their numbers in the profession. The Black Librarian in America was published to assess the climate of librarianship and examine the experience of blacks within the profession. More important, Josey desired to increase the visibility of black librarians to ensure access to America's libraries for African American citizens in every state as mandated by law.

The U.S. Civil Rights Act of 1964 banned racial segregation of public services and facilities in America. The law provided African Americans with legal access to municipal libraries, public schools, and universities throughout the United States. This law provided leverage for human rights activist and library leader E. J. Josey to promote equality in all aspects of the library profession. Yet, it would be the black librarians themselves who tested and enforced compliance through their very presence in the professional ranks. Born in the segregated South and rooted in community activism, Josey was inspired by the achievements of the national civil rights movement. His conviction to human equality compelled him to prod the ALA to take the next step to endorse racial and cultural inclusion within all state chapters. The reluctance of ALA to hasten integration of black librarians in southern states led Josey to issue a resolution in 1964 to prevent holding ALA conferences in states that did not admit black librarians as members of its state organizations.

Josey firmly believed in universal human rights, as demonstrated at the 1985 IFLA (International Federation of Library Associations) conference when he spoke against racism and the declaration of African/black inferiority as epitomized by South Africa's apartheid government. Josey drafted a resolution and called for the continuation of the cultural boycott of South Africa due to its racially oppressive government and in spite of the recent release of Nelson Mandela. Library professionals Mary and Herb Biblo recounts Josey's successful campaign in this volume of essays.

Essentially, Josey led the ALA to courageously support Council Document 97, which called for a cultural boycott of South Africa until apartheid had ended. Within the ALA and IFLA, Josey battled against the assumption of black inferiority in all of its manifestations within the profession. As a citizen of the world, Josey championed the fight against racism and elitism wherever it was encountered. During his 32 years as an ALA councilor and in much of his life, Josey was the personification of the philosophy, "act locally and think globally."

It is within this tradition of boundless compassion for global humanity that this third edition of The Black Librarian in America is presented. It is understood by the editors that the activist legacy of Josey is an extension of the African human rights movement that was born when the first African, enslaved in the new world, resisted claims of his lack of humanity. Unfortunately, this infamous allegation of "black inferiority" made its way into the U.S. Constitution and continues to tarnish the humanity of peoples of African descent today.

The 1970 and 1994 editions of The Black Librarian in America singled out "racism" as an issue to be addressed within the profession. This latest collection of 47 essays by black librarians and library supporters again identifies racism as one of many challenges of the new century. Ironically, such was the case at the dawning of the past century as noted by historian and public library advocate W. E. B. Du Bois.

The year 2011 was dubbed the International Year of People of African Descent by UNESCO, and during this special year, there is no doubt that U.S. librarians of African descent, will experience some form of racism regardless of their age, their position, or the type of library where they are employed. Unfortunately, most librarians will or have experienced at least one racist encounter on the job involving a patron, or even a colleague. Margaret J. Gibson relates an interesting encounter in her essay, "Dismiss the Stereotype! Combating Racism and Continuing Our Progress."

U.S. librarians of African descent continue to advance and contribute to the future of librarianship in spite of racial prejudice that still permeates all aspects of U.S. society, including our beloved profession. Nevertheless, black librarians rise to meet the challenge and minimize the debilitating effect of racism with strong personal character, a healthy cultural consciousness, and outstanding professional skill.

This collection of poignant essays covers a multiplicity of concerns for the 21st-century black librarian. Each essay embodies compassion and respect for the provision of information, an act that defines librarianship. The essays are personable, inspiring, and thought provoking for all library professionals, regardless of race, class, or gender. Some essays are written by library educators, library graduate school students, retired librarians, public library trustees, and veteran librarians with many years of experience from all areas of the field; others are penned by new librarians fresh out of school with great ideas and wholesome energy that will make you smile.

Part I features eight school librarians (also known as media specialists) from different parts of the country who contributed to this millennial edition. Essentially, all are in agreement that students with low academic skill levels typically come from schools with poorly equipped school libraries. Their words form a collective call to action to all librarians to help preserve the school library and assist public school policymakers in making the shift to a new and innovative model of public education employing 21st-century learning and teaching practices.

Doctoral student and former library director Silvia Lloyd writes that school administrators and classroom teachers misunderstand the mission of the school library and the role of school librarians. Even though research clearly define the connection between successful academic performance and a well-equipped school library public school administrators are reluctant to adequately fund school libraries. Similarly, retired school librarian Gloria J. Reaves reports in her essay that "many parents, educators, and lawmakers do not fully understand the importance of school libraries."

The budgets of school library media centers are often slashed or sacrificed during tight economic times, resulting in a reduction of academic resources available to public school students. Poorly funded school libraries result in poor academic preparation and chronic underachievement according to media specialist Joyce F. Ndiaye. More important, Ndiaye brings to light the age-old practice of unequal funding of schools in the same district. Ndiaye quickly adds that inequity in library funding may not be intentional but the students notice the difference.

Urban school librarians Karen Lemmons and Andre Taylor describe a dismal situation for children attending public schools in the large cities. In the midst of budget deficits, crumbling school facilities, and poor graduation rates and test scores, uncertainty is rampant. Site-based management empowers local districts or principals to determine the life or death of a school library program and the employment of the school librarian.

As municipal school systems across America suffer from reduced tax revenue, poor administration, standardized test scandals, low graduation rates, and an obsolete public education model, school librarians must document each and every activity to justify their existence from year to year. There are no guarantees, as these school librarians explain, yet they do not give up, for the education of poor black children is at stake and they are committed to their charge.

Undaunted by racially insensitive comments, low expectations, poor resources, indifferent administrators, and apathetic students, eight school librarians, thoughtfully outline the challenges facing this new century. Library school professor Pauletta Brown Bracy suggests ways school librarians can meet the unique needs of African American students. As we remember our past experience, black librarians will again make "bricks from straw" and create ways to reform or replace the current public school system that has traditionally been insensitive to the needs of black students and disrespectful of the black cultural heritage in general.

The public library has never been as important as it is today. It is many things to many people. Families and children come to participate in programs. Others come to use the computer when there is none at home. Some come to get help using technology while others check out media, download music, e-books, or magazine articles to their personal mobile devices. Patrons visit the library to browse books, leisurely read newspapers and magazines.

Job seekers come to the library to find employment; to fill out job applications online, and to file their unemployment claims. The homeless finds the public library one of few public places they can visit without the fear of being expelled because they are homeless. Also, there is a growing population of users who browse library collections remotely. They can request, place material on hold, or download electronic books and articles without ever stepping through the doors of the library.

However, as the national economy worsens, publicly funded libraries must compete with other municipal services to survive. City and county administrators will face tough decisions regarding the funding of the public library over other needs, such as trash collection or payroll for the city jail. During these hard times, public library leaders are expected to advocate on behalf of the public's need to maintain access to information in its many formats as held by the public library.

Library trustee Lucille Cole Thomas believes that the public library is important to the well-being of the community. She outlines the responsibilities of municipal library boards and explains why it is important to support public library directors in maintaining library services to the general public, especially during challenging financial times. As a black library director in a rural white community, Jos N. Holman adds another dimension to the challenge of library leadership. He notes that it is important to establish trust with your staff, the library board and exhibit strong financial management skills early. This helps the library director to gain allies and build confidence in you as a manager. Rose Timmons Dawson, director of the Alexander (Virginia) Public Library, notes that "it takes a village to raise a director" and library directors should be visionary change agents carrying the library to new heights while maintaining stability in the community.

In the tradition, young adult librarian Tamara Stewart boldly speaks out about the public library's discriminatory practices toward young people in her thought-provoking essay titled "Adultism: Discrimination by Another Name." Stewart takes the reader from the front door to the reference desk and critiques the perceptions librarians and society in general tend to have about young adults today. E. J. Josey Award winner Syntychia Kendrick-Samuel, also a young adult librarian, admits she was "terrified at the thought of working with these teens." Those "teens" were black and Latin young adult members of the Junior Friends of the Library. Kendrick-Samuel shares her enlightening experience and explains how she became a strong advocate for young adult library programming.

Librarianship is one of the few professions where clients are taught to become independent of services they seek. That is, librarians and educators teach the public to be independent and skilled information users. Bannerman-Martin and Echols note that the public librarian will continue to play an important role in the education of the general public. A similar theme is found in Brown Lawson's treatise on "servant leadership." She shares that librarians also mentor, coach, and assist each other in the fulfillment of professional goals.

Dramatic advancement in information technology, library operations, and user expectations are major concerns of 21st-century academic librarians. Keeping up with emerging technologies and their applicability for library service is a never-ending task in the academic library. Consistent attention and regular perusal of IT (information technology) news is as common as morning coffee for public service librarians, the technical service staff, and library managers. In spite of ever-evolving technologies and increasing demands of changing user populations, university librarian Ruth M. Jackson of the University of California–Riverside, cautions black librarians not to take their eyes off the prize. "The human touch," she counsels, "and the caring for the education of black youth remain the hallmarks of our discipline and profession."

This legacy of compassion is confirmed by associate professor Lisa A. Ellis through her personal interviews with black instruction librarians. In her essay, Ellis reports that "black instructional librarians are passionate about teaching and are committed to teaching the whole student." Teaching ill-equipped students, particularly if they are black, reaffirms in the black librarian a personal sense of social responsibility. Strong information gathering and analysis skills are basic fare in a world that is becoming increasingly competitive on a global scale. Black students who might need additional encouragement often get it from black librarians who are committed to the success of their students. Successful library managers Deirdre D. Spencer, Felix Eme Unaeze, and Theresa S. Boyd are from three very different academic library environments. Each shares a unique experience, yet their essays converge upon the need to reassure others that they are skilled librarians and competent managers to boot! Their librarians share the same legacy of compassion and love of library service.

Part IV focuses on the special library and features three essays from the health sciences field and two from private institutions. Medical librarian Ellie Bushhousen asserts that African American medical librarians are nearly invisible because they do not publish or participate in conference presentations as they should. The challenge of the 21st century for this group is to come out of the shadows and into the light with confidence and authority. Bushhousen reminds us that since librarians understand how information is gathered and organized, it is not difficult for librarians to work with professionals from any field—including medicine.

Special librarian Phyllis Hodges chronicles her journey from Kingsborough Community College to become assistant director at the University of Texas Medical Branch. Hodges provided tips for new library professionals, noting that in addition to a strong skill base, integrity and respect in your human relations are important attributes. Affirming Hodges' advice, health science librarian LaVentra E. Danquah identifies mentors and role models in the health sciences to inspire us to look beyond the typical places for librarians.

The role of medical and health science librarians is very important because they deliver information to medical professionals who make health-care decisions based on the information made available. Danquah shares a story of a health science librarian who was so well regarded by a medical professional that she was asked to train residents and physicians on evidence-based searching. Such an invitation is a testament to her professional skills.

The explosion of health information centers at public libraries and increased access to health information online has created a need for health-information specialists. Very little is written about African American medical and health sciences librarians in the respective professional journals. We are quite fortunate to have these impressive essays in this edition.

The final two essays in this section acknowledge the growing cultural diversity in U.S. society and tell how some private institutions deal with it. Brendon Thompson writes about diversity in the corporate library world and the success experienced by his employer. The Southern California Library (SCL) is a private community-based library with collections uniquely documenting movements of social change in Los Angeles. Michele Welsing, communications director at SCL, narrates the SCL story and its rebirth under the visionary leadership of Yusef Omowale, the third director and first black man to manage the 40-year-old community library.

Parts V and VI are slim sections containing key essays on recruitment. Deloice Holliday and Michele Fenton proudly share the success of the Indiana State Library recruitment project funded through the Institute of Museums and Library Services (IMLS) Laura Bush 21st Century Librarian Program. Archivist Steven Booth describes his recruitment experience and the importance of mentorship in his professional and personal development. The greatest lesson, Booth points out, is that we, as black librarians and archivists, are largely responsible for building our own numbers! Librarians Holliday and Fenton would agree with his conclusion.

In her call to renewed commitment to the state library organization, Em Claire Knowles of the Graduate School of Library and Information Science at Simmons College, reminds Massachusetts librarians that now is not time to rest on past achievements. Knowles challenges past and current members to maintain the link to the national organization and continue to participate in active programming as the state organization seeks to recruit new African American librarians.

Part VI opens with an interesting examination of racial prejudice in history of library and information science (LIS) programs and higher education. LIS graduate student, Angel K. Washington Durr, writes about the coming cultural shift in U.S. society, yet inside her LIS classroom, white females still outnumber any other group. Echoing archivist Steven Booth, Washington Durr realizes that we are the ones we have been waiting for. She states that only black librarians can successfully mount recruitment efforts to boost LIS enrollment. She recommends the mentoring of undergraduates, high schools students, and African American students at all levels.

Noting the glaring absence of Chicano, Asian, Native, and African American faculty and students in U.S. library and information programs, LIS Associate Professor Maurice Wheeler asserts that the hiring of African American faculty members in predominantly white institutions is usually on a token basis, but this was not always the case. He further points out that no matter how exemplary the training or credentials of black candidates, they are always subject to "insinuations that merit was not the main factor in their appointment" due the unscrupulous linking of affirmative action with lower standards.

Part VII provides a peek at the role of technology and its effect upon librarianship and access to information. Long-term access to the rich and varied Africana collections housed in the libraries of the nation's historically black colleges and universities (HBCUs) is enhanced by technology. Pioneering projects, such as the digital preservation of the black musical experience at Hampton University Library by Gladys Smiley Bell and Harvey J. Stokes, fuel the imagination and inspire other digital initiatives. Digital technologist Ira Revels, of Cornell University, monitors the ongoing success of the HBCU Library Alliance in its mission to train and educate HBCU library staff to preserve collections using state-of-the-art digitization techniques.

Metadata expert Jennifer W. Baxmeyer surveys the electronic revolution in catalog librarianship and reports that technology has changed the way all librarians do their jobs. The growing preference for electronic over print resources continues to define library service in the 21st-century library. Allene F. Hayes chronicles the shift from print to electronic resources and comments on the impact on library operations. In light of sweeping technological change, black librarians generally embrace new technologies and often hit the ground running as early adopters and regular users of cutting-edge developments.

Fantasia Thorne, like Baxmeyer and Hayes, emphasizes the importance of monitoring new technology. Thorne offers tips on how to keep up with new technology without losing sight of your primary responsibilities. She says, a librarian's ability to understand, use, and discuss new technology is impressive to users and garners the respect of colleagues and supervisors.

The final installment, "Issues and Profiles," brings together an eclectic mix of essays addressing challenges that have plagued librarianship for decades. These same issues are responsible in part for the lack of diversity within the field and maybe responsible for ALA's limited success in attracting new recruits among people of color. The provocative writing of Tracie D. Hall and Cheryl L. Branche links the origins of racial and social divisions within librarianship to the larger Western society. While the Spectrum Scholarship Initiative created in 1995 has had some success in boosting the number of African American librarians, RaShuna Brannon and Jahala Simuel points out that there is much work to do in this new century.

Valeda Dent Goodman and Johnnie O. Dent exemplify successful recruitment within a family. The mother, a public librarian, and the daughter, an academic library dean, teams up to provide an interesting look at the complex nature of library recruitment.

Taneya D. Gethers provides a history of librarianship, noting that the black librarian legacy can be traced to Africans on both sides of the Sahara. Ancient Africans secured and saved sacred information by burying scrolls in the desert sand. Gethers reminds us that self-knowledge is regarded as the beginning of wisdom. Academic librarian Carol Nurse adds a delightful piece about her short stint with a well-known library vendor indicating that library vendors are also a bit 'color-struck.'

As young librarians express their concern for technology, recruitment, and the detriment of racial prejudice, a more experienced voice, such as Emily Guss, recalls the guidance of her mentors at the Chicago Public Libraries. Well-regarded author and librarian Binnie Tate Wilkin remembers the outstanding contributions of E. J. Josey and retired librarian Satia Marshall Orange includes a touching tribute to Effie Lee Morris, the grand dame of children's librarianship.

Like the original edition of *The Black Librarian in America*, this collection of essays finds racial prejudice in the field of librarianship to be an impediment to recruitment and advancement of the black librarian. Nevertheless, black librarians must not let this reality stifle achievement of personal and professional goals. We need only to remember leaders who made a way for us fighting the vestiges of legalized racism with one hand while directing the future with the other!

Such is the "activist legacy" willed to black librarians by Dr. E. J. Josey. Linda Saylor-Marchant reminds us of this charge we have inherited. She invites librarians to visit the Live Oak Public library in downtown Savannah, Georgia, to read Josey's name on the bronze plaque there. Josey remains an example of an activist librarian who took the time to serve his community, write for the profession, and mentor the young professional no matter what color, language, or physical location in the world. I hope you enjoy this edition as much as I have in bringing it to you.

Part I

FROM THE SCHOOL LIBRARY

1

Information Literacy Instruction in K–12 Education and Barriers to Success in the 21st Century

Silvia Lloyd

The main objective of K–12 education is to prepare students for higher education or the workforce. The skills that have been identified as valuable for success in higher education and the workforce can be taught in school library media programs. These skills include self-direction, critical thinking, knowledge management, and inquiry-based learning (Business Council, 2009; Conference Board, 2006). The reality is that many students are not graduating with these skills. Students are falling through the cracks (Torgensen, 2002). Many graduate from high school are unprepared for the global economy and jobs in general (U.S. DOE Office of Vocational and Adult Services, 2009). Nationally, one of every four high school students fails to graduate on time. For African American and Latino students, that rate increases to more than one of three (Education Trust, 2008).

UNDERUTILIZED SCHOOL LIBRARIANS

The basic skills of locating information, evaluating it effectively, and using it ethically and responsibly are important in a society that values knowledge (American Library Association [ALA], 1998). Yet, when educators talk about improving instruction and increasing academic achievement, they seldom mention the benefits of school libraries or teacher collaboration with the school librarian (Loertscher, 2010). In many school libraries across the United States, underutilization of a skilled information specialist occurs. Many school librarians are being used to schedule library use for book checkout and for teacher-led instruction. A disproportionate amount of time is spent on shelving books, fixing printers, and monitoring discipline problems. When this occurs, school librarians are marginalized from classroom teachers who plan together. They are not perceived as equal partners in the professional learning community (DuFour & Eaker, 1998). In essence, the school librarian is viewed as a supplement to education and not an essential component of curriculum and instruction (Scott & Plourde, 2007).

This is a commonly held perspective that stems back to the 1950s when school teachers viewed the school librarians' role as passive, lacking integration of class work with library instruction (Craver, 1986; Michie & Holton, 2005). The role of the librarian evolved and expanded considerably after we entered the information age (American Association of School Librarians [AASL], 2007). However, the practice of using the school librarian in the limited role of someone who is only expected to promote a love of reading and to provide story hour to students in the primary grades still continues.

THE ROLE OF THE 21ST-CENTURY SCHOOL LIBRARIAN

Since we moved into the 21st century, new technologies have shifted the way we conduct research and engage in learning. New technologies require a new type of literacy (Asselin, 2004). Computers, software, and the Internet in schools are the cause of such procedural changes. With the overabundance of information found on the Internet, issues of credibility, accuracy, and currency arise when evaluating information that is easily attainable but not peer reviewed. Students need to be able to evaluate the credibility of websites by locating critical information such as the contact and date of publication. Knowing how to analyze uniform resource locators' (URL) domain extensions aids students in the identification of a website's purpose and the agenda of the author (Baker & Terry, 2007). Students need these and many other necessary skills to be considered information literate and to become lifelong learners who can manipulate information and create new knowledge beyond the scope of the classroom.

Students who are not fully engaged in the curriculum often slip through the cracks. Research shows that the teaching of higher level information literacy skills and processes is successful when taught by the librarian; after all, the school librarian is the information specialist. However, many teachers bypass the librarian and assume that they can teach students how to conduct research using print and electronic resources accessible in the classroom through the Internet. When this occurs, many students lose interest because the full process is not followed with fidelity. Smith and Hepworth (2007) found that students are able to follow the process from start to finish with the aid of the school librarian.

A great deal of literature has been written on collaboration with school librarians. Loertscher (1982, 1988, 2000) was the first to classify the behaviors of school teachers and librarians around collaborating in his eleven-step model. Montiel-Overall (2005) adapted Loertscher's taxonomy and created the Teacher and Librarian Collaboration (TLC) model, which is based on stage theory. This model identifies four facets of collaboration on a continuum from least effective to most effective:

1. Coordination: working together to arrange schedules, manage time efficiently, and avoid overlap.
2. Cooperation: dividing responsibilities among participants to create a whole new project.
3. Integrated instruction: integrating jointly planned, implemented, and evaluated instruction into library curriculum and content curriculum in a lesson or unit.
4. Integrated curriculum: expanding integrated instruction, found in the previous facet, to occur across a school or school district.

Collaboration is promoted in the federal No Child Left Behind (2002) legislation, which stipulates that classroom teachers use scientifically based research (SBR) when incorporating instructional methods. School librarians who keep abreast of the latest research in the field can be the knowledge expert on information literacy. It would be prudent for classroom teachers to consult and co-plan with this highly skilled professional on instructional methods that have been tested and proven to work when infusing information literacy into the curriculum. When integrated instruction occurs, teachers and school librarians are able to draw on each other's knowledge and skills to collectively solve complex problems (Brownell & Walther-Thomas, 2007).

THE BLACK SCHOOL LIBRARIAN

In spite of well-written theories and mandatory laws, the school librarian continues to be bypassed as an information specialist in many schools. Social and environmental issues exist in schools that prevent collaboration from occurring. Time constraints and a lack of administrative support are related to unsuccessful attempts to collaborate (Brownell & Walther-Thomas, 2002; Friend, 2000). This impasse and other systemic weaknesses in schools hinder the execution of information literacy instruction among teachers (Buzzeo, 2004). It is counterproductive when school administrators schedule class visits to the library as regularly fixed classes. The classroom teacher uses this time to either take a break or engage in independent planning time. As a result, little or no communication takes place between the teacher and the librarian.

Asking professionals to be cordial with one another is one thing, but making it mandatory that they are friendly, collegial, trusting, and engaging with one another as equal partners is a huge undertaking. Studies show that organizational culture dictates rules and regulations. This makes it extremely difficult for black school librarians, who are oftentimes the "minority in a majority organization and do not have access to the informal networks that often develop in the workplace" (Madsen & Mabokela, 2000, p. 851). The black school librarian must find clues on how to assimilate with the culture that is already established by the European majority. This may involve cultural switching, code switching, breaking down negative stereotypes, and asserting oneself as a credible leader in the school building (Madsen & Mabokele, 2000).

It would be best for the black school librarian to embrace this challenge as a legacy that has been inherited from African ancestors. Since America's beginning, Africans were creative in navigating Anglo cultural norms. After winning the Civil War, Jim Crow laws were designed to strip blacks of their dignity. Harassment, theft, murder, fraud, manipulation, exploitation, bullying, bigotry, injustice, and corruption of blacks had become not only the norm, but also the law of the land. After generations of teamwork and collaboration, blacks in America were once again victorious in changing the U.S. Constitution to include civil rights and women's rights for people of color (U.S. Department of Justice, 1964). Courage to change old ideas and practices in a dignified and peaceable manner has become the cultural norm for black America as by-products of the struggle for equality, social justice, and inclusion. Black librarians are the epitome of what teamwork and collaboration can produce, and they would do well to embrace and emulate those characteristics as cultural gems in their black heritage.

STUDENTS IN CITY SCHOOL DISTRICTS

The organizational culture in city schools is often shaped by factors such as income, race, ethnicity, and geography. Many believe that a different quality of services is provided in urban areas when compared with suburban schools (Clark, 1965; Myrdal, 1944; Wilson, 1987). Geographic location imposes segregation based on socioeconomic status. Mossberger, Tolbert, and Gilbert (2006) posit that "serious inequities persist in poor urban communities, despite decades of civil rights and fair housing legislation" (p. 584).

Warschauer (2003) offers that information literacy can be a key means to social inclusion in the 21st century. Mossberger et al. (2006) use the term digital "citizenship" to describe the ability to use information technology to participate fully in society. Inequities keep students from fully participating in lifelong learning for education, employment, health, safety, and politics. Many students in large city school districts rely on public schools to teach them these skills, although their suburban counterparts may have learned these skills at home.

Waiting until high school and college to teach these skills may be too late for disadvantaged youth who may lack access to technology, resources, and role models at home. Early mastery of inquiry-based and research-based skills could advance students of color in preparation for college, especially at a time when immigrants are taking key slots in U.S. higher education institutions (Johnson,

Burthey, & Ghorm, 2008). Although the issuance of student visas has lessened since the events of 9/11, research shows that these students continue to outperform even the highest performing students in America (National Center for Education Statistics, 2009).

In conclusion, successful collaborative practices between teachers and librarians around information literacy instruction must be examined in order to prepare students of color fully for globalization in the 21st-century workforce. When school professionals are isolated from one another, successful student outcomes decrease (Lance, 2002; Lance, Wellborn, & Hamilton-Pennell, 1993; Montiel-Overall, 2005). Elementary school librarians must find ways to collaborate with classroom teachers. This poses a greater challenge for the black school librarian who must slay old stereotypical ideas implemented by the European majority. However, it must be done in order for disadvantaged youth to become the highly intellectual, creative, adaptive learners they need to be, to access, evaluate, and apply specialized knowledge, and to be the creators of new knowledge in the 21st century.

REFERENCES

American Library Association (ALA). (1998). *Information literacy: Building partnerships for collaboration.* Chicago: Author.

American Association of School Librarians (AASL). (2007). *Standards for the 21st century learner*. Chicago: ALA.

Asselin, M. (2004). New literacies: Towards a renewed role of school libraries. *Teacher Librarian, 31*, 52–53.

Baker, D. I., & Terry, C. D. (2007). *Internet research*, 3rd ed. Boston: Thomson Course Technology.

Brownell, M. T., & Walther-Thomas, C. (2002). An interview with Dr. Marilyn Friend. *Intervention in School and Clinic, 37*, 223–228.

Business Council. (2009). *Survey of chief executives: CEO survey results*. The Business Council and the Conference Board. Retrieved from http://msnbcmedia.msn.com/i/CNBC/Sections/News_And_Analysis/_News/__EDIT%20Englewood%20Cliffs/May_09_survey_press.pdf

Buzzeo, T. (2004). Using communication to solve roadblocks to collaboration. *Teacher Librarian, 31*, 28.

Clark, K. B. (1965). *Dark ghetto: Dilemmas of social power*. New York: Harper and Row.

Conference Board. (2006). Partnership for 21st Century Skills, Corporate Voices for Working Families, and Society for Human Resource Management. Are they really ready to work? Employers' perspective on the basic knowledge and applied skills of new entrants to the 21st century U.S. workforce. Retrieved from http://www.p21.org/documents/FINAL_REPORT_PDF09-29-06.pdf

Craver, K. W. (1986). The changing instructional role of the high school library media specialists, 1950–84: A survey of professional literature, standards and research studies. *School Library Media Quarterly, 14*(4), 183–191. Retrieved from http://www.ala.org/

ala/mgrps/divs/aasl/aaslpubsandjournals/slmrb/editorschoiceb/infopower/ALA_print_layout_1_202748_202748.cfm

DuFour, R., & Eaker, R. (1998). *Professional learning communities at work: Best practices for enhancing student achievement.* Bloomington, Indiana: Solution Tree.

Education Trust (2008). *Counting on graduation: Most states are setting low expectations for the improvement of high school graduation rates.* Retrieved December 20, 2010, from http://www.edtrust.org

Friend, M. (2000). Perspectives: Collaboration in the twenty-first century. *Remedial and Special Education, 20,* 130–132.

Johnson, J. H., Burthey, G., & Ghorm, K. (2008). Economic globalization and the future of black America. *Journal of Black Studies, 38,* 883–899.

Lance, K. C. (2002). How school librarians leave no child behind: The impact of school library media programs on academic achievement of U.S. public school students. *School Libraries in Canada, 22,* 4–6.

Lance, K. C., Wellborn, L., & C. Hamilton-Pennell. (1993). *The impact of school library media centers on academic achievement.* Castle Rock, CO: Hi Willow Research and Publishing.

Loertscher, D. (1982). Second revolution: A taxonomy for the 1980s. *Wilson Library Bulletin,* 56, 412–421.

Loertscher, D. (1988). *Taxonomies of the school library media program.* Englewood, CO: Libraries Unlimited.

Loertscher, D. (2000). *Taxonomies of the school library media program,* 2nd ed. San Jose, CA: Hi Willow Research and Publishing.

Loertscher, D. (2010). Learning to read and reading to learn: Meeting the international challenge. *Teacher Librarian, 37,* 48–51.

Madsen, J. A., & Mabokele, R. O. (2000). Organizational culture and its impact on African American teachers. *American Educational Research Journal, 37,* 849–876.

Michie, J. S., & Holton, B. A. (2005). *America's public school libraries: 1953–2000.* Washington, DC: U.S. Department of Education National Center for Education Statistics.

Montiel-Overall, P. (2005). A theoretical understanding of teacher and librarian collaboration. (TLC). *School Libraries Worldwide, 11,* 24–48.

Mossberger, K., Tolbert, C. J., & Gilbert, M. (2006). Race, place, and information technology. *Urban Affairs Review, 41,* 583–620.

Myrdal, G. (1944). *An American dilemma: The negro problem in modern democracy.* New York: Harper and Brothers.

National Center for Educational Statistics (2009). *The nation's report card.* Retrieved December 2, 2010 from http://nces.ed.gov/nationsreportcard.

No Child Left Behind. (2002). Public Law No. 107-110, 115 Stat. 1425 (2001). Retrieved from http://www2.ed.gov/policy/elsec/leg/esea02/107-110.pdf

Scott, K. J., & Plourde, L. A. (2007). School libraries and increased student achievement: What's the big idea? *Education, 127,* 419–429.

Smith, M., & Hepworth, M. (2007). An investigation of factors that may demotivate secondary school students undertaking project work: Implications for learning information literacy. *Journal of Librarianship and Information Science, 30,* 3–15.

Torgensen, K. J. (2002). The prevention of reading difficulties. *Journal of School Psychology, 40,* 7–26.

U.S. Department of Justice. (1964). Civil Rights Act. Retrieved from http://www.justice.gov/crt/about/cor/coord/titlevi.php

U.S. DOE Office of Vocational and Adult Services. (2009). Adult education and literacy. Retrieved from http://www2.ed.gov/ovae

Warschauer, M. (2003). *Technology and social inclusion: Rethinking the digital divide*. Cambridge, MA: MIT Press.

Wilson, W. J. (1987). *The truly disadvantaged: The inner city, the underclass, and public policy*. Chicago: University of Chicago Press.

2

Inequality of Resources in School Libraries in the 21st Century

Joyce F. Ndiaye

I became a librarian because I've loved books and libraries since early childhood. My mission as a school librarian involves creating an environment in which today's young people can also develop a passion for reading and learning. My major worry about public school libraries in the 21st century concerns the inequality of resources within the same district. These inequalities might not be intentional, but in the district where I work, schools on the eastern side of the county, with majority Hispanic and African American students, tend to have markedly fewer library resources than the majority white schools.

I believe that the persistently lower academic achievement of students in the "majority minority" schools is inextricably linked to the fact that our libraries have been chronically underfunded for many years. The student body of the middle school where I am librarian is comprised of 39.9% Hispanics, 28.4% African Americans, 19.8% whites, and 7.8% Asians, and 63.1% come from economically disadvantaged families.

Our standardized state test scores are good, but they're lower than those of middle schools on the western, generally more affluent, side of the county, and our library resources still fall short. One western county middle school, for example, has 10.3% Hispanics, 11.4% African Americans, 70.2% whites, and 4.5% Asians, and only 10.9% of the students were considered economically disadvantaged. In school year 2009–2010, our library was given about $3,000 for books, whereas the western county middle school library received over $15,000 during the same academic year.

How does this happen? Site-based management allows this type of inequality of library resources to occur. Under site-based management, each school principal decides autonomously how to allocate the funds within the building that he or she manages. Principals who are not fans of libraries may decide to use book money to purchase new football uniforms, replace office furniture, or subscribe to expensive online reading drills. Site-based management gives them this power.

My school library has long been victimized by site-based management. When I arrived in August 2006, the average age of the book collection was 1983. Many of the books were also in bad physical condition. I worked on weeding and ran a book fair to help build the collection, but the principal insisted that there was little money to buy new books. He wanted to know instead what I could do to improve the library without having to spend money.

That fall, I saw our superintendent in the hallway near the main office. I greeted him and he promised to visit the library before leaving the building. I showed him our collection and explained our situation. As a result, we received a special grant of about $3,000 that year to purchase books. This was a wonderful gesture that I remain truly grateful for, but our school libraries deserve a systematic equitable distribution of funds.

Later that school year, we were summoned to a mandatory, emergency after-school staff meeting. An associate superintendent and the human resources director stood in front of us to witness the principal announce that he was being removed from our school. The story was that he was being removed because of gross mismanagement of site-based funds during the three years of his leadership.

Once the new principal was selected, I talked to her about the pressing needs of our library. She was sympathetic, but said that the budget was so decimated by the ousted principal that it would take at least another school year before it could recover. We experienced some small improvement during the new school year, but we still had a long way to go to reach equity with the wealthier middle schools in our division. When our students come back from sports and music events at other county schools, they sometimes report having heard our school referred to as a "ghetto school," and that epithet stings.

After one year under our new principal, the old library assistant retired. The principal and I conducted joint interviews and selected an excellent new assistant. It is an asset that she is Hispanic because we have many Spanish-speaking students who benefit from her bilingual skills. However, this asset is exploited to the detriment of the library program.

Every day, the school gets calls from Spanish-speaking parents who don't speak or understand English. Teachers, administrators, and counselors need to communicate to Hispanic parents who are not conversant in English. My assistant is pulled from library duties to translate at hearings, over the phone, for communication between students and the nurse, for parent–teacher conferences, and at formal evaluation meetings for special and limited English-proficient students. The school system has a list of approved translators that we are permitted to hire on an hourly basis for these purposes, but they have to be paid out of site-based funds. Since the library assistant is on a salary, they don't have to pay her extra, so they use her services to save money.

The library assistant is also pulled for mail distribution, photocopying services, and other nonlibrary clerical tasks even while I am in the act of teaching class. Throughout the school day, students come to the library independently to check out books, and I have to excuse myself from the class that I'm teaching in order to check books out to students waiting at the circulation desk. This is the case even though in the state of Virginia, a full-time library assistant is not an optional position on the secondary school level—it is required.

An additional strain on student access to library resources comes from the emphasis on data-driven teaching and testing. Our school library houses a general computer lab. It is used for math drills, foreign language drills, Standards of Learning (SOL) testing, benchmark testing, and midterm exams and finals. The library is locked down for weeks at a time for testing purposes. During these weeks, students are denied access to the library for most of the school day. More affluent schools have enough computer labs and laptops to allow their libraries to function normally during benchmarks and midterms.

Standardized testing is king, and if scores are not improved significantly each year, teachers and principals are reprimanded. For example, the aforementioned principal who started in the fall of 2007 was ousted in June 2010 based on student benchmark test scores. The sad footnote is that in June, the final state test scores revealed that our students passed the standardized tests with the required scores. The decision to remove that principal had been made, however, and her replacement had already been named.

Library lessons and less high-stakes computer lab tests that occur at the same time in a shared space also creates conflict. Test-takers are understandably distracted while legitimate, engaging, hands-on library instruction is going on simultaneously in the same room. We need quiet testing labs that can also be used for instructional drills. The library should be free for active inquiry-based learning.

Students who come individually to the library for independent research or to use the online catalog often can't get access to computers even when classes are just doing drills because there are only 30 computers in the library computer lab. Most of those are old and unreliable, so the five designated library computers are usually taken over by the class using the lab. Adding to the problem is that many classes have close to 35 students. One class has 37.

Our school recently underwent renovation. The cafeteria and restrooms look good. The library got new carpet and lights. We even got magazine shelving for the first time, but the bookshelves from 1971 were reused—sagging shelves and all. Bookcases that were not against the wall were repositioned, but they unattractively block student visibility and movement around the reading room.

Like all librarians, I worked hard in school to gain skills to be part of a profession that I love and to be of practical service to others. To be honest, though, I'm angry that our school district provides inferior resources to economically disadvantaged students. Though angry, I'm not totally discouraged. This year, for the first time since I started working at this school, the new principal has granted our library the nationally recommended school library budget based on our enrollment. It's beginning to make a tremendous difference, and I am ecstatic to be part of this improvement. The students are delighted to see so many new books to hold their interest. Prior to this, the library received less than half that amount in a good year.

On a daily basis, I do my best to make our school library better. I encourage students and teachers to suggest books that they're interested in. Their requests are an integral part of my collection development plan. Steadily and increasingly, our library is beginning to truly reflect their interests, information needs, and cultural backgrounds. Until county-wide measures are implemented that will comply with the spirit of *Brown v. the Board of Education*, those of us on the eastern side of the county will continue sharing our love of libraries in spite of our inferior resources.

3

Challenges of the Black School Librarian in the 21st Century: Why I Choose to Stay

Angela Washington-Blair

It's all about the students. That's why I have a career as a school librarian. When I am asked how I can work around today's self-absorbed youth with their disrespect for authority, bad attitudes, sagging pants, preoccupation with their cell phones, and a general lack of motivation for succeeding in school, I still say it's all about the students. My career as a school librarian is meaningful, and my relationship with the students is a symbiotic one. They need me, and I need them. I can show them the way, so to speak. I can help them have a growth mindset. I can show them I care about them. I can offer them 21st-century literacy skills, be a part of their college-career preparation, and be a mentor and role model. In return, they offer me not only challenges that keep me from getting bored, but also insight into their lives, humor, energy, joy, and the raison d'être for what I do each day.

I am employed as a media specialist (school librarian) by an urban high school in Dallas, Texas. Like many other schools in our city, the student body is diverse ethnically, socioeconomically (though we lean more toward the free-and-reduced lunch standard of low income), and by nationality. Thirty-seven countries are represented at our school. Consequently, we have many students whose native language is not English. It makes life interesting, and I can honestly say that I love what I do.

When I hear some of our American-born black youth say they hate to read, I cringe and sometimes get sad, knowing our history as it pertains to the right to read and get an education. We've come a long way as a people, and we cannot start the backward descent caused by ignorance. But I won't admit defeat. I roll up my sleeves and try again to inspire: to teach our history; to model good manners, protocol, and decorum; to show them how to speak properly; to somehow match each student with a book; to tell them how far we've come; to give them hope, and to truthfully let them know that without a good education, particularly post-secondary, and without being an information literate citizen, they have a slim chance for a positive future.

It is exciting to recommend books to students. I have to keep up with what's current and listen to our students. I might like the classics and cozy feel-good stories, but they don't. Our students are diverse and they have diverse reading needs. The avid readers like manga and books in series. Vampire books are a huge hit. Some of our black students ask for "drama." I get a kick out of making them explain what it is they really want. I ask if they mean Shakespeare or August Wilson or Lorraine Hansberry. They say, no, they want "baby mama drama" or "stepdad beat the stepdaughter drama." They want *Push*, and *Flyy Girl*, and *The Coldest Winter Ever*. Okay, so they like urban street lit and the "I am downtrodden" books that often mirror their lives. Maybe some of the books they want to read are not always considered to be of literary merit, but they are reading, and who am I to judge? I want them to find the pleasure in reading.

Reading for knowledge is necessary, but reading for pleasure can be transforming. So I, along with my co-librarian, suggest high-interest books to our reluctant readers. But not all of our readers are reluctant. Never let it be said that black boys do not read. Quite the contrary, some of our most voracious readers are the black males who come to the library. They discuss and suggest books with one another and are some of the top readers in our million-word reading challenge.

Being a black person in America, I recognize the fact that our race is not a monolithic group. There is no one-size-fits-all approach for us. But since I am part of that community, I have a touch on its pulse. I make it my business to know what our youth, particularly our black youth, are reading, listening to, watching, and doing. It is up to me as the school librarian, who just happens to be black, to continue to be the torch bearer, keeper of the culture, role model, advocate, ambassador, closer of the achievement gap, bridge over the digital divide, technology leader, recruiter of others to the profession, and good teacher to all students. In a highly integrated, heterogeneous school, I must continue to serve the vast variety of our students, to learn about their cultures, and welcome them into ours.

As a 21st-century school librarian, I collaborate with teachers on projects, use a variety of technology tools, and direct patrons in using the online catalog and databases. I definitely teach students 21st-century literacy skills using the "Standards for the 21st-Century Learner" from the American Association of School Librarians. It's imperative that I do so because this "net" generation of digital natives may be adept at texting, but they are often unskilled in finding reliable and relevant information, or in using and synthesizing the information. It is my task to teach them how to move beyond copying, cutting, and pasting when completing a project. It is my job to help my fellow educators assign projects that lead to intelligent questioning and critical thinking. Additionally, I am compelled to teach ethical information usage to students and staff. I also attempt to get our students involved with Web 2.0 technologies. For example, some students have written book reviews and posted book trailers to our school library blog. In our library, we offer video conference activities that get our students excited when we connect with learners in other states and Canada.

My path to becoming a school librarian has been circuitous, but worth the effort. At the University of North Texas, I had a memorable library school education with an inspiring professor, Dr. Herman Totten, and visiting professor, the late Dr. Spencer Shaw. When I became a librarian in 1986, because of my science background, I had a choice between a medical library and a school library. I have always felt the tug toward the education field in general, and K–12 in particular. So I chose the school library and haven't looked back. I worked that first year as an elementary librarian on an emergency teaching permit, but after that I had to make a decision to work on my doctorate, which I earned in 1992.

My background as a librarian is rich and varied and includes two private schools, a community college, a private college, and an architectural firm library. I even had a short stint as a library director at a historically black college and university (HBCU). But in order to be a librarian in Texas public schools, one must have a teaching certificate and a school librarian certificate (neither of which I had). Even with two graduate degrees in library science and wonderful experience working in libraries, I did not have the additional knowledge base that excellent educators have. In 2002, I returned to school and completed an alternative teacher education program. For a while I had to leave my "first love" career (librarianship) to become a full-time classroom teacher. I worked for five years as a career and technology teacher in a suburban district, teaching journalism (broadcast, yearbook, and newspaper) and pre-engineering courses. It was challenging, but certainly worthwhile, and I loved teaching in the classroom, closely interacting with the students.

The detour into classroom teaching was definitely not a waste. Not only did I develop a thick skin in relating to students, but I also gained practical experience in planning lessons, in using Howard Gardner's multiple intelligences, implementing Harry Wong's first days of school, Benjamin Bloom's taxonomy, and Grant Wiggins' understanding by design, and other researched-based effective educational practices that lead to improved student achievement. I learned about differentiation, special education, gifted education, and the Coalition of Essential Schools 10 common principles. I learned from Ruby Payne's *A Framework for Understanding Poverty*. Essentially, I learned how to be a better educator. Even students in the college courses that I teach as an adjunct benefit, because I know pedagogy. I understand how learners learn, and I know how to be an effective teacher.

Positive change agents in education come in many forms. That the United States' K–12 public educational system is in need of drastic reform is a debatable point because there are pockets of excellence out there. But anyone who has visited certain public schools in large urban areas that are labeled "failure factories" knows that the outcome for youth entering those schools is many times bleak. I am definitely not "waiting for Superman," although the award-winning documentary and book by the same name are well worth the watching, reading, and debating. I am not even waiting for any large education reform to occur to fix the problems. Individually, I cannot fix the dropout rates, the familial or societal factors, or the overall low literacy rates. I cannot on a large scale fix low test scores, lack of college preparedness, and the hopelessness many of our youth feel. I have no extra money to throw at the educational system. I cannot guarantee that no child is left behind. I cannot make sure every student has a book in his or her hands. In other words, I cannot swallow the entire ocean, nor can I eat the whole elephant. It is simply too much for one person.

Yet on the other hand, I cannot quit either. I cannot throw in the towel and admit defeat, although some days are tough. Sometimes the students just get "out of hand." Sometimes complaining co-workers are too much to bear. But no matter what, I cannot simply collect my pay and think of what I do as "just a job." In my small corner of the educational universe, I can be a positive change agent. I can be that "each one, reach one" type of advocate-educator, who happens to be a school librarian. I've made that choice and I cannot allow the panic that librarians across the country are currently feeling (as librarian positions are being drastically cut) to consume my precious time that I should use with the students. Instead, I choose to be an advocate for school libraries and to keep doing my job well.

FURTHER READING

AASL Learning Standards. (2007). *Standards for the 21st-century learner*. Retrieved from www.ala.org/ala/mgrps/divs/aasl/guidelinesandstandards/learningstandards/AASL_Learning_Standards_2007.pdf

Anderson, L. W., Krathwohl, D. R., & Bloom, B. S. (2001). *A taxonomy for learning, teaching, and assessing: a revision of Bloom's taxonomy of educational objective*. Complete ed. New York: Longman.

Coalition of Essential Schools. (2011). The CES common principles. Retrieved from http://www.essentialschools.org/items/4

Gardner, H. (1993). *Multiple intelligences: the theory in practice*. New York: Basic Books.

Gibson, S. (2010). Critical readings: African American girls and urban fiction. *Journal of Adolescent and Adult Literacy, 53*, 565–574. Retrieved from http://connection.ebscohost.com/c/articles/48996465/critical-readings-african-american-girls-urban-fiction

Guggenheim, D., & Kimball, B. (2010). *Waiting for "Superman."* [Documentary]. Produced by Lesley Chilcott. Paramount Vantage, 2011. DVD.

Marshall, E., Staples, J., & Gibson, S. (2009). Ghetto fabulous: Reading black adolescent femininity in contemporary urban street fiction. *Journal of Adolescent and Adult Literacy, 53*, 28–36. Retrieved from http://connection.ebscohost.com/c/articles/44054567/ghetto-fabulous-reading-black-adolescent-femininity-contemporary-urban-street-fiction

Meloni, C. (2007). Attracting new readers with hip hop lit. *Library Media Connection, 25*, 38–40.

Pattee, A. (2008). Street fight. *School Library Journal, 54*, 26–30.

Payne, R. K. (2005). *A framework for understanding poverty*, 4th rev. ed. Highlands, Tex.: aha! Process.

Weber, K. (2010). *Waiting for "Superman": How we can save America's failing public schools*. New York: Public Affairs.

Welch, R. J. (2007). *The guy-friendly YA library: Serving male teens*. Westport, CT: Libraries Unlimited.

Wiggins, G. P., & McTighe, J. (2005). *Understanding by design*, expanded 2nd ed. Alexandria, VA: Association for Supervision and Curriculum Development.

Wong, H. K., & Wong, R. T. (2009). *The first days of school: How to be an effective teacher*, 4th ed. Mountain View, CA: Harry K. Wong Publications.

4

The "Qualified" Black Librarian

Barbara Lynn Johnson Montgomery

In 1990, I was commuting 30 miles round trip to work each day. Desiring to work closer to home, I applied for a position in a newly built elementary school in my neighborhood school district. I did not get the job, in what would be the same elementary school my children attended. They hired someone who had not completed her master of library and information science (MLIS) degree yet. A year later I became the secretary of the parent–teacher organization (PTO). One evening during a PTO executive board meeting another black parent on the board asked, "Why is there just one black teacher at this school?" The principal answered, "I cannot find any qualified blacks," the standard response, I believe, all principals were told to give. My husband was on a district committee where this same question was asked about other schools in the district. The superintendent gave the same response, but my husband countered by saying, "You have not met my wife." A week later I was asked to interview for the media specialist position at my children's school because the media specialist was leaving. I was offered the job, which was five minutes away from home, so I could not turn it down. I would be leaving a school where I had a partially flexible schedule, teachers who believed in using the media center and the media specialist, and a principal who believed in libraries, reading, and me.

On the last teacher's workday, at my new school, I was sitting at my desk preparing for my first full day with students. I heard the media center door open and looked up to see two very official looking gentlemen, with my principal, standing in my office doorway. It seems the superintendent and the assistant superintendent had come to personally meet this phenomenal librarian. I had no idea what I was in for; but I quickly learned that men in power prefer that hiring decisions not be taken out of their hands. They also have subtle ways of making people pay for the choices they make.

I was a firm believer in giving full service. I prepared all kinds of material to give to my teachers about my services and my goals for the media center. I placed materials in each teacher's box at the beginning of the day. By the end of the day, most of the materials were either in the trash or placed back in my box. Since this school had a fixed schedule, I asked for the teachers' lesson plans so I could address their needs when classes came to the media center. The assistant principal said she would get them for me. I am still waiting. Even though these things happened, they were not the worst. The worst thing that first year was a visit, on my first day, from my daughter's second-grade teacher. She walked in smiling telling me how happy she was that I was here. I don't know how but we began talking about dogs. I told her my girls wanted a dog. She begged me to come see her dog, because they were thinking about giving it away. I told her no thank you, but she insisted, so I relented and said I would. At that moment she looked at me with a straight face and said, "Oh never mind, I forgot my dog does not like black children." She then turned and walked away. I was so shocked I did not know what to say. My daughter tried all year to tell me that teacher did not like her. Being a good mother and knowing my child was not perfect, I tried to work with the teacher. This is an aside to this story; but that same teacher was handcuffed and escorted out of school by police because she taped an African American boy to his seat.

I believe in making the best of any situation, so I worked hard and planned wonderful activities for the students at my school. I had a bank of 20 computers in the media center that I used heavily for student research. When the teachers noticed that the students looked forward to coming to the media center, they began looking at what could change. So the computers were taken out of the media center and placed in a computer lab to give the teachers another period on their planning rotation. This was not a problem; I developed other centers, created interesting lessons, and also brought in my personal home computer. An annual library sleepover at school for 90 children was the highlight of every year. Book fair profits funded author and storyteller visits. There were some wonderful teachers who supported my efforts, but most of them thought I was, as one teacher said, a "bitch." This teacher in particular told me I didn't do anything but make demands on them and their students. I was shocked because I did not know people felt that way. I simply asked her to share with her students a book by a soon-to-be-visiting author. This was a public verbal attack heard by many other teachers. The principal never approached me to address this teacher's tirade or ask me about the incident. She just never addressed it. I did call that teacher after school to ask her if there was anything I could do to help her. She told me there was *nothing* I could do for her. Unleashing that same sharp tongue on the principal was cause for her to terminate her teaching career at the end of that school year.

I tried very hard to grow professionally and became a member of the educational team of this school. I earned 30 hours beyond my master's degree to become a National Board certified teacher. I earned this honor in 2002, the first year it was offered for media specialists. These attempts at improvement were to no avail because my position, at this school, was looked upon as a planning period for classroom teachers. This was the feeling of the administration as well as the teachers.

I seldom ate in the teacher's lounge. Teachers had duty-free lunch, but I chose not to listen to them pick students apart. In the media center, I overheard a first-grade teacher talking about a home visit before a faculty meeting. She described this visit to a black child's home and complained about how nasty it was, and how she did not want to sit down there. It hurt me so badly to hear them say what they were saying that I looked at them and suggested, "There but by the grace of God go you or me." I became an advocate for children, especially black children. On picture day, I noticed teachers not wanting to touch up the black children's hair, so I took this to be my responsibility. The first-grade teachers began to realize that any black children who came to school with uncombed hair or not looking their best could come to me and I would comb their hair, wash their face, and tidy them up as best I could. These small gestures made all the difference in determining if a child had a good day or a bad day. Small acts of compassion keep some children out of trouble, at least for one day.

I want to leave you with a final story about this school. Three black teachers were sent to a Ruby Payne workshop. When they presented to the faculty they asked us what was the first thing we thought of when we heard the words "black male." A white teacher whispered in my ear "big penises." (She used the slang term.) Again, just like after the dog conversation (described above), I was at a loss for words. Another example of racial insensitivity was when a white teacher told the principal she would teach black history when we started teaching white history!

I feel that all these incidents are examples of how whites demonstrate their privilege. As a qualified black librarian in this particular school, and because of the attitude of the administration and the majority of the teachers, the students did not always benefit from the expertise of this qualified black librarian. I finally had to realize I would never be a catalyst for change in this school. Presently there are only seven black teachers in a faculty of 63 teachers, and the black and Hispanic student population continues to grow. I continue to remind myself that if everything in life were easy, we would never witness the great strength we possess.

Today I am a Ph.D. candidate at the University of South Carolina School of Library and Information Science. My research agenda examines the impact of the lack of library service upon the literacy of the generation of African Americans before *Brown v. the Board of Education* Supreme Court decision.

5

The Black School Library Media Specialist as Cultural Intermediary

Ayodele Ojumu

Cross (1989) defined "cultural competence as a set of congruent behaviors, attitudes, policies that come together in a system, agency, or among professionals and enable that system, agency, or those professionals to work effectively in cross-cultural situations" (p. 28). Although this definition was written to improve the quality of health care that children of color receive, it is also applicable to K–12, urban education. The student population in urban schools is becoming more heterogeneous, while the teaching force remains very uniform. A "cultural mismatch" currently exists between students and teachers, which is reflected in the nationwide, low performance of students (Garrett, 2009). Teachers of color, who possess firsthand knowledge with culturally responsive pedagogy, are critical to turning this epidemic around. Black library media specialists can be particularly efficacious in this mission.

We hold a unique position in schools. We are the "conveyers of information" as well as the "facilitator of relationships as well as partnerships" (Press & Diggs-Hobson, 2005). Our professional ethic is based on sensitivity, honor, and respect. We are unbiased due to our service to all members of the school community. We are interested in the human side of education by remaining cognizant of the patterns and nuances of behavior. We use these skills to serve as an intermediary for students.

Most black library media specialists are products of public, urban education. This enables us to truly identify with our students. When we see them, we see ourselves. We are able to relate to the "code switching," as I like to call it, that students must perform to ensure success in the school environment. We have learned to conduct ourselves with a level of comfort in spite of the differences that exist between ourselves and the status quo. Students come to know that we share the same plight they do: persevere and accomplish goals by any means necessary. We encourage them via verbal and nonverbal interaction. We translate instructional requirements and expectations in terms students can relate to. Culture, in this sense, becomes the link that bonds us to students. This makes our relationships with students much more personal. One of the most valuable strengths that black school library media specialists possess is a oneness with all students of color. Through pride in our own heritage, we value the heritage of others.

As the student populations in urban settings become progressively more international and multilingual, so too does the urgency for educators with culturally responsive pedagogical practices. The ability to understand the multitude of cultures that students bring to school is vital for guaranteeing student academic success. Black library media specialists can be instrumental in reaching students of color in addition to closing the achievement gap.

REFERENCES

Cross, T. (1989). *Towards a culturally competent system of care: A monograph on effective services for minority children who are severely emotionally disturbed.* Washington, DC: Georgetown University Child Development Center, 1989. ERIC Document Reproduction Service No. ED330171.

Garrett, T. (2009). A teacher educator's journey: Reflections on the challenges of teaching culturally relevant classroom management. *Teaching and Learning*, *23*, 111–120.

Press, N., & Diggs-Hobson, M. (2005). Providing health information to community members where they are: Characteristics of the culturally competent librarian. *Library Trends*, *53*(3), 397–410.

6

Swimming Against the Tide: Library/ Media Centers in Urban Schools

Karen Lemmons and Andre Taylor

The school library media specialist (SLMS) who works in an urban school district faces several challenges. More often than not, the urban school district in which he or she works has a budget deficit, low state test scores, low graduation rates, old school buildings, limited resources, and other challenges. Funding in urban schools impacts the ability of a school librarian to start and sustain a library. Money is allocated based on the student population, programs in the school, and other criteria.

At the school level, the principal determines where and how the funds from the district will be used. This funding is not usually allocated for the library. State assessment scores indicate that students in urban schools score lower than students in other school districts. Some urban high schools have graduation rates below 50%. Most school buildings in urban school districts are at least 20 years old or older. Declining enrollment often results in reduced state and federal funding. This means fewer programs and a reduction in resources and services. Crime, poverty, and high unemployment in cities impact schools, too. As a result, the SLMS often faces the possibility of the district or principal closing his or her library program, losing his or her job, or being reassigned to the classroom.

In spite of these challenges, the SLMS is in an exciting position to help raise state test scores and improve student achievement. In order to achieve these goals, the SLMS must be proactive by staying abreast of information, cultivating relationships, utilizing print and electronic resources, and integrating technology.

The SLMS knows the research that cites the importance of certified SLMSs and effective school library programs. *School Libraries Work*, a research foundation paper, was published by Scholastic Research and Results and was first released in 2004. This foundation paper brought findings from a variety of organizations and from nearly two decades of empirical studies and cites the measurable impact school libraries and library media specialists have on student achievement (Scholastic Research and Results, 2008). The American Association of School Librarians (AASL) conducts an annual survey of school libraries to advocate the importance of school librarians and effective school library programs on student achievement.

The SLMS can participate in the survey, access the results of the survey, and share the information to advocate for his or her library school program. Furthermore, the SLMS can collect evidence for his or her program by documenting how he or she impacts student achievement and supports the school's curriculum. The SLMS can collect the evidence and maintain the information in a binder, or he or she can create an electronic portfolio. During the annual evaluations, the SLMS will have evidence to support the need for keeping the library program in the school's budget.

The SLMS knows the state curriculum standards, the information literacy standards (AASL, 2007), and the technology standards (ISTE, 2007) and integrates these standards when teaching students and collaborating with teachers. The Common Core Standards, an initiative that establishes national standards in mathematics and English language arts, have been adopted by over 50% of the states and is another resource that the SLMS should be familiar with.

School data provide information the SLMS needs to help him or her improve student achievement. Knowing the school assessment data, the school improvement plan, and any content area action plans that have been developed targets specific skills and content areas in which students need improvement. In addition, the SLMS can provide print and electronic resources that can help strengthen students' academic skills.

Becoming a team member in the school is essential in cultivating relationships. The SLMS should volunteer to serve on the school improvement team, on any core content area committee, or on other school committees. Working with the school's parent organization can provide the support the SLMS may need for his or her library program. In addition, forming partnerships with the local public library and other institutions can expand resources and services to students.

Furthermore, the SLMS can cultivate relationships with other teachers by talking with and listening to teachers. The SLMS can have formal and informal conversations with the teachers to learn what lessons, concepts, and projects they are teaching in the classrooms. The SLMS can volunteer to collaborate or coordinate with the teacher by providing additional resources and support. Sometimes this collaboration can be challenging because of scheduling conflicts. In some urban schools, the elementary SLMS does not have time to meet formally with teachers. The elementary SLMS can either supplement the lessons, concepts, or projects when the students are in the library, or the SLMS and teacher can arrange to team teach if the schedule permits. In urban high schools, some teachers will ask the SLMS to help them with a project or unit of study. Other times, the SLMS should volunteer to assist the classroom teacher with resources, technology tools, or other support.

Equally important is joining the local and national school library associations. Becoming a member of these organizations, the SLMS will form new relationships and expand his or her network and learn more information and about resources to use and share with students and staff. Attending the local and national conferences also provides opportunities for the SLMS to cultivate relationships and broaden his or her information base. Last, but not least, the SLMS must become an activist for his or her program. He or she needs to know his or her local and national representatives and senators to contact them on educational issues that will impact his or her school. Advocate, advocate, advocate! The SLMS should encourage other stakeholders, students, parents, and teachers to advocate for the school library program, too.

The AASL document *Empowering Learners Guidelines for School Library Media Programs* (AASL, 2009) describes four roles of SLMS: instructional partner, information specialist, teacher, and program administrator. As an instructional partner, the SLMS collaborates with classroom teachers to develop assignments that are matched to academic standards, including critical thinking skills, technology and information literacy skills, and core social skills and cultural competencies. In the information specialist role, the SLMS uses technology tools to supplement school resources, assists in the creation of engaging learning tasks, connects the school with the global learning community, and communicates with students and classroom teachers. The SLMS introduces and models emerging technologies as well as strategies for finding, assessing, and using information. As a teacher, the SLMS empowers students to be critical thinkers, enthusiastic readers, skillful researchers, ethical users of information, and digital citizens. The SLMS as program administrator ensures that all members of the learning community have access to resources that meet a variety of needs and interests.

Stephen Krashen (2004), professor emeritus at the University of Southern California, educator, linguist, and activist, stresses the need for schools in high poverty areas to have access to a school library with good books and a certified library media specialist to run the library. The SLMS can work actively to form partnerships with stakeholders and other organizations to get the resources students need to be lovers of reading and lifelong learners.

The SLMS must use all the skills and knowledge mentioned above to survive and thrive in an urban school library media center. In addition, the SLMS must have other skills. For example, the SLMS must be flexible to handle the many changes in administration, policies, and procedures. With a limited or no budget, the SLMS must be creative and resourceful in seeking funds for print and electronic resources to meet students' recreational reading and information needs, as well as curriculum and instructional needs. If the library media center needs additional desktop computers and laptops, the SLMS can apply for and write grants to address these needs. By taking advantage of the many free Web

2.0 tools, like blogs, wikis, free audio, video, and creative web-based tools, the SLMS can help students achieve academically while at the same time teach new technology skills.

Last, but not least, the SLMS must be a person who loves children and young adults and loves working with them. Students are a challenge and, as someone has stated, they are "wired differently." However, students are human and sometimes they have other concerns that can impact their learning. Sometimes students need an adult who will listen, give them a hug, or value them as human beings. The SLMS, with all his or her skills, talents, and resources, can be the very adult who addresses the needs of the whole child.

REFERENCES

American Association of School Librarians. (2007). Standards for the 21st century learner. Retrieved from http://www.aasl.org/ala/mgrps/divs/aasl/guidelinesandstandards/learningstandards/standards.cfm

American Association of School Librarians. (2009). *Empowering Learners: Guidelines for School Library Media Programs*. Chicago: American Library Association.

International Society for Technology in Education. (2007). Digital-age learning NETS for students. Retrieved from http://www.iste.org/standards/nets-for-students.aspx

Krashen, S. D. (2004). *The Power of Reading Insights from the Research Second Edition*. Westport, CT: Libraries Unlimited.

Scholastic Research and Results. (2008). *School libraries work*, 3rd ed. Retrieved from http://www2.scholastic.com/content/collateral_resources/pdf/s/slw3_2008.pdf

7

❖ ❖

Winning the Future with 21st-Century School Libraries

Gloria J. Reaves

President Barack Obama in the January 2011 State of the Union Address spoke often and adamantly about innovation and education. In one instance, he said: "Maintaining our leadership in research and technology is crucial to America's success; but if we want to win the future, if we want innovation to produce jobs in America and not overseas, then we also have to win the race to educate our kids" (Obama, 2011).

In this second decade of the 21st century, there continues to be an urgency to upgrade U.S. education and career pathways so that students can compete in the developing global economy. In K–12 schools, the buzz about infusing 21st-century skills into the curriculum is getting louder in some instances but remains amazingly faint in others. One of the greatest challenges of black librarians in the 21st century is raising the volume of the buzz, then getting the right people to hear it, understand it, and appropriately act on it. Historically, the fate of school libraries has followed a pattern of thriving in affluent communities where people of influence deftly advocate for their children. They have waned in communities where people have been marginalized by societal ills, where food and shelter are of the utmost priority. Today, this pattern continues. The black librarian, now more than ever, must use intellect and knowledge along with the skills and resources of the profession to help schools educate children for the 21st century.

In the introductory chapter of the *World Is Flat*, Thomas Friedman (2005) relays his discovery of the leveling global playing field and its threat to U.S. competitiveness in the business and job markets. *Time* magazine in 2006 ran a series of articles calling for the United States to replace the outdated agrarian model of education with one more conducive to meeting the demands of the 21st century (Wallis, 2006). The Partnership for 21st Century Skills has developed an educational framework they feel will help students successfully navigate the future. Within the framework are categories of skills that entail Learning and Innovation, Digital literacy, and Life and Career (Trilling & Fadel, 2009). School libraries and school librarians can support this 21st-century education initiative by helping students develop digital literacy skills, which include information literacy, media literacy, and ICT (information, communications, and technology) literacy.

Information literacy, in brief, is the ability to recognize an information need, the ability to locate and evaluate the needed information, and the ability to effectively use the acquired information. In the 21st century, the school librarian is a professional educator with multifaceted and continuously evolving roles that stimulate creativity and innovation in learners. The school library is a learning environment that provides the guidance of such skilled personnel, as well as access to books and a variety of print, digital, and online resources. Librarians not only work with students in the physical space of the library, but also in classrooms and other educational spaces. They collaborate with teachers, varied school personnel, and parents on the best ways to help students with class and homework assignments or research projects, select materials for reading enjoyment, and find appropriate answers to personal questions. These activities model teamwork and communication, which are important 21st-century workplace skills.

School librarians guide teachers and students through the process of making sense of vast amounts of information floating around out there, including how to evaluate Googled websites for accuracy and reliability. Librarians, often with the input of students and the school community, develop websites that provide access to informational resources 24/7. They enable teachers and students to locate, understand, organize, and use information to solve problems and produce useful knowledge.

In a December 10, 2006, *Time* magazine article titled "How to Bring Our Schools Out of the 20th Century," Claudia Wallis makes a point that, in my opinion, undergirds the importance of media literacy education. She also quotes a Dell executive, Karen Bruett:

> Becoming smarter about new sources of information in an age of overflowing information and proliferating media, kids need to rapidly process what's coming at them and distinguish between what's reliable and what isn't. "It's important that students know how to manage it, interpret it, validate it, and how to act on it," says Bruett.

In July 2010, a conservative blogger posted a video of excerpts from a speech made by Shirley Sherrod of the U.S. Department of Agriculture, which made her remarks seem racist. As a result, she was denounced by the public and fired from her job. Later, the speech was viewed in its entirety and proved not to be racist at all; she had actually done a good and heroic deed, which was not revealed in the excerpts. According to the Center for Media Literacy, "media literacy is characterized by the principle of inquiry—that is, learning to ask important questions about whatever you see, watch or read" (Thoman & Jolls, 2004). As global citizens, we are to use information ethically and be able to identify when that does not happen. The American Association of School Librarians (2007) standards for the 21st century state:

> Ethical behavior in the use of information must be taught. In this increasingly global world of information, students must be taught to seek diverse perspectives, gather and use information ethically, and use social tools responsibly and safely. (p. 2)

Critical to the process of preparing students for 21st-century productivity is district and local school administrators' understanding of the connection between skills learners need and how they acquire them for success academically, in careers, and in life. As a school librarian and educator in an urban school system for nearly two decades, I have often witnessed libraries being closed and certified librarians being eliminated in schools in poorer sections of the city, where they are most needed. It is a continuous cycle of setbacks for students who are struggling to catch up academically and reach a level that will enable them to be productive citizens in a global community. This inequity in education has the potential to adversely impact all of us.

Although the following quote from the previously referenced *Time* magazine article was made in a different context, it conveys my sentiments of what can happen when children do not receive an adequate education:

> This is a story about the big public conversation the nation is not having about education, the one that will ultimately determine not merely whether some fraction of our children get "left behind" but also whether an entire generation of kids will fail to make the grade in the global economy because they can't think their way through abstract problems, work in teams, distinguish good information from bad or speak a language other than English. (Wallis, 2006)

School libraries are also about helping students develop basic literacy skills. U.S. students are challenged to become innovative and globally competitive; yet a large percentage of students do not read well. A local District of Columbia newspaper recently reported a correlation between high illiteracy rates and high unemployment rates in the nation's capital (Rowley, 2011). Many citizens, parents, educators, and lawmakers do not fully understand the importance of school libraries in enabling children to become good readers, which is a necessary foundation for lifelong learning. In conveying results of research addressing the issue of libraries and literacy, the Center for International Scholarship in School Libraries (CISSL, n.d.) at Rutgers University stated: "These researchers conclude that well stocked libraries, managed by a qualified school librarian, who actively promotes literacy and coordinates resources, provide the essential infrastructure for developing literacy" (p. 5).

The school librarian is the logical choice for leading the charge to infuse 21st-century digital literacy skills into the curriculum and for guiding the school community in the team-building and collaborative work it takes to realize results. When students are good readers who are empowered with information and media literacy skills, they also acquire ICT literacy, defined as "using digital technology, communications tools, and/or networks to access, manage, integrate, evaluate, and create information in order to function in a knowledge society" (ICT Literacy Panel, n.d.). All stakeholders benefit when the school educational leader works with the librarian and the school community to design a program that enables learners to navigate vast amounts of information and convert it to useful knowledge. This type of informed, visionary, and collaborative leadership is important in developing quality schools capable of educating present and future generations. Harold Howe, former U.S. Commissioner of Education, said it best when he said "What a school thinks about its library is a measure of what it thinks about education" (Credaro, 2007). I wholeheartedly agree, yet not only a school but also a school system and ultimately a nation.

> CISSL takes the position that schools without school libraries cannot educate this generation in a way that prepares them for 21st-century study and work, and being part of the increasingly digital, global society. Cutting school libraries is not the solution: School libraries, now more than ever, are integral to quality learning and teaching in 21st century schools. (CISSL, p. 6)

If the United States is to "win the future," schools must maintain 21st-century, multidimensional libraries that engage, enlighten, and empower learners. The time is now!

REFERENCES

American Association of School Librarians (2007). *Standards for the 21st century learner*. Chicago: American Library Association. Retrieved from http://www.ala.org/aasl/sites/ala.org.aasl/files/content/guidelinesandstandards/learningstandards/AASL_Learning_Standards_2007.pdf

Center for International Scholarship in School Libraries (CISSL). (n.d.). *School libraries, now more than ever: A position paper*. New Brunswick, N. J.: Rutgers University. Retrieved from http://cissl.rutgers.edu/CISSL_POSITION_PAPER_revised.doc

Credaro, A. B. (2007). Now we've got the Internet, why do we still need school libraries? Retrieved from http://warriorlibrarian.com/CURRICULUM/libcomp.html

Friedman, T. (2005). *The world is flat: A brief history of the twenty-first century*. New York: Picador.

ICT Literacy Panel (n.d.). Definition of ICT literacy. Digital transformation, a framework for ICT literacy. Educational Testing Service. Retrieved from http://www.ets.org/Media/Tests/Information_and_Communication_Technology_Literacy/ictreport.pdf

Obama, B. (2011). Remarks by the president in state of union address. Washington, DC: Congressional Record: January 25, 2011 (House), pp. H457–H462]. Retrieved from http://www.gpo.gov/fdsys/pkg/CREC-2011-01-25/pdf/CREC-2011-01-25-pt1-PgH457-6.pdf

Rowley, D. (2011). RIF elimination equates to higher illiteracy in D.C. *Washington Informer* (March 10–16). Retrieved from http://www.washingtoninformer.com/pdfs/11-03-10/index.html#

Thoman, E., & Jolls, T. (2004). Media literacy: A national priority for a changing world. Center For Media Literacy. Retrieved from http://www.medialit.org/reading-room/media-literacy-national-priority-changing-world

Trilling, B., & Fadel, C. (2009). *21st century skills: Learning for life in our times*. San Francisco: Jossey-Bass.

Wallis, C. (2006). How to bring our schools out of the 20th century. *Time* (December 10). Retrieved from http://www.time.com/time/magazine/article/0,9171,1568480,00.html

8

Meeting the Needs of African American Students in the School Library Media Program

Pauletta Brown Bracy

Irrefutably, the school library media program (SLMP) is an integral part of the K–12 educational enterprise. A second, lesser known fact is that the school library media specialist (SLMS) is a teacher. These two premises are requisite for this discussion about the exigent role of the SLMP in the education of African American children. Teaching is both intrinsic and fundamental to the profession of school librarianship. As stated in the "Mission and Goals" statement of the American Association of School Librarians (AASL, n.d.), SLMSs are expected to participate as active partners in the teaching and learning process. Today, the education landscape is challenged by greater demands of accountability and the realities of changing demographics. In this high-stakes environment of testing and accountability for student learning at all levels, scores have become the bases for monitoring school progress and making major decisions about school funding. The emphasis on quantitative school performance eclipses concern for the student who through testing carries a burdensome responsibility for the outcomes. In too many classrooms, testing and test preparation have replaced teaching and learning (Banks & Banks, 2007). In spite of objections to this kind of assessment, it remains the celebrated manifesto of the standards movement. Nonetheless, in any school setting, faculty, staff, and administration all share responsibility in this accountability milieu. As for all educators, SLMSs must be willing to both adapt familiar teaching practices and seek innovative methods to accommodate *all* learners.

In exploring the specific role of the SLMS in *best* accommodating the needs of African American learners and creating environments conducive to student success, some important viewpoints on pedagogy and selected research about teaching African American students are summarized to enlighten SLMSs and others about their consequential roles in ensuring success for all students.

PEDAGOGY

Grounded in pedagogy and imbued with a commitment to children's learning, teachers and SLMSs conceivably should embrace the professional disposition that *all students can learn*. General consensus affirms the resolute variable of culture in the education of African American students. Delpit (1995) asserted that any discussion about education and culture should acknowledge the individual child and his or her learning needs in the most expedient means. The danger of ignoring this variable is inevitable conflict between home culture and school culture, which could lead to misaligned teaching and learning styles at odds with community norms.

Ladson-Billings (1994) studied effective teaching for African American students and how the teaching fostered academic success and maintained positive identity. She defined culturally relevant teaching (CRT) as a pedagogy that empowers students intellectually, socially, emotionally, and politically by using cultural referents to impart knowledge, skills, and attitudes in which teachers recognize the differences among children. In CRT, teachers see themselves as part of the community; believe all students can succeed; help students make connections between their community, national, and global identities; structure social relations in the classroom and extend them into the community through fluid teacher–student relationships; and encourage a "community of learners" approach in which students learn collaboratively, teaching one another. Gay (2010) asserted that culturally responsive teaching is validating and affirming because it teaches *to* and *through* the strength of students. In addition, it acknowledges the legitimacy of the cultural heritages of different ethnic groups as worthy content of formal curricula; builds bridges of meaningfulness between home and school experiences; uses a variety of instructional strategies that are connected to different learning styles; and incorporates multicultural information, resources, and materials in all the subjects and skills taught in the schools.

In issues of equity in assessment involving diverse students, Irvine (2003) offered three principles that illuminate the influence of culture in learning:

1. The management of knowledge from acquisition to communication through verbal and nonverbal language is influenced by culture;
2. Culture is critical in both learning and teaching; and
3. Assessment of knowledge is also related to culture as culturally responsive teachers reject the efficacy of standardized testing, asserting that it lacks relevance to the everyday lives of African American students.

Arguing for an educational system that is sensitive to black culture, Hale (1986) proposed a model early childhood curriculum for young black children in which the teacher is someone who shares, understands, and participates in black culture. Her strategies for teachers include attention to body language, as black children are proficient in nonverbal communication; modeling standard English; equal talking time in which teacher talk is approximately comparable to child talk; group learning through hands-on contact with the teacher and in small group learning with peers; a variety of learning activities, including movement, games, prose, and poetry; and music in the classroom and permeating the curriculum.

SELECTED RESEARCH

A prolific researcher on cultural themes in the schooling of African American children, Boykin (1983) offered an "Afro-graphic" approach, a distinct cultural ethos based in part on West African philosophy articulated by Nobles (1972). The black cultural ethos (BCE), which characterizes how African Americans perceive, interpret, and interact with the world, is comprised of nine dimensions: spirituality, harmony, movement, verve, affect, communalism, expressive individualism, orality, and social perspective of time.

Boykin, Lilja, and Tyler (2004) conducted extensive research on the theme of ethos. Throughout some studies, elements of the "mainstream" Euro-American ethos culture (including individualism and competition) are compared to those of the BCE. Five investigations on teachers' practices and perceptions, classroom dynamics, learning strategies, home values, and student preferences speak compellingly about the vital role of culture in education. These findings are summarized below.

Among white teachers, competitive and individualistic students were viewed as significantly more motivated and achievement-oriented than those who displayed communal and vervistic behaviors (Tyler, Boykin, & Walton, 2006).

Many teachers expose students to learning activities and behaviors that reinforce mainstream cultural values, although research has shown student preference to the contrary (Boykin, Tyler, & Miller, 2005).

Students in the communal learning context significantly outperformed students in the individual learning context in assessments that measured immediate and long-term retention of information (Boykin, Lilja, & Tyler, 2004).

Students and parents held the greatest learning and working preferences for communal and vervistic behaviors over individualistic and competitive behaviors. In contrast, teachers had higher preferences for individualistic and competitive learning behaviors in the classroom (Tyler, Boykin, Miller, & Hurley, 2006).

Cooperative learning versus competitive and individualistic classroom learning was most endorsed by all students; however, African Americans reported stronger preferences. White students held stronger preferences for both the competitive and individualistic learning situations (Ellison, Boykin, Tyler, & Dillhunt, 2005).

Within the aforementioned attributes and research findings, implications are clear for SLMSs. As collaborators, SLMSs work with teachers in delivering instruction and also assume teaching roles in information literacy instruction and use of technology. In working with African American students, SLMSs must be *pedagogically dispositioned.* This concept explicates six requisite behaviors for effective teaching. They must:

- Adopt the precept that all students can learn.
- Embrace the notion that culture is a means to successful teaching.
- Infuse home and community in teaching and learning.
- Cultivate a caring teacher–student relationship.
- Affirm challenging expectations that lead to success.
- Respect the individual differences of students and teach to them.

Equipped with culturally relevant dispositions and behaviors, SLMSs are poised to engage African American students in meaningful learning experiences that lead to academic success.

REFERENCES

American Association of School Librarians (n.d.). Mission and goals statement. Retrieved from http://www.ala.org/ala/mgrps/divs/aasl/aboutaasl/missionandgoals/aaslmissiongoals.cfm

Banks, J., & Banks, C. M. (Eds.) (2007). *Multicultural education: Issues and perspectives*, 6th ed. San Francisco: Jossey-Bass.

Boykin, A. W. (1983). The academic performance of Afro-American children. In J. T. Spence (Ed.), *Achievement and achievement motives: Psychological and sociological approaches*. (pp. 324–371). New York: Freeman.

Boykin, A. W., Lilja, A. J., & Tyler, K. M. (2004). The influence of communal vs. individual learning context on the academic performance in social studies of grade 4–5 African-Americans. *Learning Environments Research, 7*, 227–244.

Boykin, A. W., Tyler, K., & Miller, O. (2005). In search of cultural themes and their expressions in the dynamics of classroom life. *Urban Education, 40*, 521–549.

Delpit, L. (1995). *Other people's children: Cultural conflict in the classroom*. New York: New Press.

Ellison, C. M., Boykin, A.W., Tyler, K. M., & Dillhunt, M. L. (2005). Examining classroom learning preferences among elementary school students. *Social Behavior and Personality, 33*, 699–708.

Gay, G. (2010). *Culturally responsive teaching: Theory, research, and practice*. New York: Teachers College Press.

Hale, J. E. (1986). *Black children: Their roots, culture and learning styles*. Baltimore: Johns Hopkins University Press.

Irvine, J. J. (2003). *Educating teachers for diversity: Seeing with a cultural eye*. New York: Teachers College Press.

Ladsons-Billings, G. (1994). *The dream keepers: Successful teachers of African American children*. San Francisco: Jossey-Bass.

Nobles, W. W. (1972). African philosophy: Foundations for black psychology. In R. L. Jones (Ed.). *Black psychology* (2nd ed., pp. 18–32). New York: Harper and Row.

Tyler, K. M., Boykin, A. W., Miller, O., & Hurley, E. (2006). Cultural values in the home experiences of low-income African-American. *Social Psychology of Education, 9*, 363–380.

Tyler, K. M., Boykin, A. W., & Walton, T. R. (2006). Cultural considerations in teachers' perceptions of student classroom behavior and achievement. *Teaching and Teacher Education, 22*, 998–1005.

Part II

FROM THE PUBLIC LIBRARY

9

What Does Black Librarianship Look Like in the Proverbial Information Age?

Linda Bannerman-Martin and Sandra Michele Echols

Public libraries today play an integral part in the community and in the exchange of information and knowledge. The role of the public library continues to evolve to meet the informational and social needs of its customers. The work of black librarians, especially in urban communities, is increasingly varied as it expands to keep up with electronic government information disseminated through the World Wide Web, especially in response to the Electronic Government Act enacted in 2002.

Today's public libraries are changing as a result of the era of new technology and knowledge, combined with the legislation enacted in 2002, resulting in the public library as a community information center. In addition, tough economic times today have proven pivotal. As evident in the days of Vivian Harsh's work (Burt, 2009), the role of black librarians has always encompassed the traditional roles of all librarians: collection development, acquisitions, cataloguing and classification, circulation, reference work, preservation, and conservation. However, throughout history, black librarians have maintained close cultural ties to their community, protected historically cultural information from loss and damage, and hence, have added the newly coined term "culture keeper" to the responsibilities of black librarianship. As culture keepers, they remain true and steadfast to the commitment to serve their communities and also advocate for equal access. With the equal right to use comes protection and preservation of information and knowledge to be shared with their communities.

The E-Government Act of 2002 (PL 107-347) was established in an effort to "promote use of the Internet and other information technologies to provide increased opportunities for citizen participation in Government" (American Library Association, 2011). Increasingly, libraries are well positioned to partner with government entities to meet constituents online, where they can voice their opinions, influence decisions, democratize information, and transform citizens from passive observers to active participants in a more inclusive conversation. As a vehicle for citizen engagement, libraries help build trust and maximize transparency of government while expanding their civic agency role in local communities. Basically, e-government endeavors to provide customers with access to government services 24 hours a day; seven days a week.

How will this act affect the role of the black librarian in public librarianship? Black librarians in the proverbial information age are agents of change who provide customers with several types of materials from the libraries' vast collections and are also positioned to provide assistance with electronic government sites, which borrows from the role of a social worker during the industrial age. During this era black librarians provided not only books, but also community information to spur racial justice and competition, assisting with literacy, employment, education, skill building, and entitlements. Prejudices still exist and, combined with today's tough economy and high unemployment rate caused by the stock market crash in 2008, many black public librarians are finding themselves "counseling" customers concerning their daily living, financial, and social needs and acting as de facto social workers. Gone are the days of merely providing information solely based on a reference question, research topic, or location of a book. Questions customers have may involve accessing information related to social services. Access is simplified as a result of the E-Government Act of 2002, allowing entry to government sites that are directly related to social services. For example, information concerning the application process for the Supplemental Nutrition Assistance Program (SNAP), formerly known as the Food Stamps program, is available not only through the U.S. Department of Agriculture website, but also through local and state government websites. Recent studies have shown that Internet use has increased tremendously not only to search the web or retrieve e-mail, but also to tap into other resources (seeking employment) and the use of government sources with guided assistance from librarians, as indicated in the numerous studies conduct by the Pew Research Center's Internet and American Life Project.

As noted by E. J. Josey:

> The information industry has the technology to control information, but its price tag on information distribution and its profit goal create a bias in what information is made available and how it is dispensed. Only the nonprofit organization, the library, dedicated to a total community service goal with trained experts, librarians, running the operation can provide the full scope of information for the total population in a fair and objective manner. (cited in Berry & Oder, 2009, p. 23)

Reliability must be an integral role for the 21st-century black public librarian. Skills from the past must be combined with the present to assist customers with obtaining adequate information concerning an array of topics from obtaining basic education skills to job information and how to utilize the information available on the World Wide Web, coinciding with the traditional roles that all librarians provide in the form of collection development and acquisition, cataloguing, classification, reference work, and preservation, and especially with the newly recognized role as culture keepers (Berry & Oder, 2009, p. 2). As changes in technology become more prevalent and accessible, the innuendo, question, discussion, and controversy remain among librarians. Will the information age cause black librarianship in the 21st century to react and perform more in the role of a social worker? The answer is no. They have and will augment the field by enhancing the role of the librarian.

Despite its changing dynamic, especially the reduction of blacks entering the profession, the core aspects of black librarianship remain, which involve developing unique ways to make information available and useful. They still introduce and teach library patrons how to evaluate and use sources. The move from the industrial to the information age presents some challenges for black librarians. History has shown that the role of the black librarian has not only been to provide books to customers but also to outreach to the community in various ways. The commitment to improve library services through introduction of new ideas, programs, and services is not an unfamiliar task for the black librarian within the urban public library. They proactively provide materials in different media and promote, advertise, and support co-sponsorship, and afford the community the limitless potential the library has to enhance life. Outreach within black public librarianship is a role that was perfected by Vivian Harsh, a black librarian from Chicago's Bronzeville section. As noted by Laura Burt in the article titled "Vivian Harsh, Adult Education, and the Library's Role as Community Center":

> Vivian Harsh was a pivotal figure in both Chicago's Black community and the field of library science for her collection and outreach work. She was the first African American branch head in the Chicago Public Library. In her time as Hall library director from 1932 to 1958, not only did Harsh shepherd her branch through the Depression and World War II, but she also established the Hall Library as a vital community center. (Burt, 2009, p. 234)

In conclusion, past experiences, though harsh, and coupled with perseverance and commitment to the continuous struggle for equality, have brought the black librarian to the present age of information and technology stronger, with the advantage of being able to assist customers with prompt, reliable information and assistance. Their most important role, therefore, continues to be even more prevalent: to introduce, teach, train, and assist with maneuvering through the government information maze, as well as impart the critical value of e-government resources and the impact of possibilities access has on helping to improve customers' lives.

As Marcum (1996, p. 192) stated, "changes are taking place in the library world almost faster than anyone can measure and certainly faster than anyone can predict." Along with these changes, the use of electronic government sites is pivotal for the advancement of black librarianship and how this act affects customer service in the 21st century. The challenge for black librarians adopting e-government principles within the community library setting becomes being able to equip the customer with enough information to help prioritize social versus basic needs information and being ready and willing to enhance their bibliographic instruction skills by increasing their knowledge of and remaining updated with e-government resources. The E-Government Act of 2002 requires black librarians to be flexible, trustworthy, and reliable with the information they disseminate to their customers.

REFERENCES

American Library Association (2011). Legislation and Information Policy, 2002. Retrieved from http://www.ala.org/ala/issuesadvocacy/advleg/federallegislation/govinfo/egovernment/egovtoolkit/legislation/index.cfm

Berry, J., & Oder, N. (2009, July 6). E. J. Josey, legendary activist librarian and leader, dies at 85. *Library Journal.* Retrieved from http://www.libraryjournal.com/article/CA6669152.html

Biddle, S. F. (Ed.) (1993). Culture keepers: Enlightening and empowering our communities. Proceedings of First National Conference of American Librarians, September 4–6, Newark, NJ: Black Caucus of the American Library Association, ca. 1993.

Burt, L. (2009). Vivian Harsh, adult education, and the library's role as community center. *Libraries and Cultural Record, 44*, 234–255.

Marcum, D. B. (1996, Fall). Redefining community through the public library. *Daedalus, 125*, 191–205.

10

Servant Leadership and the Importance of African American Mentors

Rhea Brown Lawson

Leadership has many definitions. Within those varied definitions are similar terms such as organization, vision, influence, and servant. My own thoughts about leadership and my definition of a leader encompass those terms. Unlike leadership approaches that espouse a top-down hierarchical style, I advocate for and subscribe most closely to servant leadership. Developed by Robert K. Greenleaf in 1970, servant leadership is a leadership philosophy and practice that is still relevant today (Greenleaf, 2002). It emphasizes collaboration, trust, empathy, and the ethical use of power. In this approach to leadership, the leader is at heart a servant first and holds as his or her primary objective to enhance the growth of *individuals* in the organization. Servant leadership coalesces nicely with a lifelong philosophy that I have adopted from my favorite poet and author, Maya Angelou (Del Boccio, 2011, p. 1), "When you learn, teach, when you get, give." Throughout my career I have benefited greatly from professionals who generously shared their wisdom with me so I find it very rewarding to help others reach their goals, challenge themselves, and actualize their full potential.

Servant leaders listen very carefully to their employees. Doing so allows them to identify how best to support employees and helps them be successful in their roles. Servant leaders create work environments that are professional, support creativity and innovation, and, most importantly, encourage employees to feel comfortable approaching top leaders in the organization for guidance and feedback.

Assuming the role of mentor comes easy for the servant leader. Mentoring is a one-on-one developmental relationship between a more experienced individual—the mentor—and a less experienced individual—the mentee. Through regular or periodic interactions, the mentee relies on the mentor's guidance to gain skills, enhanced perspectives, and experience. The mentor simply wants to help—to give back. He or she provides advice, shares knowledge, and guides the mentee into paths that will be most beneficial to his or her career development. A mentoring relationship can be very rewarding and is often a two-way street, with each of the participants learning from the experience.

In general, servant leaders and mentors are critical roles for African Americans who have achieved top leadership positions in their chosen profession. In the particular case of librarianship, where 90% of the profession are white and 8% are African American, the number of African Americans in influential leadership roles is small (American Library Association [ALA], 2005). Data collected between 1990 and 1998 indicate that nearly 9 of 10 public, academic, and school librarians are white (ALA Office for Research and Statistics, 1998). A 2006 membership survey conducted by ALA revealed that only 5% of the respondents were credentialed African American librarians (ALA Office for Research and Statistics, 2006). And, a 2011 membership survey update reveals that the library profession's demographic percentages still remain largely unchanged (ALA Office for Research and Statistics, 2011). These statistics help amplify how great the need is for African Americans in positions of leadership and influence to embrace the tenets of servant leadership and be willing to serve as mentors.

Finding a mentor can be difficult in librarianship if one's preference is to have a mentor who shares one's ethnicity or cultural background. There may not be professionals of color in your organization or those whom you feel comfortable approaching. That is why I often take the initial step of saying hello to another African American professional, introducing myself and striking up a conversation at conferences. It is conceivable that a librarian can go through his or her entire career, or many years in a career, without the benefit of having a mentor. The good news is that it is never too late; a mentor/mentee relationship can develop at any stage during one's career. Also, mentors do not have to belong to the same organization or even live in the same state. The two people need only be a good fit for each other and find a way of operating that is comfortable for both. It is also possible to have more than one mentor during one's career, and leaders may have a number of mentees.

When you are in a leadership role, time can often become the enemy because you have so little of it and even less of it to spare. I can almost hear you saying, I would really like to serve as a mentor and be more of a servant leader, but I just don't have the *time*. I don't think we really have a choice in the matter. It is incumbent on us to reach back to share our knowledge and wisdom with others needing encouragement, guidance, and professional connections. Need I remind you of the paths that have been forged and difficult sacrifices made by those who came before us so we could enjoy the opportunities we have today? Enough said.

So how does one serve as a mentor? There are no hard and fast rules except presenting yourself as available and being willing to share your wisdom. Fortunately, technology makes staying in touch easier. Listed below are eight roles a mentor might engage in. You will find that you will change roles or merge roles as appropriate for different situations or with different mentees.

1. **Teacher:** As teacher, the mentor shares with the mentee the skills and knowledge required to perform tasks successfully; shares his or her experience as a seasoned professional, and the wisdom gleaned from past mistakes and helps the mentee realize that no one is perfect.
2. **Guide:** Here, the mentor helps navigate through the inner workings of the organization and deciphers the "unwritten office rules" for the mentee. This information is usually the "kernels of knowledge" that one only acquires over a period of time. The inner workings of the organization are simply the "behind the scenes" dynamics, or "office politics," that are not always apparent, but are crucial to know.
3. **Counselor:** The role of counselor requires the mentor to establish a lasting, trusting, and open relationship. In order to create a trusting relationship, the mentor needs to stress confidentiality and show respect for the mentee and vice versa. Both should agree to not disclose any personal information that is shared between them. The counselor role also encourages the mentee to develop problem-solving skills. The mentee must learn to think through problems rather than always depending on the mentor to provide the solution. The mentor can develop the problem-solving skills of a mentee by advising the mentee to first attempt to solve the problem before seeking assistance.
4. **Motivator:** Motivation is an inner drive that compels a person to succeed. Mentors usually perform the role of motivator when there is a need to motivate a mentee to complete a difficult assignment or to pursue an ambitious goal. Through encouragement and support, mentors can motivate mentees to succeed. One of the most effective ways to encourage mentees is to provide frequent, positive feedback. Positive feedback is a great "morale booster." It removes doubt and builds self-esteem that results in a sense of accomplishment.
5. **Coach:** Coaching primarily involves providing different kinds of feedback as the situation demands: positive feedback to reinforce behavior and constructive feedback to change behavior. Both types of feedback are critical to the professional and personal growth of the mentee. Feedback should be specific and based on direct observation of the mentee (not secondhand information). When giving constructive feedback, the mentor should be descriptive about the behavior and not use labels, such as "immature" or "unprofessional." The mentor should neither exaggerate nor be judgmental.
6. **Advisor:** This role requires the mentor to help the mentee set realistic learning objectives and develop an action plan that outlines what knowledge, skills, and abilities are needed to reach the objectives. As the old saying goes, "If you don't know where you are going, you don't know how to get there." The mentor needs to think about where the mentee wants to go

personally and professionally and help set the goals. The goals should be specific, time-framed, results-oriented, relevant, reachable, and flexible to accommodate the changing dynamics of the society.

7. **Role Model**: As a role model, the mentor is a living example of the values, ethics, and practices of the profession. Mentees may even imitate their mentors from time to time. Teaching by example may be a mentor's most effective developmental tool. The mentee will learn as he or she observes how the mentor handles situations or interacts with others. The mentor needs to be careful how he or she comes across to the mentee. The mentor needs to strive for high standards of professionalism, solid work ethics, and a positive attitude.
8. **Door Opener:** This role primarily involves helping the volunteer establish a network of contacts within and external to the organization. The mentee needs a chance to meet other people to spur personal and professional development. As a door opener, the mentor can introduce the mentee to the mentor's contacts to help build his or her network structure. The mentor also opens doors of information for the mentee by directing him or her to resources that may be helpful. (Plone Foundation, n.d.)

Because of the time and wisdom you share with others, you "seed" the way for more of us to be successful and to become great leaders.

REFERENCES

American Library Association, Office of Research and Statistics (2005). *Diversity counts.* Retrieved from http://www.ala.org/ala/aboutala/offices/diversity/diversitycounts/acs2005_aladiversity.pdf

American Library Association, Office of Research and Statistics (1998). Racial and ethnic diversity among librarians: A status report. Retrieved from http://www.ala.org/ala/research/librarystaffstats/diversity/index.cfm

American Library Association, Office of Research and Statistics (2006). 2006 membership surveys. Retrieved from http://www.ala.org/ala/research/initiatives/membership surveys/ALA

American Library Association, Office of Research and Statistics (2011). March 2011 demographics update. Retrieved from http://www.ala.org/ala/research/initiatives/member shipsurveys/ALA_Demographic_Studies_March2011.pdf

Del Boccio, R. (2011). When you learn, teach. When you get, give. Maya Angelou Inspirational Quotes on Success. Retrieved from profitablestorytelling.com/33395/personal-development/success-quotes/when-you-learn-teach-when-you-get-give-maya-angelou-inspirational-quotes-on-success/

Greenleaf, R. K. (2002). *Servant leadership: A journey into the nature of legitimate power and greatness*. Mahwah, NJ: Paulist Press.

Plone Foundation (n.d.). *Eight different roles a mentor can assume.* Retrieved from http://www.evspedia.ro/wiki/8-different-roles-a-mentor-can-assume

11

Becoming a Leader within the Library Profession

Rose Timmons Dawson

In 1939, five young African American men individually entered the Alexandria Library. They each asked for a library card; upon being denied, they politely went to the shelves, got a book, and sat down to read. For this, they were eventually arrested.

In 2009, I had the pleasure to celebrate the 70th anniversary of this little known event. It was somewhat emotional for me because as the first African American director of the Alexandria Library, I recognized the debt I owed those trailblazers.

The real issue today is not just African Americans becoming librarians. The Spectrum Initiative took care of that; the real pressing matter before us is that after the accomplishments of library trailblazers such as E. J. Josey, Clara Stanton Jones, and Effie Lee Morris, we should aspire to the leadership ranks. As with most things, climbing the library corporate ladder does not come without its challenges.

Many librarians seek top management level positions but for some reason are unable to attain them. Based on my career, I closely examined those factors that played a critical role in a children's librarian moving through the profession and eventually landing one of the more desirable directorships within the public library world.

As with anything, African American librarians need to be strategic if we are to position ourselves for library jobs at the highest level.

To capture or position oneself into a major leadership role, there are a number of things that are critical. In examining my career, there are five things that have helped shape me as a librarian and assisted in my successful transition from entry level children's librarian, project manager, change agent, deputy director, and ultimately to director.

In hindsight, there five factors helped me meet this goal:

1. Value of mentors: It takes a village to raise a director.
2. Professional involvement: Getting involved and staying involved.
3. Beyond the MLS degree: Making the executive leadership programs work for you.
4. Mobility: In order to move up, you need to be willing to move on.
5. Leading change: Necessity to stay ahead of the pack.

VALUE OF MENTORS

Mentors are a necessity. But, it is not only a mentor within the organization that is necessary. Mentors within the community are also important.

Regardless of the position, I have always had wonderful mentors. During my first position as a children's librarian in the Palisades community with the District of Columbia Public Library, I was the first African American to ever hold that position. The Palisades, a community that was 98% white, is located on the other side of the popular Georgetown neighborhood and flanked between McLean, Virginia, and Glen Echo Park, Maryland. Although my educational credentials were considered impeccable, with undergraduate and graduate degrees from the University of North Carolina, longtime patrons had difficulty accepting this new, younger, browner face than the 30-year veteran I had replaced. However, it was the customer I was serving, the children, who became my strongest supporters.

For example, after being on the job for two weeks, when a parent came to the library they would request my predecessor or the part-time librarian. Upon finding they weren't there, they would leave or say they would come back later when the part-time librarian was scheduled. One day when a young fourth-grade girl came in to work on an assignment, I made certain suggestions after conducting a very thorough reference interview. We had a great time and when her mother came to pick her up and barely interacted with me, I was not bothered because the young girl was so excited and happy when she left. The next week, I was shocked when the same parent came to the library before her daughter arrived to talk with me privately. She wanted me to know that her daughter had a learning disability and the homework assignment I had assisted her with had resulted in her first "A." She thanked me and left. I think that parent gave me "neighborhood cred." After that exchange, other parents embraced the new librarian. This parent and one other were my community mentors. Parents came into the library asking for me by name, and whenever outside the library, the children made sure the librarian was included. Never discount the different directions from which one can receive support.

I actually had two mentors within the branch who played a pivotal role in the library administration and kept me informed concerning the "wonderful" job I was doing in the branch. Not only that, they often defended me to the branch manager, who was recognized as being somewhat difficult. In January 1986, I decided to initiate a celebration of Dr. Martin Luther King's birthday. I created special programs to take to the elementary schools. I was very pleased with my efforts. During that time, there were very few premade activities, so everything had to be original. I had shared my program with the staff and they were all very impressed, except for the branch manager. The manager came to me and asked why I was doing the program. Since the school had not asked for it, he thought, given the community and the small number of African American students at the school, that it wasn't necessary. When I told him it was part of my job to introduce children to subjects and not always do what was requested, he directed me to either do something else or cancel the outreach visits. Thanks to the support of my mentors within the branch and out in the community, I felt empowered to do the program. Needless to say, it was the most popular program I ever did for that community, and the schools requested a black history month program for every class the following month.

PROFESSIONAL INVOLVEMENT

State library memberships serve as the perfect precursor for serving on the national level. My participation within the local state library association was a great training ground to combine my limited work experience and book knowledge. It is also a great networking opportunity. The District of Columbia Library Association (DCLA) provided leadership opportunities such as mock Newbery/Caldecott committees, membership committee experience, and recruitment.

In 1991, I became the first African American librarian to manage the children's division of the Martin Luther King Memorial Library. I am certain that participation on the local level helped me to acquire this position. It was during this time that I actively pursued participation within the American Library Association (ALA), Black Caucus of the American Library Association (BCALA), and the Association of Library Services to Children (ALSC). Feeling that I had solidified my work experience with my formal educational training made this move a real logical next step. Working on the national level is an opportunity to give back to the profession. It also presents an opportunity to increase your marketability and networking opportunities when considering your career options. I will admit, I had tried to gain committee assignments before and a chance to serve did not come easily.

Since that time, ALA has created a number of entities to help improve access to committees. Aggressive recruitment from the New Members Roundtable, the creation of the Spectrum Initiative, followed by strategic plans that focused heavily on diversity have expanded our level of participation, but more still needs to happen.

When I was unable to gain an appointment to a children's services committee, I accepted a nomination request to run for council. Recognizing that I could probably not win such a seat but wanting the name recognition and the chance to get my name out there to show that I was willing to work were the driving forces to do it. Interestingly enough, I did become a councilor with a four-year term. This appointment provided a sneak peek into the governance of ALA and was one of the best things to ever happen to me. I strongly encourage librarians to do this. Who knows, win or lose, it may result in an appointment to a coveted committee assignment, since the incoming presidents would have seen your name on the ballot and read your credentials and philosophical beliefs.

BEYOND THE MLS

ALA and Public Library Association (PLA) conferences have proven to be full of amazing workshops that have been invaluable over the years. In the 21st century, virtual training and webinars leave no room for staff to lack training in any area. The creation of the Emerging Leaders Program gives librarians at a certain point in their careers an early leadership opportunity.

After being in the profession for more than 10 years, librarians should consider executive leadership programs to enhance and reenergize their credentials. I think the creation of more formal leadership training, such as that offered by American Library Association/Allied Professional Association (ALA/APA) and the Simmons Ph.D. program, was an important step toward this goal.

In 1995, through yet another mentor, I was given the opportunity to participate in the George Washington University Executive Leadership Program and earned a certified public manager credential. This type of program over the years has become critical in educating potential library directors in the expectations of county and city managers when looking to interact with their department heads.

I also participated in the Urban Libraries Council (ULC) Executive Leadership Institute (ELI). Based on research that said library directors were going to retire in huge numbers during a certain time frame, ULC took the lead in trying to groom individuals to replace them. This program was an eye opener and offered first-class training and a chance to see the big picture of running a library.

MOBILITY

Upon completing this program, I credit my mentors with finding a position that they felt best suited my skills. Although the position was intriguing, yet challenging, it required relocating from that which I knew. I must admit, I hesitated. However, there are clearly times when we need to move out in order to move up. It is critical that we not allow ourselves to stagnate as we try to outwait someone who "claims" they will retire in a few years. Do not hesitate to pursue all of your options.

LEADING CHANGE

Do not get content once you've acquired a top administrative position. Stay ahead of the pack. At this stage in the game, you should be mentoring others. Continued professional involvement at all levels and a willingness to share your experiences and function as a trainer shows real leadership.

Becoming a leader within the library profession comes with its challenges, but if you plan strategically, it is well worth the effort.

12

Making the Grade as an African American Library Director in a Majority Community

Jos N. Holman

Fifteen years as a black library director in two Midwestern majority communities constitutes what many would consider an accomplishment in public libraries. Librarians I meet at conferences rarely ask the racial makeup of the community I serve. No doubt many presume I work in a community primarily composed of African Americans. Frankly, I have yet to enjoy that privilege.

Instead, I have utilized particular approaches to working in majority communities to avoid historical racism based on black stereotypes. Oftentimes these racial stereotypes are perpetuated by staff members who want and expect you to fail. So how do you make the grade as a black library director in a majority community? I share the following as a sample of my experiences in my own attempt to make the grade.

Obviously there are a variety of factors, strengths, and skills that produce success for black library directors in majority communities. Though it is impossible to examine all aspects of the above, my examination in this straightforward way reflects generally historically racist attitudes and stereotypes.

Historically, racism has embodied an element of mistrust when it comes to anything of value to whites. Therefore, it is extremely important that early in their tenure, black library directors establish an element of trust regarding financial matters. Demonstrating a thorough knowledge of finance and budgeting goes a long way in establishing trust between a library director and his or her staff. Sharing detailed information about revenues, expenses, and the organization's financial status helps staff members build confidence in the skills of a black library director. It also helps with transparency in the organization, especially in financial matters. When black library directors establish a consistent correlation between the day-to-day decision making and financial resources, they demonstrate core administrative efficiencies that bring about cooperation. In time cooperative staff members influence doubtful staff of the director's efficient leadership. Though all library directors are charged with maximizing financial resources, black library directors are held to a greater scrutiny in all things financial. Gaining trust in this area is foundational to success in other areas.

Historically, racism has labeled black people as shiftless, lazy, and looking for any way out of work they can find. Therefore, whites in the Midwest who have little real-life experience with blacks often have a substandard expectation of black library directors. After silently wondering, "Are they really qualified?," majority co-workers look for signs of nonproductiveness. There is a universal truth that says that 89.9% of life is showing up. Black library directors must hit the ground running by displaying commitment at work in attendance and dependability. Dispelling racist stereotypes, they must prove their dependability by being on time and present for each day's work. Not only do black library directors have to show their fortitude in attendance, they must show they are prepared for the day's work. This preparation includes being prepared for every meeting, following up on staff communication, and keeping up with administrative paperwork.

As a black library director, adhering to the highest standard of ethics, honesty, and integrity achieves more mileage with your superiors and library staff than anything else. Displaying integrity in guiding the operations of the library as it relates to policies, services, and other library resources helps library staff know a black library director is truthful to his or her responsibilities. The gracious display of this integrity instills confidence in the operational decisions made by a black library director. It also alleviates the idea that a black library director is acting solely on selfish motives and ambitions. When people know that you will not only tell the truth but also stand by it in every decision and interaction, there is less speculation about who they are dealing with. Also, new black library directors must quickly confirm the capability to maintain confidentially and privacy in all work-related matters, but especially personnel matters. The inability to maintain confidence and privacy of personnel issues will thwart all efforts to be a successful leader. This holds true within the workplace and outside it as well.

Finally, integrity is seen in your willingness to admit mistakes. Ready acknowledgment of a mistake facilitates the probability to earnestly move past the mistake toward the resolution of unintended consequences. If black library directors fail to admit mistakes and be accountable for their actions, staff members will refuse to be accountable as well. This leads to a very unproductive organizational culture.

Another racist approach for black library directors is based on the idea they are unqualified for the job and therefore don't know what they are doing. Often this is manifested when someone thinks a black library director didn't have the valid qualifications and was given a job for conscience sake or appearances. Exhibiting a comprehensive knowledge and understanding of job responsibilities is paramount to your success. When staff members think a black library director doesn't know what he or she is doing, their lack of confidence will manifest itself in several ways. Sometimes there are outright verbal challenges or attacks. Often there is unnecessary questioning of statements and actions. Then there is unified resistance against much needed policy changes because staff members think you don't know what you are doing. For black library directors, making sure that staff are able to see that you understand your role as director, with all the responsibilities that encompasses, has to happen early in your tenure. Staff members need to have confidence in your capabilities to help them develop confidence in your vision and leadership. Once that confidence is established, the same integrity will prove invaluable for black library directors.

As a black library director in a majority community, there are several key relationships that must be cultivated and sustained. These relationships are the same for other (white) library directors. The major difference is that historical racism factors in for the black library director, especially in a majority community. Why? Because it is likely that many individuals the new director interacts with will have had limited, if any, exposure to blacks in positions of leadership and authority. For many library staff, this is the first time they are accountable to a person of color. Naturally, there is a curiosity about the skill set of the new library director. However, staff overlook the fact that the new library director is an experienced professional with similar goals of service. This often repeated scenario is why key relationships are enormously important.

Obviously the first established relationship is with the library board. Newly hired black library directors should never forget they serve at the pleasure of their library board. Development of a mutually respectful and supportive relationship between the director and the library board is essential to the library's success. All library directors need to understand and accept that they report to the board but are not equal to board members. The library board hired the library director for his or her professional expertise in the administration of the library. Black library directors cannot take a subservient role but must maintain a professional approach in supporting the board through their communication and work ethic. When this occurs, a mutually beneficial level of dependence and trust between the director and the board will see the library through unexpected trials and challenges.

The greatest challenge for new black library directors may be in building direct relationships with the staff. It is essential in the development of staff relationships that fairness and consideration of individual strengths be shown. More important, the staff must believe the director advocates on their behalf in terms of pay, benefits, policies, and work conditions. Once staff members believe they are being fully considered, they become more open to the vision and leadership of a black library director. This openness becomes the basis for the continued development of professional relationships. *As a reminder, both the board and staff need to remember that staff report only to the director, not the board.*

Black library directors working in majority communities must realize that building relationships with the at-large community is paramount to the daily success of the library. Black library directors need to be visible and involved in the community so they become "the face of the library." Business owners, elected officials, and educational leaders need to know not only who the director is but also how the library is doing. Being actively involved in the community will naturally provide opportunities to "tell the library's story" to people who will ultimately confirm whether or not the library is supported. Also, utilizing good customer service approaches with customers who ask to "speak to the library director" provides a direct sense of leadership to patrons and proves the library exists for their benefit.

Starting out as a children's librarian, I didn't have to think a lot about children's perceptions. My creativity, kindness, enthusiasm, and "kid spirit" served as the basis for working with them. I like to think I would be perceived as being successful as a library director because of my expertise, professionalism, and job experience. However, in most cases, I have surprised many people by excelling beyond their minimalist set of expectations for a black library director. Am I making the grade? I believe so. But I do hope that one day, I will have more flexibility entering a new directorship, and that historical racism doesn't have to be the guiding principle for how I approach the job.

13

❖ ❖

The Challenge of Designing and Promoting Public Library Services for Teens of Color without Losing One's Sanity

Syntychia Kendrick-Samuel

As a public librarian specializing in teen services, my profession has charged me with the responsibility of advocating the "support of the defense of the rights of youth to equal access of information, resources, and services in all libraries" (Vaillancourt, 2000, p. 85). Yes, constant vigilance is required on my part to actively meet the needs of an often unwelcomed demographic at the public library, namely teenagers. Being a librarian of color who works in a racially and ethnically diverse community, I've given myself the responsibility of making my place of employment and the profession of librarianship attractive to teens of color. It is my view that as a black librarian, I'm in a unique position because I have a cultural link to most of the teens I serve. For minority teens of other backgrounds such as the West Indies or Latin America, I still share the experience of growing up as a minority in U.S. society.

Some may argue that this is 2011 and we have an African American president, and it is time to stop thinking in terms of color. Teen services should be colorblind. I would argue the opposite. A few short years ago, in 2006, there was the Jena 6 case of Jena, Louisiana, where six African American teens were charged with attempted murder of a white classmate. If it weren't for the national outrage over the trumped-up charge of attempted murder against a white classmate and the subsequent funds from private citizens and special interest groups for competent legal defense, those African American teens would have probably served long undeserved jail sentences. I cite the Jena 6 case to highlight that the United States is far from being the haven of equality and blind justice. Combine prejudice with the physiological and psychological changes that come with being a teenager, and one can just imagine—or remember—the tumultuous effect that can have on the young adult of color's mind, attitude, and behavior. The teens' librarian can play a role in helping adolescents navigate this difficult time by offering programs and opportunities for teens to let "their" voices be heard in their communities.

YOUNG ADULT PROGRAMMING: THINK SOCIALLY CONSCIOUS PROGRAMMING

As stated earlier, being culturally relevant to the community I serve is important to my professional mission as a teen librarian. When planning programs, I constantly ask myself: "How can I attract teens to the library to engage in productive activities?"

The Search Institute, a nonprofit, nonsectarian organization whose mission is to provide "leadership, knowledge, and resources to promote healthy . . . youth, and communities," identified 40 developmental internal and external assets that contribute to the positive development of teens ("Discovering what kids need to succeed" 2011). Included in those assets are empowerment, support, positive values, positive identity, and social competencies. The public library can become an active participant in molding our young people into productive individuals now and in the future.

Junior Friends groups are an excellent tool to help mold and shape young people in a positive manner. I'm fortunate that prior to my appointment as the young adult librarian, a Junior Friends group had been started in 1996 by Nancy Bertrand. After she left the library, adult programming librarian Stacey Smith-Brown took the reins of the Junior Friends and continued to cultivate the group. When I was hired as the young adult librarian in 2004, supervision of the group was added to the young adult librarian's job responsibilities.

I was both excited and terrified at the thought of working with these teens. But I really shouldn't have been nervous. True to the description on the membership form, these 6th through 12th graders were really "ambitious teens" who promoted library programs and "voiced their ideas while developing valuable leadership and organization skills."

The Junior Friends is a subdivision of the Friends of the Library, and they elect their own officers each year and serve as library volunteers; I keep track of their hours, which can be used for community service credit. It has been a joy working with these teens and developing a professional relationship with them and even their families. In regard to programming, these mostly Latino/a and black kids sponsor various library events year round. In 2009, they won the *Voices of Youth Advocates* magazine's most valuable program runner-up award for their annual Kwanzaa celebration.

At the Kwanzaa feast called "Karamu," the Junior Friends write and act in their own plays based on Kwanzaa principles; they also do crafts with the youngsters who attend. The feast is the most popular part of the program. Members of the group and the library donate food items for the feast each year. For the past six years, the parental liaison to the group, Elsie Souffrant, has provided the bulk of the food, cooking up delicious Haitian comfort food. In 2010, I won the first ever Nassau County Young Adult Service Division's Teen Programming Excellence Award for my supervisory work in the Kwanzaa Karamu feast.

Other programs sponsored by the Junior Friends include the Black History Celebration. Members portray famous people of African descent; they talk in character and dress the part for the audience. This past year, we had Zora Neale Hurston, Langston Hughes, Dr. Henry Louis Gates, Jr., Ruby Dee, Edwidge Danticat, and Prince Rahman grace our stage! The Junior Friends also sponsor a yearly talent show, and a Latina member of the group is in the process of planning the first ever Spanish Heritage Month program. Over the years individual members of the group have won the local B.E.S.T (Bringing Excellence in Service by Teens) award sponsored by the Nassau and Suffolk County Library Associations. The B.E.S.T award is given yearly to a deserving teen who has truly enriched his or her local library through dedication and service.

I also have offered what I call "Straight Talk" programs where members of the community, ranging from former convicts to practicing litigators, come and speak to teens and their parents about how to avoid the pitfalls of life, know their rights, and make good life choices.

This past winter, thanks in part to a small grant that I won from the Margaret A. Edwards Trust, I was able to create an "Empowerment Academy" that ran for five consecutive weeks. It was designed to boost the self-esteem, creativity, individualism, and sense of community responsibility in 6th through 12th graders. Educators, authors, a Junior Friend alumnus, and a local museum presented the programs. Both teens and their parents attended and expressed great satisfaction with the opportunity to participate.

THE OCCASIONAL RANT MAY BE NECESSARY

A few weeks ago I went on a rant at my graphic novel discussion group, when some of the teens were resistant to reading *Yummy: The Last Days of a Southside Shorty* by Greg Neri. This disturbing book, sadly based on real life events, was a bit too "black" or "ghetto" for some of the black kids present. This was my opportunity to get on my soapbox and preach self-love, the need to avoid classism, and so forth. Yes, some of the kids were bristled by my response, but every one of them showed up for the discussion, having read the book, and these bright kids were prepared for a thoughtful, intelligent discussion. My point is this, had I been of another race, would *Yummy* have been up for discussion? If yes, could I have responded to the kids remarks of self-hatred in such a potent manner? I really don't know the answer because I am what I am, an African American who sees the beauty in her culture and other minority cultures and who tries to instill that same feeling in the younger generation.

I have often heard it said "Well, you do realize that if you want to advance in your career, you'll have to leave that place?" Recently I read Philip Roth's latest book *Nemesis*; the main character is a Jewish American physical education teacher who purposely chooses to work in a Jewish community. Why? He wanted to serve as a role model for the Jewish kids, letting them know that yes, they too (despite stereotypes about the physical prowess of Jewish Americans) can become a physical education teacher one day. For me, that same principle applies. In Long Island, New York, librarians of color are far and few between. Of course like other professionals, career advancement is an always present objective. Who wouldn't want an increase in monetary compensation via job promotions? For me though, I realized that I can make a difference and still aim for advancement at my current job. As a black librarian working in a predominantly black community, I've struck gold! Perhaps because of being exposed to Mrs. Kendrick-Samuel, a few of the teens that I serve will add "librarian" to their list of potential future professions! If that were to happen, then all my ranting and remaining ever socially conscious would have been worth it.

REFERENCES

Discovering what kids need to succeed" (2011). Retrieved from http://www.search-institute.org/developmental-assets.

Vaillancourt, R. J. (2000). *Bare bones young adult services: Tips for public library generalists.* Chicago: American Library Association.

14

Adultism: Discrimination by Another Name

Tamara Stewart

As dedicated black librarians, we humbly stand on the shoulders of giants like Dr. E. J. Josey, Dr. Eliza Atkins Gleason, and Clara Stanton Jones. Many of us chose this profession because of our passionate belief in freedom, equality, and service. Nowhere is this belief more evident than in public libraries.

Public libraries embody the democratic ideals we hold dear: freedom to read and learn, equal access to resources, and quality service to all. Unfortunately, despite our best efforts, public libraries and public library service don't always live up to our lofty goals. Although public libraries strive to provide great service to all, the truth is that we do a better job of providing service to some than others. Discrimination, both intentional and unintentional, continues to be a problem in 21st-century public libraries.

DEFINITION AND SCOPE OF ADULTISM

One of the most prevalent forms of discrimination that exists in today's public libraries is the "adultism" being perpetrated against teens. In his seminal article titled "Understanding Adultism: A Key to Developing Positive Youth-Adult Relationships," Bell (2003) provided a definition for the concept of "adultism":

> The word adultism refers to behaviors and attitudes based on the assumption that adults are better than young people, and entitled to act upon young people without their agreement. This mistreatment is reinforced by social institutions, laws, customs, and attitudes. (p. 1)

The good/bad news is that librarians have plenty of company in a society that frequently fails to treat teenagers with the same patience, concern, and respect that we accord to adults and senior citizens. As a young adult librarian for six years, I frequently witnessed adultism firsthand and occasionally fell prey to it myself. At its most extreme, adultism in public libraries shows up in the form of public libraries literally closing their doors, rather than deal with teens, as happened at the Maplewood Public Library in New Jersey a few years ago (Kelley, 2007). In his recently published article "Representations of Youth in Local Media: Implications for Library Service," Bernier (2011) asserted that young adults are routinely depicted in a negative light in the media and thoughtfully analyzed the potential implications these negative portrayals have for library service to teens.

When teenagers show up at our doors or in front of the reference desk and we make them feel unwelcome, or serve them less respectfully than we do adult patrons, that is adultism. Adultism in public libraries is also seen in far too few libraries with dedicated spaces for teens; the lack of enthusiastic, dedicated professionals to serve young adults; and few programs targeted to appeal to teen audiences. Interestingly, although many of our colleagues feel justified in their discriminatory behavior against teens, they are much more tolerant and supportive in their attitudes and behaviors toward younger children.

PART OF THE PROBLEM VERSUS PART OF THE SOLUTION

What does discrimination against teens have to do with black librarians? Simply put, we know how it feels to be disrespected, and we have a responsibility to combat discrimination in our organizations, wherever it exists. The battle can be daunting at times, given that many of us are still facing professional discrimination ourselves. We can start by looking in the mirror and asking ourselves if we're part of the problem, then making a commitment to being part of the solution. Bell (2003) suggested asking oneself questions like these to help uncover unconscious adultist behavior:

- "Would I treat an adult this way?"
- "Would I talk to an adult in this tone of voice?"
- "Would I make this decision for an adult?"
- "Would I have this expectation for an adult?"
- "Would I limit an adult's behavior in this way?" (p. 7)

As professional librarians, we take pride in our core values, which include access, the public good, service, and social responsibility (American Library Association, 2004). We have a long tradition of being in the forefront of social change that empowers people and levels the playing field. Consequently, we have an obligation to confront the issue of adultism within our institutions, setting a good example for the larger society in the process. Spielberger, Horton, and Michels (2007) pointed out that library youth development programs can potentially benefit youth, libraries, and communities. Increasingly, public libraries are recognizing the value of cultivating the net generation, a large cohort of not-so-distant-future voters and taxpayers, in whose hands the future of our profession and public libraries will soon rest.

Now that we've identified the work that needs to be done, we can turn to the process of how to make that change a reality. Bell (2003) offered some great guidelines librarians can apply that should help us foster a more positive relationship with the young people we serve:

- Listen to young people. Really listen.
- Ask questions. Ask what they think about everything.
- Validate their thinking. Welcome their ideas.
- Lay back. Curb your inclination to take over. Support initiatives of young people.
- Be willing for them to make mistakes.
- Provide training for them to take on greater levels of decision making and leadership.
- Always respect all young people, no matter what their ages, and expect them to respect each other at all ages.
- Have high expectations of their potentials, and positively assess their current abilities.
- Do not take out your anger about them on them.
- Give young people accurate information about the way the world works. Never lie to them. (pp. 9–10)

I would add that it is a good idea to learn young people's names and use them whenever possible. Bell also importantly reminds us to be patient with ourselves when we unconsciously slip into our old adultist habits because it will take time to undo them. The ability to extend grace and compassion to others starts at home.

The disrespect of young adults is a prevalent social attitude that insidiously infiltrates our libraries and can undermine our best efforts to provide equal access and quality service to all. If you observe a colleague rudely chiding a teen patron, don't just let it slide. Make time to have a coaching conversation with your colleague and point out the harm in his or her approach. Speak to your administrators about staff training in the area of youth development. It is our responsibility as protégés of Dr. E. J. Josey to take a stand for what's right. In Dr. Josey's own words: "The potential leader of tomorrow may not have a computer at home and your library is the educational agency which introduces him to this new device. There are so many of our young people who need to be influenced by librarians and be influenced by libraries" (Josey, 2009). In order for youth to be influenced by librarians and libraries, however, we must first ensure that they are welcome and respected when they cross our thresholds.

REFERENCES

American Library Association. (2004). ALA policy manual: Section two: Positions and public policy statement: core values, ethics and core competencies, Subsection 40.1. Retrieved from http://www.ala.org/ala/aboutala/governance/policymanual/updatedpolicymanual/section2/40corevalues.cfm

Bell, J. (2003). The Freechild Project. Understanding adultism: A key to developing positive youth-adult relationships. Retrieved from http://www.nuatc.org/articles/pdf/understanding_adultism.pdf

Bernier, A. (2011). Representations of youth in local media: Implications for library service. *Library and Information Science Research, 33*, 158–167.

Josey, E. J. (1998). California Black Librarians Caucus. Speech by E. J. Josey. Delivered at the National Sankofa Council on Educating Black Children Conference on April 5, 1998, in Merrillville, Indiana. Retrieved from http://clbc.org/2009/07/speech-by-e-j-josey/

Kelley, T. (2007). Lock the library! Rowdy students are taking over. *New York Times,* January 2. Retrieved from http://www.nytimes.com/2007/01/02/nyregion/02library.html

Spielberger, J., Horton, C., & Michels, L. (2007, January 2). New on the shelf: Teens in the library: Summary of key findings from the evaluation of public libraries as partners in youth development, a Wallace Foundation initiative. Retrieved from http://www.wallacefoundation.org/knowledge-center/Libraries/Pages/New-On-The-Shelf-Teens-in-the-Library.aspx

15

Public Libraries in the 21st Century: Challenges and Solutions

Lucille Cole Thomas

"The public library is a keystone of democracy—its one of the great levelers in our society . . . " (Littman, 2010). It provides services that equalize opportunities for individuals and organizations. With the rapid changes of providing information and changing demographics, libraries must change to meet the needs of the communities. Economic and technological developments are reshaping and redefining how libraries do business. The Internet is a major tool for communication and job-related tasks. Public libraries are one of the major providers of Internet access to the public. How are librarians and library boards of trustees, the policy-making groups, embracing these challenges and providing solutions?

PUBLIC LIBRARIES CONTRIBUTE TO THE ECONOMY

> Brainpower is the new currency of success in the 21st century. And libraries are often cities' best assets in building up the brainpower of the community.
>
> —Julian Castro (2010)

Brainpower is one asset the library contributes to economic development. Public libraries support local communities by providing:

- assistance to small businesses
- literacy skills for children and adults
- opportunities to learn new technical skills
- space for community groups to meet

According to Tanzi Merritt (2010) in *Public Libraries & the Local Economy*:

- 300,000 Americans receive job-seeking assistance at a public library daily.
- 2.8 million small business owners and their employees use the library every month to access resources to support their business.
- 5,400 libraries offer free technology training classes, and 14,700 people attend these classes daily—a retail value of $2.2 million.
- Public libraries circulate as many materials daily as FedEx ships packages worldwide.
- In a single year, Americans visit a public library more times than they attend live sporting events or go to the movies.

Seminars on home buying and real estate planning are popular programs. The concept of "community information hub" provides a community portal—one-stop access to a variety of community resources.

The homeless frequent the library. For obvious reasons, strict rules must be enforced. Although many problems arise, the library does serve as a sanctuary for many.

DIVERSITY AND PUBLIC LIBRARIES

Trustees have an obligation to make policies that recognize all ethnic groups in the community. The library staff offers a conceptual framework that encompasses library services and programs for diverse populations—ethnic, cultural, physically challenged, and aging—that implement the policies. Gathering information about the demographics of the community is a first step. Although general information is readily available, a community survey is helpful in updating the needs of the current population.

Staff Diversity

The library policy should ensure that access, selection, and advancement opportunities are available to all applicants and employees based on their knowledge, skills, and abilities without regards to race, color, religion, or age. The director of human resources may serve as the equal opportunity officer. Staff training should include cultural sensitivity.

Collections

Information collected in the survey can serve as a guide in material selection for the library. Multicultural media, such as films, foreign language books, and other library materials, are essential. Collections should be built on sensitivity to tolerance, equity, and the history of the culture of all populations in the community.

The criteria for selection should include suitability of subject and style for intended audience, historical significance, and relation to existing collection. The library director and professional staff are responsible for the selection of library materials. Picture books featuring characters that reflect people in the community and materials in their native language are appreciated.

Programs

Programs that reflect the importance of the ethnic and cultural groups in the community should be a priority. At intervals, an informal survey can provide information regarding special needs and interests. Users and nonusers of the library may be invited to serve on program planning committees. A multiethnic calendar is a means of creating program ideas for festivals and historic events highlighting ethnic accomplishments.

Education

The 21st century presents many challenges for education. The United States ranks 25th among developing countries in reading; it is estimated that the cost of illiteracy to business and taxpayers is $20 billion per year. The educational careers of 25% to 49% of U.S. children are imperiled because they do not read well enough. Many of these children are underserved and underrepresented in the community. What can libraries contribute to solve the problem? The public library is an "out-of-school environment" that contributes to the advancement of learning skills. This is a free service available from cradle to grave. As an approach, there should first be an awareness that low reading levels, high dropout rates, and lack of preparation for employment exist. Many libraries are implementing the programs, and more, as addressed in this chapter, and more.

> Reading is the gateway skill that makes other learning possible.
>
> —Barack Obama (2005)

At the annual meeting of the American Library Association, Obama stated: "At the dawn of the 21st century, where knowledge is literally power, where it unlocks the gates of opportunity and success, we all have responsibilities as parents, as librarians, as politicians, and as citizens to instill in our children a love of reading so we can give them a chance to fulfill their dreams." (2005).

Summer Reading Programs

Partnered with school systems, libraries attract large numbers of children. The children select books that interest them without the restrictions of assigned reading. Observations reveal that preschool and summer reading activities encourage children to spend more time with books.

Lifelong Learning

For seniors who want to continue learning, the library offers books, DVDs, lectures, and many more programs. The Books by Mail program allows the disabled to receive library materials without leaving the comfort of their homes. Technology provides many online opportunities.

English as a Second Language (ESL) Programs

Groups may be designed to give participants a chance to carry on informal conversations and improve their listening skills. One-on-one tutoring is available.

Information Literacy

Librarians' skills include the ability to teach users how to locate information and how to evaluate the information. What is the background of the person who wrote the article? Is the information slanted? When was the historical article written? Is the information up to date? Answers to these questions enable the writer to make informed decisions.

LIBRARY ADVOCACY AT LOCAL, STATE, AND NATIONAL LEVELS

Advocacy means supporting a cause of action. Librarians can't do it alone. For the public library, this means the efforts are strengthened when a partnership is formed among librarians, trustees, volunteers, and community organizations. The trustees should be knowledgeable about the political environment, demographics of the community, laws and regulations, and needs of the community. The librarians are familiar with the programs and services and in a position to interpret the true value of each. Being a part of a library association network—local, state, and national—is paramount. Participation in National Legislative Day is an opportunity to visit your legislators in Washington. All must communicate the message of library value on a regular basis.

FUNDRAISING AND PUBLIC LIBRARIES

Adequate funds are required to provide for the needs and interests of communities. Fundraising and advocacy are intertwined. Librarians and trustees have a joint responsibility. Everyone on the library staff can share the responsibility by telling library stories. The message should be refined to tell how the library resources benefit the individual. Trustees establish policies to encourage gifts in the form of bequests, trust funds, or cash donations, which are considered important sources of additional revenue.

Fundraising best practices include:

1. Set a calendar for cultivation events—donor luncheons, recognition for donors
2. Establish a donor database
3. Delineate clearly that private donations are above and beyond public funds
4. Provide public recognition and publicity for all gifts
5. Schedule media coverage for fundraising events and recognition ceremonies

When librarians and library trustees work together to institute these and other best practices, the library is the beneficiary. Many libraries have turned to grant writing as a means of connecting with funding sources. A staff member or a paid consultant may be responsible for writing proposals.

Establishing a library foundation is an option for public libraries. Foundations provide a variety of revenue sources to supplement tax support. The focus is usually on capital projects, collections, programs, and services that are funded through public dollars. A library foundation is a separate legal entity formed for the purpose of enhancing and extending library programs and services. Planned giving opportunities make it possible for donors to make gifts to the library and receive financial and tax benefits. The donor may restrict gifts. The foundation board, library board of trustees, and library staff must work closely together to ensure success. Foundations focus on the entire system; friends groups provide financial support for their local branches.

SUMMARY

In the 21st century the public library is faced with a multiplicity of challenges. Librarians and library trustees are working together, with the assistance of technology, to provide solutions. Across the country, public libraries are engaged in a broad spectrum of programs and services that benefit all ages. The discussion in this chapter has focused on the contributions in three areas: the economy, diversity, and education. Many libraries are contributing in other areas. Fundraising and advocacy enable libraries to supplement local, state, and federal support.

REFERENCES

Alire, C. (2009, Sept.). *Fifty-two ways to make a difference: Library advocacy throughout the year.*

Burlingame, D. F. (Ed.) (1995). *Library fundraising models for success.* Chicago: American Library Association.

Castro, J. (2010). Economic prosperity: Making cities and counties stronger. In *Partners for the Future: Public Libraries and Local Governments Creating Sustainable Communities.* Urban libraries Council, p. 11

Kniffell, L. (2011). 12 ways libraries are good for the country. *The Voice for American Libraries, 12*, 2.

Littman, S. D. (2010 July 20). *Greenwich Times.*

Merrit, T. (2010, Sept. 10). Public libraries and the local economy. *Citizens Participation, Economic Development.* Lexington Kentucky Public Library Annual Report. Shevawn Akers, editor.

Obama, B. (2005, August). Bound to the word. *American Libraries*, 48–52.

Part III

FROM THE ACADEMIC LIBRARY

16

National and International Challenges of Black Librarianship in the 21st Century

Ruth M. Jackson

Libraries have rapidly evolved within the past 10 years from primarily print resource facilities with clearly defined user services to learning centers and information hubs in which users have high expectations of how they will be provided access to the world's publishing output of both scholarly information and popular culture in an almost dizzying array of formats. In identifying the challenges to black librarianship in the 21st century, we must first examine the framework of libraries at large in the various sectors of U.S. society and then the several influences that are impacting the library and information science discipline as it evolves into the realm of the librarian as scholar and information broker.

Among the key factors that will significantly influence the role of 21st-century libraries and librarians and the staffs that they manage are (1) paradigm shifts predicted to occur during the next five to ten years in publishing models, technologies, and mechanisms for providing access to popular, scholarly, scientific, and economic information and communications; (2) the impact of the web in transforming the ways in which information technology systems are built for delivery of information services; and (3) the demand among information seekers (students, faculty, researchers, the public at large) for libraries to provide "one-stop shopping" via single sign-on, discovery tools, and outreach programs.

Prevailing trends also indicate that there will be a greater mixture of information seekers of all ages, cultures, and economic backgrounds who will rely on libraries as the gateways and preservers of culture, economic, and scientific and health care information across a spectrum of delivery and access options. The population shift predicted to occur by 2050, when it is expected the diversity composition of the population base potentially served by libraries will have dramatically changed from the current almost 75% non-Hispanic white to 53%, will also exert a profound influence on service demands and use patterns.

As a result of the information explosion, sparked by the transformation of both scholarly and cultural information to digital format, libraries of all types (academic, research, public, school, and special libraries) have worked to reposition themselves to easily integrate wired and wireless devices and networks, print and digital collections, and flexible learning spaces within their facilities, as well as access through handheld devices, to the diverse populations they serve.

Mass digitization projects through commercial firms (e.g., Google, Microsoft), the Open Content Alliance, and development of local platforms to digitize and curate historical and intellectual assets hold much promise for enhancing access to information. And they will hopefully provide, in time, more cost-effective means of mass digital collection storage and preservation. However, the cost of information has not yet decreased in this evolving environment. Therefore, within our national professional associations, we are beginning to grapple with the concept of the possibility of U.S. society evolving into a division between the information rich and the information poor, given the projected cost of access to information in the digital age.

In an article celebrating the history of black librarianship published in the summer issue of *Library Trends* in 2000, Alma Dawson notably stated: "[T]hroughout their history, African American librarians have been pioneers, visionaries, risk takers, hard-workers, innovators, organizers and achievers" (p. 49). In the midst of the information transformation of the 21st century, African American librarians should play a role no less important than those of the contributions chronicled in Dawson's article. We currently face several new challenges in this regard, however.

In the 21st century, one major challenge to black librarians, whether they are leading academic libraries or contributing as reference librarians in the bulwarks of our public library system, is to work to ensure that the human touch and caring for the education of black youth remain the hallmarks of our discipline and profession. As we enter the 21st century, we will surely accelerate the building of multifaceted digital and print collections and technology infrastructures to enhance user access to services that can easily accommodate on-site traditional resources and provide access to digital information that users are seeking for rapid information transfer via self-paced digital delivery systems. At the same time, we must not forget that reading and learning form the basic building blocks of truly educated and functioning individuals who are able to contribute positively to society. In this new environment, children and youth will still need to have sustained access to public and school library reading programs. Collaborative initiatives formed by the K–12 education system and the nation's libraries should continue to forge relationships with parents through innovative teaching and learning programs. This is particularly true for the underserved and the populations of urban communities.

Black librarians are faced with an unprecedented challenge resulting from a long-term and continuing decline in the number of young African Americans who choose to enter the library and information science field by pursuing the requisite MLS degree. We must identify the reason for this downturn if we are to keep our numbers strong and vital and continue to play a pivotal role in helping the nation to shape the 21st-century information and educational environment. The 2011 report from the American Library Association (ALA) Office for Accreditation documented that 31 of the 52 ALA-accredited graduate schools of library information science experienced a decline in minority student enrollment between the fall semesters of 2009 and 2010 of 126 graduate students (American Indian/Alaskan Native; Asian/Pacific Islanders; black, non-Hispanic, and Hispanic) as compared to a 278 gain the previous year (American Library Association, 2011).

Although fluctuations do occur in these annual reports, the decline has been a long-term trend among African Americans. At the forefront of national efforts to increase the number of African Americans and other underrepresented groups entering the field and the discipline has been the Laura Bush 21st-Century Librarian Program funded through and managed by the Institute of Museums and Library Services (IMLS). Recruitment barriers most frequently cited by the 29 respondents to a survey I conducted for this chapter, who are among members of the Black Caucus of the American Library Association (BCALA), were low salaries in our field as compared to other professions and disciplines, a lack of knowledge about the field, and the cost of obtaining the graduate degree. These factors were viewed by the respondents as key contributors to the long-term recruitment decline and challenge.

We must also find additional ways to remove the glass ceiling that still exists among major academic research libraries in the United States and resists having African Americans serve as library deans, directors, and vice presidents for information resources. The projection is that a significant number of leaders within the membership of the prestigious Association of Research Libraries (ARL) will be leaving their positions for retirement within the next five years. A pivotal question is how many African Americans will be successfully recruited to fill these positions? Among this cadre of the largest academic and research libraries in the United States (116 or more), there is currently a dearth of African Americans who have assumed leadership roles at the highest level of administration.

We should ask the question whether there is an adequate number of librarians of color in the pipeline who are being groomed, mentored, or are on track to compete for these positions. The ARL has invested significant sums in its Initiative to Recruit a Diverse Workforce Program, with approximately 119 African American librarians participating since 2002–2003. The question that remains is what has been the career path of these individuals since their participation in the ARL program? Longitudinal studies should be made to determine where the graduates of these programs go following their participation to ensure that the programs are achieving their mission of preparing a new breed of librarians from diverse and underrepresented groups to serve as the new leaders of our field and discipline.

A major challenge and an opportunity exists for the librarians of our historically black colleges and universities (HBCUs) to ensure that their libraries continue to function as learning and research hubs within their parent institutions. Library budgets across the nation are generally among the first to be cut within an organization when budget reductions occur. With the current decline in the nation's fiscal base, we must be careful that our libraries in HBCUs will continue to be prime components of the academic enterprise in that the HBCUs currently produce the highest number of undergraduates who go on to pursue their doctorates in various fields at majority universities. We would like for this pattern and trend to continue, and the libraries of the HBCUs are a major part of this past success. The libraries of HBCUs have a responsibility to continue their recent efforts to galvanize the digitization of their substantial special collections and archives about African American history, even in the current budget decline. These resources are unique, and having them readily available in the open access web environment will serve as an important stimulus in furthering research and scholarship about African American history and culture for publication and distribution on national and international scales. Vigorous opportunities should continue to be explored by the HBCU libraries through foundations and federal agencies, such as the National Endowment for the Humanities and the IMLS, for funding to develop collection links with majority research universities holding extensive African American archival resources and with the universities of the southern African nations. Such partnerships are important to enhance and increase the presence of black librarians and diversity library programs within such agencies as the IFLA, the United Nations Educational, Scientific, and Cultural Organization (UNESCO), and the U.S. Information Agency (USIA) as black librarians have much knowledge and many skills to offer as field consultants.

Finally, a major challenge exists as to how we can reach young black people at an earlier stage of their development (high school and the undergraduate years) to interest them and expose them to the joys and benefits of pursuing a career in which they will have an opportunity to participate in shaping the new information environment. We should consider models similar to those used in the medicine and engineering fields, where summer programs are made available to African American youths to explore various learned careers. We should consider, as we plan recruitment strategies, what can be used to attract more African Americans to the field of medical librarianship and those who have backgrounds in the science, technology, engineering, and mathematics fields where higher salaries are the norm. My impression is that opportunities in the new information management environment also exist for African Americans to pursue studies in information systems currently offered by our graduate schools of library and information science or information studies. Our representation in the highly marketable subfields of library and information science and information systems is not currently well represented in the national recruitment pool.

I would say to young potential librarians that this is an exciting time to enter our discipline. Libraries are on the cusp of creating new models of scholarly communications and open access. Library professionals and leaders need to continue to take responsibility for monitoring changes in national and international copyright laws, for influencing federal legislation that impacts funding for libraries, and for ensuring that fair use principles are protected for the benefit of scholarship and learning, and at the least cost of access to users, to avoid creating a society of the information rich and the information poor. Librarians need to continue even more so to be the guardians, preservers, and gateways to human culture and new knowledge in the digital age.

We need young, committed, and bright librarians to assume the pioneering roles of Virginia Lacy Jones, the imminent founding dean of the former Atlanta University School of Library Science who contributed so much during her lifetime to the education of black librarians; Charles Churchwell, who broke the race barrier as the first African American to be appointed to the position of dean of an ARL Library; E. J. Josey, the prolific scholar and writer and who served as a moral compass to the ALA on diversity and international librarianship issues; and Robert Wedgeworth, who yielded significant influence on the future directions of the ALA as the first African American to serve in the capacity of executive director. Black librarians have much to contribute to our field and discipline. We must continue to work strategically to address and debate these challenges and to seek ways to expand our contributions and impacts on the local, national, and global scales.

REFERENCES

American Library Association, Office of Accreditation (2011, May). Statistical Reporting Summary of Changes in ALA-Accredited Programs, Fall 2009–Fall 2010. Retrieved from http://www.ala.org/ala/aboutala/offices/accreditation/Statical%20reports/summarychanges.cfm

Dawson, A. (2000, Summer). Celebrating African American Librarians and Librarianship. *Library Trends*, *49* (1), 49.

Day, J. C. Population Profile of the United States: National Population Projections. In U.S. Census Bureau. Population Profile Maine Overview Profiles. Retrieved from: http//www.census.gov/population/www/pop-profile/natprojet.html (p. 1)

17

❖❖

Academic Art Librarianship and the Black Librarian

Deirdre D. Spencer

This chapter reflects on 25 rewarding years as an academic art librarian. Although the library profession is dominated by women, ethnicity occasionally complicates the challenges faced by women of color as administrators and supervisors. In administrative matters such as departmental and intralibrary relations, resource management, automation, and facilities oversight, the black female librarian negotiates a divide between pleasant authority figure, who carefully presents her authority, while addressing challenges rarely confronted if identified with another gender or race. As the bibliographer and manager of a special research collection, patrons recommend acquisitions but sometimes also question your handling of them. Reference, instruction, liaison, and outreach efforts require steps to ensure an approachable, cooperative, flexible, and welcoming demeanor.

The field of art librarianship is not often associated with African Americans or ethnic minorities, although the demographic is changing as a result of diversity and mentoring efforts within the profession. Still, head librarians of major art research collections count few blacks among their ranks. Upon entering the profession over 25 years ago, I accomplished my 10-year career goals within three years, beginning as an assistant art and architecture librarian at a large southern university in the late 1980s, and two years later becoming the head art librarian of a major midwestern university. Having earned the bachelor's and master's degrees in art history before applying to library school, I was prepared academically for the demands of my positions. An internship in academic art librarianship and courses in personnel administration prepared me professionally to meet my duties, but the pioneering experience of a young black female academic art librarian presented occasional challenges of a different nature, requiring patrons and colleagues to reconsider any preexisting notions of academic librarians, black women, or art library professionals.

In Albert Boime's 1990 classic monograph *The Art of Exclusion: Representing Blacks in the Nineteenth Century*, one chapter in particular, titled "The Question of Black Competency," is appropriate to this discussion. At issue was the capacity of former slaves to assimilate into American society "by entering trades and the learned professions." Post-Reconstruction segregation restricted blacks' spheres of influence in their own communities and institutions. Nearly 150 years later, after the civil rights struggles of the 1950s and 1960s, the controversies over affirmative action, and after the election of an African American president, questions of black competency and legitimacy persist.

Blacks in positions of leadership in predominantly white environments may experience tacit resentment or challenges to their authority in the execution of their duties. Clearly, questioning authority is ingrained within academic culture, yet questioning black female authority within the academic milieu may acquire tones of questioning the legitimacy of one's existence in a position of responsibility to manage resources that affect academic production. These rare encounters provide opportunities for the library professional to demonstrate skill, knowledge, and diplomacy. Most valuable are external networks of colleagues in university and corporate management, who provide a sounding board, support, situational analysis, and strategic planning to address the complexities of institutional and individual racism if or when they occur. In my experience, the key to avoid potential complications is to frankly assess situations and their potential impact, plan ahead, and pleasantly deliver excellent customer service that exceeds patron's expectations and is sufficiently flexible to accommodate exceptions.

Reference and research services are offered to the university community and the broader public through direct contact and remote electronic access. We also receive referrals from public libraries. A black female head of an art history research collection may be unexpected; therefore, negotiating the reference interview with a surprised patron requires the librarian to put that person at ease. Smiling, nodding, listening, gently probing for clarification, conveying one's knowledge of the collection, and sincere follow up with the patron break potential barriers and inspire patron confidence. Early in my career reactions from patrons upon initial encounters included surprised looks, puzzled gazes, and questions such as "How does one get a job like this?" "What educational preparation do you have?" and "Do you have an art history background or a library degree?" Although these questions may be probes for career information, one momentarily considers race and gender and whether such questions would be asked if one identified with another race or gender. Are these questions to assess one's competency and legitimacy? Does it matter? One's response is to pleasantly recite the litany of one's education and experience and quickly demonstrate expertise in response to their query, hopefully resolving any question of competency and recruiting another fan for the library.

Related to reference is bibliographic instruction, which is offered at varying levels of complexity. The bulk of our instruction classes are for undergraduate students, whom we instruct in how to navigate the myriad electronic bibliographic, text, and image databases in addition to library services. Engaging them in the learning process is sometimes challenging. During the introduction I share my background so they will view me as a resource. I make jokes to keep them engaged, thus enabling me to appear approachable and knowledgeable. Weeks after the sessions I receive e-mails and visits requesting research assistance when they are ready to work on their topics. I discuss their ideas with them, map out arguments, and facilitate their skill with the resources on their own terms. As a black female, I position myself as an academic nurturer who facilitates knowledge of the discipline by helping others (including a struggling student who credits my help for his entry into the senior honors program). My experience as an art history doctoral student has expanded my knowledge of resources and complex research strategies, which I share with patrons of all levels.

As a bibliographer and collection manager my duty is to ensure an extensive art historical research and teaching collection that reflects changes within a Eurocentric discipline. In recent years, the fields of art history and visual culture have expanded beyond Eurocentric norms and the traditional Western canon. Instead, artistic production among ethnic groups of the African, Latin American, and Asian diasporas, as well as contemporary art from the continents of origin, is receiving scholarly attention. Within the past two decades the emergence of critical theory and the construction of class and gender within the realm of art history have altered the discipline. As a black female art librarian and scholar I am invested in the perpetuation of scholarship that speaks to our issues, alongside more traditional studies. By providing print and electronic access to new art historical resources, I help facilitate the expansion of new scholarship and perpetuate its inclusion into the canon.

Collection development is one of the most rewarding aspects of the profession because you and your users shape the collection according to your informed judgment and financial resources. As a black female collection budget manager, one must sometimes maintain a firm position in relations with vendors in order to act in the best interest of the collection and budget. Coercive tactics by vendors are unacceptable, and budget managers of any gender or race should receive respect. Working collaboratively with vendors encourages the development of new services such as automated selection and account management and shelf-ready processing as well as price negotiations that benefit libraries.

In conclusion, I would like to comment on a common occurrence with art libraries, whether academic or museum: sharing building space with your primary clientele. As a black female administrator in the building, close proximity to our academic department ensures swift and unrelenting accountability to our users and building occupants. For example, during the early 1990s, I used faculty requests for a free campus book delivery service to pilot a project that is now a popular, library-wide service. New services such as this one were piloted by fine arts library staff, and it is important to nurture cohesive relations with one's staff. The black female supervisor must tread lightly but firmly in communicating service goals and delivering them through our staff. As a black female outreach and liaison librarian, projection of friendly confidence in our resources and services and a willingness to cooperate within and across disciplines help to promote good relations and necessary support for the library and the black librarian.

REFERENCES

Boime, A. (1990). *The art of exclusion: Representing blacks in the nineteenth century.* Washington, DC: Smithsonian Institution Press.

Curry, D. A. (1994). Your worries ain't like mine. African American librarians and the pervasiveness of racism, prejudice and discrimination in academe. *Reference Librarian, 45/46*, 299–311.

Fisher, E. M. (1991). *Modern racism in academic librarianship towards black Americans: A California study.* Pittsburgh: University of Pittsburgh.

Jones, E. J., Nelson C. O., & Berry, J. (1999). Culturally competent librarianship. *Library Journal, 124*, 14.

Kemp, R. (1994). The secrets of my success; an African American librarian. *Wilson Library Bulletin, 68*, 35–37.

18

Managing Historically Black Colleges and University Libraries during Economic Recession: Challenges and Expectations for Library Deans and Directors

Felix Eme Unaeze

Many academic libraries on college and university campuses have experienced some budget cuts during both normal and tight economic times. Now that there is an economic downturn in the United States, many academic libraries are facing serious budgetary problems, and libraries at historically black colleges and universities (HBCU) are not exempt from this situation.

Mezick stated that "Libraries, by function, are an integral part of the college experience. They are a place where necessary resources are provided and research assistance can be obtained" (2007, p. 561). It is generally known that academic libraries and academic librarians play an integral role in the college experience of students.

Libraries have often been labeled as a "bottomless pit" simply because they consume a lot of money in the acquisition of resources needed by their users, and they do not generate substantial funds to sustain themselves. Instead, they depend on their various campus operating budgets or other funding sources, such as student technology fees, to meet their daily operations costs. However, the purported money they consume is spent in the acquisition of resources that are badly needed by their users for their educational needs, including training, learning, and research.

Deans and directors at HBCU libraries face a monumental task in finding the funding required to manage their respective libraries, especially during this time of economic recession. As a result, they have to develop various strategic plans and other methods to manage their libraries effectively. Academic libraries are expected to do more with less during difficult economic times, especially when users are out of jobs and with increased enrollment on college and university campuses, with the aim to learn new skills to position themselves for future jobs. Subsequently, for the aforementioned reasons, HBCU libraries will experience an upsurge in their user statistics.

Finally, considering the numerous challenges and opportunities that exist for library deans and directors at HBCU campuses, this chapter explores various critical ways of managing, finding funding, and building partnerships for HBCU libraries during an era of economic recession.

Some more recent works have address some of these issues. Mezick explained:

> Today, academic libraries can no longer be complacent about their "good" status. There is growing pressure on all academic library managers to be more accountable for how they use limited resources and to achieve institutional outcomes perceived as important by college and university stakeholders. Such stakeholders include students, faculty, and academic staff and administrators; as well as accreditation agencies. (2007, p. 56)

Howard stated:

> Academic libraries have been beset by changes that have led some observers to wonder whether they have a future at all. Their budgets have been hit hard even as the cost of buying and storing information . . . continues to climb. Search engines have replaced librarians as the go-to source of information for most researchers. (2011, para. 2)

Sanders further expounds:

> Thus, in studying a university library, the institution and its various intricacies also must be studied. Gauging the effectiveness of libraries may be achieved by measuring them against the Association of College and Research (ACRL) Libraries Standards. These allow libraries to access library effectiveness in the categories of collections, organization of materials, staff, service, facilities, budget, operations, and overall administration. The libraries at the historically black colleges and universities (HBCUs) often have difficulty in achieving these standards because of their history of inadequate funding. Yet, with the shortages of funds administered by the deans/directors, amazingly the librarians perform quite admirably towards meeting the needs of their diverse faculty, students, and other clientele. (1994, pp. 162–163)

GROWING FINANCIAL WOES AT HBCU LIBRARIES

The United States and most countries of the world are currently facing serious economic and financial downturn. This has caused many countries, including the United States, to take some drastic actions in the dispensation of their funds. This has affected many public and private sectors of the country, including colleges and universities. It is even worse at HBCUs. Academic libraries are one of the first areas their respective institutions look at when they are asked to return some money to their state governments. This situation puts every library dean or director in a difficult position in making budgetary decisions. The leaders of academic libraries will attest that when their colleges and universities face a serious financial crunch from state or federal government, and when asked to refund some money from their dwindling budget, the library will be one of the first areas to be considered to cut. This situation is worse in HBCU institutions, where libraries face severe financial pressure while making decisions in reference to the acquisition of resources including technology, staffing, and facilities management.

As noted in the 2010 Association of College and Research Libraries (ACRL) report, "Value of Academic Libraries: A Comprehensive Research Review and Report":

> Academic libraries have long enjoyed their status as the "heart of the university." However, in recent decades, higher education environments have changed. Government officials see higher education as a national resource. Employers view higher education institutions as producers of a commodity—student learning. Top academic faculty expects higher education institutions to support and promote cutting-edge research. Parents and students expect higher education to enhance students' collegiate experience, as well as propel their career placement and earning potential. Not only do stakeholders count on higher education institutions to achieve these goals, they also require them to *demonstrate evidence* that they have achieved them. The same is true for academic libraries; they too can provide evidence of their value. Community college, college, and university librarians no longer can rely on their stakeholders' belief in their importance. Rather, they must demonstrate their value. (Oakleaf, 2010, p. 11)

In order to demonstrate those values, librarians must discover what their stakeholders expect from the library. For example, in the "State of Libraries at HBCUs":

> in 2005 the Association of College and Research Libraries (ACRL) President's Program Committee commissioned a study in which a group of provosts and chief academic officers were asked what was wanted from the library. The findings indicated, among other points, that they wanted their libraries to be good with regards to quality, accreditation, academic success, and faculty and student satisfaction. The respondents also indicated that they want to see the libraries be better used and more engaging. (Nyberg & Idleman, 2005)

THE BENEFITS OF PROFESSIONAL DEVELOPMENT

Deans and directors of HBCU libraries should utilize the opportunity and encourage their staff to attend professional development trainings, conferences, workshops, and webinars. Recently the HBCU Library Alliance facilitated workshops for HBCU library deans and directors in Atlanta, Georgia. Loretta Parham of the Atlanta University Center addressed "Fundraising Strategies for HBCU Libraries." Dr. Consuella Askew, associate dean for public services, Florida International University Libraries, facilitated a session on "Data Speaks: Using Data to Effectively Make Your Case." The two workshops were informative, educative, and assisted HBCU library deans and directors about grant writing and fundraising skills. Library deans or directors who could not be present wisely sent their associates or other relevant staff members to ensure pertinent information was captured for implementation.

HBCU library deans and directors should take advantage of what the HBCU Library Alliance has to offer in terms of conferences, workshops, webinars, and training in order to strengthen their leadership skills and the skill sets of their library staff. Professional development opportunities for support staff help to build a sense of belonging among staff who thereby become strong advocates for the library program.

THE MISSION OF THE HBCU

HBCUs are a source of accomplishment and great pride for the African American community as well as the entire nation. The Higher Education Act of 1965, as amended, defines an HBCU as:

> any historically black college or university that was established prior to 1964, whose principal mission was, and is, the education of black Americans, and that is accredited by a nationally recognized accrediting agency or association determined by the Secretary [of Education] to be a reliable authority as to the quality of training offered or is, according to such an agency or association, making reasonable progress toward accreditation. HBCUs offer all students, regardless of race, an opportunity to develop their skills and talents. These institutions train young people who go on to serve domestically and internationally in the professions as entrepreneurs and in the public and private sectors. (U.S. Department of Education, 2010, para. 1)

THE ROLE OF THE HBCU LIBRARY ALLIANCE

The HBCU Library Alliance is defined as a

> consortium that fosters excellence in HBCUs and their constituencies through the development, collaboration, coordination and promotion of programs and activities designed to enhance the resources and services of its members. The HBCU Library Alliance was created in 2002 by deans and directors of HBCU libraries and is com-

prised of over 100 member institutions. Membership in the HBCU Library Alliance is institutional and is open to libraries so designated by the White House Initiative on HBCUs. (HBCU Library Alliance, 2011)

LEADERSHIP AND MANAGEMENT SKILLS EXPECTED OF HBCU LIBRARY DEANS AND DIRECTORS

University administrators expect their dean or director to handle daunting and challenging issues and responsibilities. In spite of the fact that libraries are expected to do more with less during a tight economy, the demands of students and other users increase exponentially every day. Library deans and directors are held responsible for the leadership and management of their libraries and in keeping them as the "hub" of academic activities on campus.

Over the past decade, technology has greatly impacted and influenced the nature of library services and the role of the library in the academic community. Library deans and directors should take the additional responsibility of identifying and training the staff that will be responsible for and directly operating the complexities of library technology and other emerging technologies.

The role of the HBCU library dean or director has expanded beyond the usual administrative, budgeting, and coordinating (ABC) roles. They provide leadership as it relates to accreditation, recruitment and retention, marketing, overseeing, and maintenance and upkeep of their facilities. They are also responsible for providing leadership for the library as it relates to students, faculty, and staff.

The dean or director at a HBCU must possess administrative foresight while managing daily complex operations of the library. The HBCU library dean and director should possess strategic planning experience and be proactive, motivated, analytical, and service oriented.

During a tight economy, HBCU library deans and directors should explore alternative ways of managing their libraries successfully as it relates to resources, including technology, budgeting, staffing, and facilities management. "Effective leaders who manage complex organizations" such as the library "often rely on the skills and the abilities of subordinates at all levels in making or carrying out decisions. By encouraging the involvement of subordinates in decision making" (Moon Pharma, Inc., Corporate Values, Ethics, and Vision, p. 5), senior library administrators will build staff morale, encourage shared leadership within the organization, and establish staff empowerment within all departments. This means that HBCU library deans and directors should encourage and practice participative decision making throughout their libraries.

"Leadership is the ability to get work done with and through others while winning their respect, confidence, loyalty, and willing cooperation" (Plunkett, 1992, p. 325). Leadership is further defined as "stimulating people to be high performers. It is directing, motivating, and communicating with people, helping guide and inspire them toward achieving team and organizational goals" (Concepts of Management: Management & Functions). As chief spokesperson of their libraries, HBCU library deans and directors should possess good oral and written communication skills so they can articulate the perspective and goals of their libraries to the larger academic community. They must also possess the vision to lead their libraries effectively into the future.

Metz (2001) noted that today, effective library leadership requires an extraordinary ability to maintain a delicate and continually shifting balance in the management of technical, financial, and human resources to serve the academic mission of our colleges and universities.

Leaders must make judicious decisions that blend the strengths of the past, the demands of the present, and the uncertainty of the future, and they must do so continually—often within an organizational environment that is also challenged to evolve.

GUIDELINES FOR A TOUGH ECONOMY

HBCU library deans and directors should be fully aware of the strengths and priorities of their library to help guide it through difficult economic times. Some suggestions for HBCU library deans and directors are:

- Undertake a periodic SWOT analysis of their libraries to acquaint themselves with the *S*trengths, *W*eaknesses, *O*pportunities, and *T*hreats of their entire organization.
- Perform a strategic planning session in order to set priorities to meet the library mission and goals as well as the mission and goals of their institutions and various accrediting agencies.
- Join partnerships with other libraries and build a reputable consortium. By joining a consortium, you will be able to acquire some resources in a cost-effective way that would otherwise be expensive if you were to do it alone.
- Encourage professional development of your staff and encourage the integration of techniques and emerging technologies in you library.
- Seek other funding sources and participate in grant writing and grant-writing workshops.
- Establish a good working relationship with the university development office and your Title III office.
- Collaborate with other departments on campus. Bear in mind that the library affects every part of the university.
- Market the library effectively to various campus constituencies and become the chief advocate of the library to the university community and administration.
- Be friendly and approachable, keep an open-door policy, and be mindful of the diverse population of the campus.

- Establish or maintain a Friends of the Library group. This group will assist in fundraising and other issues that may be helpful to the library.
- Constantly review the mission and vision statements of your library to be sure that they are consistent with the mission and goals of the university.
- Make sure that there is proper accountability of goods and services that are offered by the library and that your library meets the audit requirements of the state and university.
- From the student perspective, establish regular communications with the student government association.
- Finally, maintain very close contact and good rapport with your supervisors, especially the provost/vice president of academic affairs.

HBCU libraries have experienced a much more difficult time than non-HBCU libraries related to resources, funding, staffing, and facilities management for many reasons. These difficulties have increased during this most recent economic recession. In spite of these obstacles, HBCU library deans and directors should not be distracted by unpleasant campus politics and work hard to turn every challenge into an opportunity. HBCU library deans and directors should concentrate on creating a welcoming and friendly learning environment that will accommodate all learning styles. Finally, every HBCU dean and director should align his or her library program with his or her institution's missions and goals and assist the institution in meeting the requirements of its accrediting agencies to ensure a quality educational experience is had by all students.

REFERENCES

HBCU Library Alliance (2006). About us. Retrieved from http://www.hbculibraries.org/index.html

Howard, J. (2011, May 8). Tomorrow's academic libraries: Maybe even some books. *Chronicle of Higher Education*. Retrieved from http://chronicle.com/article/Tomorrows-Academic-Libraries-/127393/

Metz, T. (2001, January). Wanted: Library leaders for a discontinuous future. *Library Issues, 21*(3), 2–3.

Mezick, E. (2007, September). Return on investment: Libraries and student retention. *Journal of Academic Librarianship*, *5*, 561.

Moon Pharma Inc. Retrieved from http://www.mpharma.ca/docs/Corporate%20Values%20-%20Ethics%20and%20CSR%20Vision.pdf

Nyberg, S., & Idleman, L. (2005, September). The state of libraries at historically black colleges and universities: A comparative analysis using data collected through the Academic Libraries Survey (Introduction by Loretta Parham). Atlanta University Center, Inc. Chair, HBCU Library Alliance. Retrieved from http://www.hbculibraries.org/docs/Stats-report.pdf

Oakleaf, M. (2010). Value of academic libraries: A comprehensive review and report. Executive summary. Association of College and Research Libraries. http://www.ala.org/ala/mgrps/divs/acrl/issues/value/val_report.pdf

Plunkett, W. R. (1992). *Supervision: The direction of people at work*, 6th ed. Needham Heights, MA: Allyn and Bacon.

Sanders, L. H. (1994). *The commitment of dean of libraries at a predominantly black university*. Lanham, MD: Scarecrow Press.

Unknown Author. Concepts of Management: Management & Functions. Retrieved from http://www.solutionwand.com/web/concepts-of-management/

U.S. Department of Education (2010, July). White House Initiative on historically black colleges and universities. Retrieved from www2.ed.gov/about/inits/list/whhbcu/edlite-index.html

19

❖ ❖

Managing the Academic Library: The Role of the Black Librarian Leader in Three Different Institutional Environments

Theresa S. Byrd

LIBRARIANSHIP A SERENDIPITOUS CAREER

Academic librarianship is a career that has suited me and one I have enjoyed and been committed to since I became a librarian at the age of 23. I was fortunate to be a part of the first American Library Association (ALA) accredited graduating class at North Carolina Central University in 1976.

I was born and raised in a blue-collar family with hard-working parents who stressed education. In my youth, my mother was a housewife and my father was a factory supervisor. I grew up in Philadelphia, Pennsylvania, and visited the Free Library of the Philadelphia branch libraries in my neighborhood. But librarianship was not a career I had thought about. In fact, I did not personally know anyone who was a librarian. My selection of librarianship as a career was a combination of academic preparation, a full Mellon scholarship, and serendipity.

In the 1970s, there were two historically black colleges and universities that offered a master's degree in library science: Atlanta University (AU), a private institution; the other North Carolina Central University (NCCU), a state institution. AU was headed by Virginia Lacy Jones and NCCU was headed by Annette L. Phinazee. AU is closed now, but NCCU flourishes. These two schools trained many of the black librarians in this country, especially those who worked in the South. NCCU had a rigorous residential program that trained the whole student, from library school courses, to the proper way to dress and wear your hair, to the importance of being punctual. I am extremely grateful for the type of mentoring that I received at NCCU under Dr. Phinazee's leadership.

WORKING IN THREE DISTINCT ACADEMIC LIBRARIES

I have served in a leadership role in three distinct institutions. Regardless of the type of institution, I have found that serving as a leader meant managing the library's personnel, budget, facilities, services, and policies and serving as an advocate for the organization on campus. Upon graduating from library school, I immediately began working at the Parham Campus of J. Sargeant Reynolds Community College (JSRCC), the suburban campus of a multicampus institution, in Richmond, Virginia. JSRCC is the third largest of the Virginia Community College System's 23 institutions. I liked the broad mission of the two-year public community college that offered adult students, ranging in age from 18 to 80, a low tuition rate and served all in the community.

I held a variety of positions in the Parham Campus Library but ultimately became the director of learning resources. During my early years at the Parham campus of JSRCC, I did not receive any mentoring. I did, however, form strong relationships with my black colleagues at the downtown campus and occasionally connected with the black librarians at Virginia Commonwealth University. Despite the lack of mentoring, I eventually became active in the Virginia Library Association, and this exposure allowed me to network. Then John C. Tyson became the university librarian at the University of Richmond, and he and Clarence Chisom, a founding member of the Association of College and Research Libraries (ACRL) African American Studies Librarians Section (AFAS), introduced me to the ALA and the Black Caucus of the American Library Association (BCALA). Recollection of John brings to mind how proud the black librarians were of him when he became the state librarian of Virginia at 40 in 1990. He was the second black librarian to serve in this role. In 1986, Ella Gaines Yates became the first black librarian and woman to serve as the state librarian of Virginia.

In Virginia, I learned the politics of the profession. Because the profession tracks, it is also very difficult to make the switch from community college library to a four-year institution. But I did with the assistance of a number of white female university librarians. The Virginia years were good years for me. I was appointed by Governor Douglas Wilder to serve two terms on the State Networking Users Advisory Board. I chaired the Virginia Community College System's task force on library automation for 23 institutions at 35 libraries. In addition, I chaired the Virtual Library of Virginia (VIVA) Consortium Steering Committee for the commonwealth's 39 institutions at 52 campuses.

My involvement with VIVA provided me with the opportunity to meet at different types of institutions across the state. I really liked the campus environment of small, liberal arts institutions, and after completion of my doctorate I decided to seek employment in this type of institution. In 1998, I became the director of libraries at Ohio Wesleyan University (OWU).

OWU, which was founded in 1842, is the type of institution that multiple generations of family members have attended. OWU is a private, residential

Methodist institution in origin and one of the elite liberal arts schools where the curriculum focuses on imparting broad education and developing critical thinking skills. The emphasis is on teaching, not research. The student body is homogeneous, class sizes and teacher–student ratio are small, and the cost of attendance for the year as of 2011is $47,784.

OWU and small liberal arts schools have excellent libraries. The OWU libraries were the "heart of the campus," both in terms of collections and programming as well as location. Because of my success with the library, the president and executive officers asked me to take over the Information Technology Department and to become the chief information officer and director of libraries at OWU in 2004. The merging of information technology and libraries was a trend in small liberal arts institutions. I was in charge of libraries, information technology, audiovisual, the help desk, administrative computing, academic computing, and digital initiatives.

I represented OWU locally and nationally. I was a member of OhioLINK and served as the private institutions directors' representative to the state directors' library advisory committee meetings. I also served two terms on the OHIONET board, including one year as board chair. I was a member of the Five Colleges of Ohio Consortium directors' group, a member of the Oberlin Group (an elite group of 85 liberal arts institution library directors), and the Council of Library and Information Resources' (CLIR) chief information officers.

As director of libraries at OWU, I do not recall race being an issue, perhaps because I was a seasoned, experienced administrator and I understood the profession and the academy. I also had learned at JSRCC how to navigate the white academic world. The other reason is that being head librarian is different from being a staff librarian. Overall, my experience as a black, female chief information officer was positive. I found my information technology colleagues, especially in the CLIR chief information officers group and EDUCAUSE, to be great. But it will come as no surprise that there were men who, despite my accomplishments, struggled with a black woman librarian in the chief information officer role. I guess I did not have enough machismo for them. My treatment, however, mirrors that of other women in the information technology profession.

After 12 years at Ohio Wesleyan, I wanted to work in a university. I currently work at the University of San Diego (USD), a Roman Catholic private residential doctoral/research institution. Like OWU, the student population is homogenous and the cost of attendance for the year as of 2011 is $49,902. The university emphasizes teaching and scholarship at the undergraduate and graduate levels. USD, which is perched on a pristine canyon, is constructed in the beautiful 16th-century Spanish Renaissance architectural style. I have found USD to be typical in operation and structure to other higher education institutions that I have worked in and am enjoying my work and involvement with the university community.

I have always worked in majority institutions. To succeed I had to acknowledge the cultural differences between blacks and whites and hone my emotional intelligence skills. I learned in my first job that a key to surviving in a library organization where I was the only black librarian was to make friends with black colleagues in other departments in the institutions, such as student services, as well as to be an active member of the institution and local community. As a head librarian, I have found my relationships with colleagues, many of diverse ethnic backgrounds who hold similar position locally and nationally, to be my support system.

I have been very active with the ACRL. My involvement has included serving on the ACRL board twice, serving as chair of the ACRL Budget and Finance Committee and as a member of the ACRL Board Executive Committee, and working on the national conference committees. I also developed the ACRL Dr. E. J. Josey Spectrum Scholar Mentor program, which focused on ACRL assisting ALA with recruitment of diversity to the profession.

RACE, ELITISM, AND ACADEMIC LIBRARIES

Regarding women and people of color as library professionals, the country and profession have made progress since the 1950s and 1960s. Yet the idea of a black head librarian is an oxymoron for some. After 22 years of serving as a library leader, I still get asked the question from white colleagues: "Is this [head librarian] a new role for you?" Although I have been successful as a librarian, I often wonder how my career would have turned out if I had started my career in an institution other than a community college. Would I be where I am today? I have to admit that I think not. Though careers are situational, I believe that if I had started work in a small or large college or university library, the culture and hierarchy of these institutions would have prevented me from excelling to the director level.

Racism and segregation are strong themes in the chapters written about the leaders in Josey's *The Black Librarian in America.* Although the role of the black librarian in the profession has improved on university campuses today, racism still exists. A new trend is the practice of limiting black librarians' involvement in their home library and the profession to positions in access services, diversity librarian, or black studies librarian. Also, committee involvement is limited to the diversity committee. I call this practice the "ghettoization" of minority librarians in majority institutions. These librarians have good jobs in prestigious institutions but they are cut off from the mainstream organization and opportunities for advancement. When majority, prestigious institutions hire minority librarians in these roles and fail to mainstream them, it appears that either they solely want to claim a diverse staff or that these are the roles they believe are appropriate and they are comfortable with allowing minority librarians to have in the organization. Moreover, in academic libraries, the tenure decision can be heavily influenced by schmoozing or likability rather than meritorious work. When this happens, the candidate of color always loses. I want to challenge all library leaders to be courageous enough to address these issues. After 40 years, the profession should have eliminated such capricious and biased behavior.

Academic libraries and research libraries are very elitist and they track by last place of work. Of course, everyone denies this practice, but it is true. For management positions in certain types of institution, it is a matter of pedigree, not effective skills, that is the important factor. This latter practice is race neutral. A white librarian who is not a member of the club she wishes to join will not get hired either. This is where I say shame on librarians, who are mostly women, for maintaining this elitist environment.

THE FUTURE OF BLACK ACADEMIC LIBRARIANS

The work of Dr. E. J. Josey and others in breaking down barriers in the library profession and library associations has paid off. There are black library directors in all types of higher education institution libraries, including the Association of Research Libraries (ARL) institutions. There are black library administrators, both male and female, who are leading and thriving in majority institutions. As a member of this group, I know our accomplishments would not have been possible without the work of the trailblazers who went before us. The ARL's Leadership and Career Development Program and the ALA Spectrum Initiative are preparing the next generation of minority librarian leaders. The future looks bright for these librarians, as long as we are vigilant activists by continuing to work through the BCALA, ALA Council, ALA executive board, and division boards to bring about change and eliminate barriers to the success of minority librarians.

20

More than Just a Drop in the Bucket: Black Instructional Librarians Teaching for Academic Success

Lisa A. Ellis

As American society changes due to new technologies and globalization, institutions of higher education have had to implement new teaching and learning practices to address student success, especially among underserved college students. Working collaboratively with college administrators and faculty, instructional librarians have the opportunity to participate in a variety of instructional programs, to teach information, communication, and technology (ICT) literacies. With the formal articulation of Information Literacy (IL) Competency Standards by the Association of College and Research Libraries (ACRL) nearly a decade ago, instructional librarians were prompted to develop new curricular offerings ranging from first-year programs coupled with English writing courses to full-scale credit courses in information studies, all of which sought to directly teach IL, and in the process, indirectly foster communication and technology abilities (ACRL, 2000).

Instructional librarians, many of whom are black (defined as African, African American, or a product of the African Diaspora), understand the importance of helping students, especially those underserved, to develop a high proficiency of ICT abilities, not only to attain academic success, but also to foster career success and lifelong learning. The absence of statistical data regarding the teaching activities of black instructional librarians in academia makes it difficult to evaluate their efforts.

To gain knowledge about the teaching activities of black instructional librarians, I conducted a series of focus groups and personal interviews with a group of black instructional librarians with 10 to 41 years of teaching experience at both public and private institutions. Through rich conversations, shared stories, and candid discussions, the source of their keen insight, teaching philosophy, and practices, in and outside the classroom, was discovered. These librarians are confident, assured, and motivated by the responsibility of educating a new generation of learners. Significantly, these librarians noted how former students thanked them for having a positive impact on their college experience. Overall, black instructional librarians should be valued for their distinctive contribution to student success in academia and beyond.

Former K–12 teachers, computer instructors, and young adult librarians in the public library, these librarians were ready to make the transition to instructional librarians. Some librarians interviewed were reference librarians who admitted having a practice conducive to teaching. Evidently, there are cogent and well-established reasons for linking reference and instruction that help to explain the facility for adaptation (Ellis, 2004). Whether working with others one-to-one or in group situations equated with classroom instruction, these librarians described themselves as outgoing individuals who were committed to teaching and found great purpose in instructional librarianship.

When asked to explain their teaching philosophies, black instructional librarians noted the benefits of teaching IL abilities as a part of their common curricular objectives. For many instructional librarians, including those of color, teaching course-related lectures, what is commonly known as "one-shot" instructional offerings, is more the norm than the exception. They described in detail teaching such abilities as: thesis or topic formulation, database searching from Boolean to the use of proximity operators, and evaluating sources and content, as well as correctly citing sources. However, a number of black instructional librarians I interviewed taught semester-long credit courses in information studies. For these librarians, they described their teaching philosophies in all-encompassing or holistic terms. One librarian stated, "teaching life-long learning skills and how to navigate issues related to information . . . [and the] global society of which they are a part." Concurring with this philosophy, another librarian expounded on this and noted: "Students are taught how to . . . think critically about how this information world affects them . . . , and how they can, through knowledge and awareness, [have] impact."

Black instructional librarians discussed teaching in transformative terms. They continuously challenge students to think critically, question established principles upheld by a dominant few and to formulate an understanding that is "open and receptive to others" by taking into account divergent points of view. Of high importance to black instructional librarians is teaching respect in the classroom in order to have civil discussions on information topics that promote communication skills of speaking and listening. As one librarian observed, "the classroom is a safe-haven to discuss issues." Many report it is important to inspire students to "think outside the box to be truly engaged and apply critical thinking skills that are more elaborate than one defined answer checked off in a box." As one librarian succinctly noted, "students have grown accustomed to lecture-style courses where the professor uses PowerPoint, assumes the role of 'sage on the stage,' with little to no interaction from the students who are rigidly or robotically taught." Recently, questions have been raised about whether college students are sufficiently challenged to have learned something at the end of their college careers beyond socialization skills (Arum & Roksa, 2011). Another librarian related that: "10% of the population will be doing the thinking for the other 90%; another 40% will be needed to follow orders in a manner which requires training not education. Knowing this, students are presented with making a conscious choice in taking responsibility for deciding the role of education in their lives."

Whether or not black instructional librarians teach library credit courses or not, those interviewed were unanimous in their view that library credit courses should be required of all college students. In fact, as one librarian claimed, it is not unusual for upperclassmen to comment, "I wish I had this course earlier in my college career." Fortunately, much has been written in the library literature advocating for the offering of credit courses in academic libraries (Owusu-Ansah, 2004). These courses would appropriately fit in with other general education requirements, giving students the necessary foundation to increase their potential for learning and understanding at an advanced level. Although course content should include aspects of IL, wide-ranging topics on information involving communication and technology certainly could be accommodated. When asked why there are not more library credit courses, particularly with credit hours comparable to other discipline courses, black instructional librarians speculate the reasons could be political and logistical. Perhaps librarians are reluctant to accept a lengthy teaching assignment in addition to their current responsibilities. Regardless of the obstacles, the rewards of teaching information literacy skills to students are immeasurable.

In working with underserved students, black instructional librarians share numerous stories about the importance of offering additional encouragement to build confidence and self-esteem in students. Today, many underserved students include non-traditional older students returning to school after a long absence. Library use via computer technology is often the most significant change they encounter. As a result, a fear of technology makes some of these students a bit anxious and a challenge to teach.

To help students overcome this fear of technology, one librarian suggested using analogies to demystify computers and databases (e.g., cellphones are small computers). Others suggested pairing these students with tech-savvy students for collaborative work. Additionally, it is effective to use real-world issues for assignments and incorporate theory only as grounded in practice. It is also useful for underserved students to consider projects that they are not only interested in pursuing, but also allow them to find their unique voice for expression. Such assignments as self-assessments and contemplative practices (e.g., journaling) may be initially confounding to underserved students who are not accustomed to commenting on their learning. With proper guidance and established trust by instructors, these reflective practices can promote self-efficacy and contribute to critical thinking skills in all students (Fritson, 2008).

Black instructional librarians emphasized their ability to form relationships with students. Librarians who are sincerely supportive of students can perceive learning challenges and intuitively address the individual need of a student among the collective. Routinely, these librarians spent hours outside the classroom working one-on-one with students. Such activities are indicative of a commitment to teaching, instilling confidence, and developing strong information literacy in underserved students. Mentoring and relationship building are certainly factors contributing to the increased retention of underserved students and, likely, all students (Redon, 2006).

Through my work with this group of black instructional librarians, I have found that they are passionate about teaching and are undoubtedly committed to educating the whole student and challenging them to excel above their own expectations. I am confident that they represent the best qualities of instructional librarianship and provide the basis for a bright future for black instructional librarians in higher education.

REFERENCES

Arum, R., & Roksa, J. (2011). *Academically adrift: Limited learning on college campuses*. Chicago: University of Chicago Press.

Association of College and Research Libraries (ACRL) (2000). Information literacy competency standards for higher education, ACRL. Retrieved from: http://www.ala.org/ala/mgrps/divs/acrl/standards/informationliteracycompetency.cfm

Ellis, L. A. (2004, February 1). Approaches to teaching through digital reference. *Reference Services Review*, *32*, 2, 103–119.

Fritson, K. K. (2008). Impact of journaling on students' self-efficacy and locus of control. *InSight: A Journal of Scholarly Teaching*, *3*, 75–83.

Owusu-Ansah, E. K. (2004, January 1). Information literacy and higher education: Placing the academic library in the center of a comprehensive solution. *Journal of Academic Librarianship*, *30*, 1, 3–16.

Redon, L. I. (2006, October). Reconceptualizing success for underserved students in higher education. Symposium on Postsecondary Student Success. Retrieved from: http://nces.ed.gov/NPEC/pdf/resp_Rendon.pdf

Part IV

FROM THE SPECIAL LIBRARY

21

Medical Libraries, Information Technology, and the African American Librarian

Ellie Bushhousen

Today's information landscape is dynamic and full of promise and new directions. Search engines, global positioning systems, and social media have altered how people think about locating, accessing, storing, and using information. Medical information, whether for the health care provider or consumer, inhabits a large portion of the digital landscape. Patients, along with their families and caregivers, struggle to find trusted sources for health news and trials. Health care practitioners stagger under the weight of trying to stay abreast of journal articles, systematic reviews, and clinical trial results. In addition, both sets of medical library patrons are retrieving medical information on handheld devices, such as smart phones, tablets, or electronic readers. When I considered the topic of this chapter—challenges facing the African American medical librarian—I decided the focus should be on how African American librarians can become adept with the tools and formats of this new information environment.

Stereotypes have a way of restricting movement or progress because the image or story is passed from person to person as "the way it is." In a 1988 essay that appeared in *American Libraries*, Patrick A. Hall captured the conundrum stereotypes create: "most black librarians and other minority professionals are trapped in the awkward position of trying to make people 'comfortable' with them as professionals while reserving enough energy to perform their jobs well" (p. 900). Librarians chafe at the image of an older, white woman with her finger pressed firmly to her lips to "shush" patrons. Similarly, if asked to describe an individual who is "tech savvy," many people would describe a white male in his teens or 20s. The mainstream media perpetuate both stereotypes because the images provide a visual cue for an audience: people can readily grasp what the image represents when they see it. In an earlier, less virtually connected world, stereotypes were easier to maintain because no one could refute their veracity on a large scale. America in the 21st century, however, has an African American president. In addition there are scores of other African American leaders, such as Dr. E. J. Josey, founder of the Black Caucus of the American Library Association, who have demonstrated perseverance and accomplishment despite society's limited expectations. Today's African American medical librarians must push personal boundaries and dispel the stereotypes regarding prowess with technology. Today's librarians are increasingly called on to use smart phones, mobile readers, and other handheld devices, as well as to be able to identify trends and reliable sources for mobile applications. Being on the margin of discussions about emerging trends in handheld and personal information technologies is a disservice, not only to us professionally, but also to our patrons, particularly those from ethnically and culturally diverse populations.

Medical librarians everywhere are encountering an unprecedented wave of digital resources. In addition, many content providers are developing mobile portals as more people own and utilize handheld devices. A report released in July 2010 by the Pew Internet & American Life Project stated that "minority Americans lead the way when it comes to mobile access—especially mobile access using handheld devices." The report noted that in 2010, 87% of African Americans owned cell phones and that African American cell phone owners "*take advantage of a much wider array of their phones' data functions*" (Smith, 2010, emphasis added). Specifically, the report noted that African American cell phone owners use nonvoice functions such as text and instant messaging, e-mail, and access the Internet via their handheld device. One possible reason for this, the report notes, is that white cell phone users may also own a desktop or laptop computer to perform nonvoice functions and, therefore, are not confined to using a sole device.

African American medical librarians must stay abreast of trends and developments in the digital information pipeline. This is not just for their own edification, but to continue to provide service to their patrons. The next generation of medical librarians and medical information consumers are digital natives—if they are using the applications and tools available on these devices, the African American medical librarian must be well versed and adept with them, as well to provide a richer library experience and enhance his or her own career trajectory.

Two of this country's premier national library organizations, the American Library Association (ALA) and the Medical Library Association, have groups that provide professional support and mentorship for African American librarians. The Black Caucus of the ALA and the African American Medical Librarians Association are communities that gather in cyberspace and at face-to-face conferences to exchange ideas and consider future directions. One of these future directions might include focusing on enhancing and improving African American medical librarians' facility with existing and emerging technologies. Today's youth take these tools for granted because they are the "born digital" generation.

Another librarian online community for networking and support that may be of interest is the Black Librarian Nation.

Two other organizations African American medical librarians may want to investigate are the National Society of Black Engineers and Black Data Processing Associates. It is not a stretch to see the potential for medical librarians to collaborate with information technology (IT) and engineering professionals and students to develop useful portals of health information for diverse populations. Librarians understand how information is gathered and organized; IT professionals and engineers know how information can be formatted and packaged for dissemination. Combining these strengths can bolster both professions and communities.

Our challenge, therefore, is to make the effort to become more visible and to speak with authority on the merging of IT, medical information, and library services. African American medical librarians must seek out opportunities for exploring and using these tools and assisting our patrons to be viewed as engaged and taken seriously by our colleagues. Just as important, we must write about these experiences for others to read and learn from. Most medical and hospital libraries are part of, or have a connection to, an academic campus. This connection provides access to professional resources that can further careers and expand professional horizons. African American medical librarians must make our presence known by publishing in peer-reviewed journals that focus on special or medical libraries. Our research should include case studies of our progress in mastering multiple information technologies, creative ways to use these tools with medical content, and how we are sharing this knowledge with our patrons. These efforts often lead to invitations to present at conferences or workshops, where we can share our experiences and expertise with our professional peers. As we put ourselves in the public arena, we also become role models and mentors for African American students across all disciplines. Each of us knows how disheartening it is to not see ourselves well represented in the intellectual community. African American medical librarians are in the unique position of being individuals who walk in multiple paths—information professionals, ethnically and culturally diverse, and increasingly adept with current and emerging technology. There is much to be shared from this abundance of experience.

REFERENCES

Hall, P. A. (1988). Yassuh! I's the reference librarian! *American Libraries, 19*, 900–901.

Smith, A. (2010). Mobile access 2010. Pew Internet & American Life Project. A Project of the Pew Research Center. Retrieved from http://www.pewinternet.org/Reports/2010/Mobile-Access-2010.aspx

22

Achievements of Selected 21st-Century African American Health Sciences Librarians

LaVentra E. Danquah

The achievements of African American health sciences librarians have had limited exposure in the library profession. Irrespectively, they continue to make meaningful contributions in service to the profession. Cynthia Henderson's (2000) comprehensive review on the roles of black health sciences librarians provided a conceptual framework for this chapter. This work highlights the activities and achievements of selected African American health sciences librarians. Specific attention is given to professional activities, success strategies, and foresights about the profession. Ideally, the featured librarians will unfold a story of successful, embedded professionals committed to a greater purpose.

The Medical Library Association (MLA) states: "The health sciences librarian believes that knowledge is the sine qua non of informed decisions in health care, education, and research, and the health sciences librarian serves society, clients, and the institution by working to ensure that informed decisions can be made" (2010, para. 2). Health sciences librarians are immersed in information-intensive, organizationally complex health care environments. They serve as administrators, managers, coordinators, educators, subject specialists, and clinical librarians who hold positions in consumer health and patient education centers, hospitals, health care agencies, information services industries, pharmaceutical companies, public libraries, colleges, and universities (Brettle, 2008; McKinnell, 2008; Wood, 2008). African American librarians are as much a part of these exchanges as their counterparts. My intention in this chapter is to encourage greater efforts to document and publish the diverse works and contributions of health sciences librarians of color.

AFRICAN AMERICAN HEALTH SCIENCES LIBRARIANS

Cassandra Allen, Division of Specialized Information Services, National Library of Medicine (NLM)

Cassandra Allen is an influential voice in medical librarianship with notable career achievements. Functioning within the Division of Specialized Information Services, Cassandra has conducted numerous outreach initiatives with special populations. She has worked closely with the National Medical Association (NMA), the oldest and largest professional association of minority physicians, to provide training on NLM resources. In addition, she assisted this group with implementing NLM's Information Rx program, which encourages physicians to direct patients to MedlinePlus.gov for quality, filtered consumer health information.

Her efforts toward increasing diversity are marked by chairing NLM's first Diversity Council and receiving the NIH Diversity Champion award. More recently, Cassandra received the Black Caucus of the American Library Association's Distinguished Service to the Library Profession award. With nearly 25 years of medical library experience, Cassandra expressed the importance of stepping outside your comfort zone to grow professionally. With this notion in mind, she actively networks and volunteers on committees because she believes librarians should never stop learning.

Triza Crittle, Louis Stokes Health Sciences Library, Howard University

Triza Crittle speaks with excitement as she describes the clinical librarian services she is heading at the health sciences library. As a result, she provides library instruction for minority physicians and health care providers. Triza is mobile and believes library instruction must follow. She explains the rapidly moving clinical environment and time constraints of physicians: "Sometimes, I'm stopped in the [hospital] hallway and a physician might ask about an article they've been meaning to contact me about. I'll take out my smart phone and immediately send an e-mail so that he can remember to send me the information about the article, and receive it in a timely matter . . . they're thrilled." Triza explains the value of being visible, going out to where your users need you. She is keenly aware of the influence of digital natives and how their use of technology will continue to impact how we delivery library services, including instruction. Triza has her sights on establishing a mobile and flexible clinical librarian program. The plans and strategies she has outlined suggest she is headed in the right direction.

P. J. Grier, National Network of Libraries of Medicine, Southeastern Atlantic Region

P. J. Grier is constantly asking: "What's over the horizon?" A self-described early adopter, P. J. is schooled in clinical informatics and information science. He has definite ideas on how and why librarians must join the conversation on current health care reform by demonstrating their expertise. Because of the continued maturation of electronic health record systems, health information exchanges, accountable care organizations, demands on interoperability, global standards, and vocabularies, P. J. believes there is a dire need to manage health information effectively. Unlike information technology (IT) professionals who focus primarily on the "technology" part of IT, informaticists, including librarians, are experts at information delivery, information retrieval, and human–computer interactions. For example, librarians are well versed in how users access information, as well as technical and structural barriers to access due to poorly designed user interfaces. This depth of knowledge and experience allows librarians to partner with health care IT professionals in providing better information systems products to users. Just as important, P. J. acknowledges that librarians must initiate their involvement and cannot wait for an invitation.

Cindy Gruwell, St. Cloud State University

What greater acknowledgment of one's professional expertise than to have the internal medicine residency director invite you to train internal medicine residents and physicians on evidence-based searching during an intense workshop at the University of Puerto Rico. It happened to Cindy Gruwell, a former health sciences librarian at the University of Minnesota, St. Cloud. Cindy also found a niche in publishing; for nearly eight years she served as the co-editor of "Navigating the Net," a column in the *Medical Reference Services Quarterly*. She has written a number of articles and received a highly favorable review for her co-edited publication *Diversity in Libraries: Academic Residency Programs* (Cogell & Gruwell, 2001).

This work is a solid contribution to the literature on racial and ethnic diversity in academic libraries and a unique opportunity to encounter the voices of the new generation of minority librarians entering the profession, as well as those of the new generation of minority leadership in academic libraries (Garcia, 2002).

Cindy began her career in an academic residency program at the University of Minnesota and is convinced that the connections she made plus a good mentoring relationship helped shape her career decisions. At St. Cloud University, she currently serves on a number of influential university committees, which gives her a platform to promote library services and demonstrate her expertise. For those who are hesitant about health sciences librarianship because they do not have a science background, Cindy encourages them to have no fear and embrace the challenge.

Sandra Martin, Shiffman Medical Library, Wayne State University

"Having a voice matters," according to Sandra Martin, co-founder of MLA's Association of African American Medical Librarians Alliance (AAMLA) Special

Interest Group. As an associate director, Sandra prides herself on linking people with their health information needs. This includes creating an informed health information consumer. With myriad amounts of health information on the web and multiple access points through mobile devices, Sandra affirms the importance of training users on how to identify quality health information. Just the same, understanding the library's role within the context of the larger organization is paramount. Operating effectively in a team-based environment is a standard professional expectation. Sandra emphasizes the significance of being creative in an information-rich environment with shrinking library budgets. She believes this should not intimidate one from entering the profession; those who are creative with a keen sense of career direction and a voice will do just fine.

Neville Prendergast, Rudolph Matas Library of the Health Sciences, Tulane University

As a science teacher in Jamaica, Neville Prendergast often perused the library in search of scientific information. Admittedly, he enjoyed his quests for information, which led to his career as a health sciences librarian. His background in science helped smooth the transition into health sciences librarianship. He had "visions of moving up" after participating in the Association of Research Libraries (ARL) Leadership and Career Development Program (LCDP), and move up he did. Prior to his current medical library directorship, Neville served as a health sciences librarian at Buffalo and associate director at Washington University in St. Louis. To date, Neville proactively cultivates relationships with faculty to promote the library's rich collection of resources and to stay abreast of faculty members' needs.

A proponent of networking, Neville maintains close contact with colleagues from the inaugural class of the LCDP. In addition, he mentors library science students for ARL's Initiative to Recruit a Diverse Workforce. When asked about creating successful mentoring relationships, he explained the importance of scheduling time to communicate, setting learning and development goals, and evaluating progress. Sharing one's knowledge, information, and contacts when necessary are equally important.

CONCLUSION

The achievements of African American health sciences librarians are sparsely documented with limited exposure. Yet the vignettes presented here portray a group of dedicated individuals who are committed to advancing knowledge and discovery in the health sciences. Actively promoting the achievements of librarians from underrepresented groups offers several benefits. First, it suggests the inclusion of library professionals from diverse populations. Second, it can serve as a tool for recruiting a diverse library workforce. Most important, it creates synergy among colleagues, fostering new ideas, initiating collaborative projects, and exploring different ways to approach traditional services. Frankly, this level of energy must be sustained if we are to continue our work for a greater purpose.

REFERENCES

Brettle, A. (2008). Current status and future prospects. *Health Information and Libraries Journal, 25* (Suppl. 1), 32–34.

Henderson, C. (2000). The role of the black health sciences librarians. In E. J. Josey & M. L. DeLoach, M. L. (Eds.), *Handbook of black librarianship* (pp. 683–696). Lanham, MD: Scarecrow Press.

Cogell, R. V., & Gruwell, C. A. (2001). *Diversity in libraries: Academic residency programs.* Westport, CT: Greenwood.

Garcia, V. (2002). Review of the book *Diversity in libraries: Academic residency programs. Journal of Academic Librarianship, 28*, 259–262.

McKinnell, I. (2008). Challenges for the next 25 years. *Health Information and Libraries Journal, 25* (Suppl. 1), 47–48.

Medical Library Association (2010). Code of ethics for health sciences librarianship. Retrieved from http://www.mlanet.org/about/ethics.html

Wood, S. (2008). *Introduction to health sciences librarianship.* New York: Haworth Information Press.

23

❖ ❖

Why Did I Become a Special Librarian?

Phyllis Hodges

The reasons I became a special librarian are: I enjoy people, I am a good listener, I am good at locating information, I am good at threading parts of a request to find the answer, and I like working with aggregate databases. It just so happens that these qualities are necessary for a librarian, or as we are also known, an information specialist. I am defining special librarians as individuals who research, deliver, manage, and archive materials or information for public or private patrons related to the fields of art, music, insurance, finance, nonprofit, medical, law, and museums in a collection environment.

It's worthy to note that the primary library skills taught in graduate library schools are general collection development, reference interviews, archiving, cataloging, and retrieval of information from databases, and these are all transferable to many different fields. For example, the collection process of reviewing written or electronic material for distribution depends on the type of subject. The resources may be chronicled work, an individual article, or a group or series of periodicals. Formatting the data to read online requires cataloging the source by subject, author, date, or keywords, and writing it in html, pdf, or jpeg format or on a CD-ROM for electronic use. Delivery of the information can depend on availability or cost. Aggregate data systems allow for multiaccess to a host of resources, decreasing the delivery time. Therefore, special librarians can utilize these same skills to maintain and manage material and access for our customers.

Currently, I am working in the fundraising department of a university in the Development Office as an assistant director of prospect research. It is important that the information provided has value for the development team in order to make strategic fundraising decisions. My clients are the development officers and the university's executive leadership. I make use of some of the same library skills learned from my years in the profession to ascertain information on potential funders and their interest in the university.

MY JOURNEY

My journey into the field of librarianship began when I was 16 years old working in the Bayside branch of the Queens Public Library as a summer intern. I was introduced to the concept of being a page and reshelving the returned books. The tasks were basic and I enjoyed reading the book jackets of the various publications—fiction, biography, sciences, and children's books. At that time I did not consider employment in that environment, yet I did enjoy the solitude. For the next few summers I worked odd jobs to pass the summer vacation time, and when I read the Sunday *New York Times*, I found myself looking for filing jobs or technical library positions. During this time, I was not aware of the specific discipline called *library science* nor was I aware of the scope of services for information gathering.

By the time I completed my associate's degree in biology with an interest in forensic science at Kingsborough Community College, I was working part time at night in the file room in the library at an investment firm on Wall Street. For me, the pay was good and the hours worked for my class schedule. While I was there, I learned about financial documents and the Lexis/Nexis databases and the importance of the New York Stock Exchange and the ticker tape machine. I also learned about corporate documents and their relevance to financial investments.

Eager to learn more and gain more experience, I accepted a full-time position at Value Line Investment Services. My family background or the black community where I was raised had not exposed me to corporate business protocol or politics, but being a fast learner I was able to grasp another rung on the ladder of my library experience. A dear friend, Joann Adams, the only other African American women in our department, schooled me on the expectations of the staff and how to handle quarterly deadline pressures. Although she is not a librarian by education and training, her insights into how to work as a team member, even when no one looked like me, are still my guides to this day. These insights include these basic principles: learn your job, build your skills, become a valuable asset, be professional, and expand your knowledge of the subject matter.

Later, I took a bold step and answered an ad for a library manager position in a legal department, with no formal training in this discipline. I ventured into Shearson Lehman's law department in the World Trade Center, organizing a room of books and training attorneys how to use Lexis/Nexis on a small red computer—the Ubique system was all the rage. My tenure there further taught me the importance of working hard in a professional setting and how to deliver information in a timely fashion.

While completing my undergraduate work at John Jay College of Criminal Justice and working full time, I realized that I needed more knowledge with case law, "Sheperdizing," and Westlaw Key citations that attorneys would request. I accepted a position at Richards & O'Neil and was under the leadership and mentorship of Paulette Toth. While working at the law firm, I also worked part time in the evening at various New York corporate libraries, opening up another level of experience in a different special library—corporate libraries.

Corporate libraries integrate both library and project management skills. The librarian provides the client with relevant information, but also has the task of interacting with one or more outside sources to obtain information. Often the information request is specific to a larger project and time sensitive, and the librarian has to manage the client's expectations of the availability and delivery of the information. Keeping track of the outside sources contacted, staying within an agreed cost parameter, delivering the product on time, and ensuring the information is relevant form the corporate librarian's creed. Thus, interpersonal skills are extremely important in all library transactions, but they can be especially important in a corporate library.

While attending Pratt Institute in the library science master's degree program, I continued to cultivate my library skills and accepted a position with the United Negro College Fund in their Capital Campaign, researching funding streams. After graduation from Pratt Institute, I accepted a position at the National Urban League as the director of research, again researching and managing sources for fundraising.

While working at these various jobs, I participated as a member of the New York Law Librarians, Special Library Association (SLA), New York Chapter of SLA (NYSLA), and the New York Black Librarians Caucus. My volunteering with other professionals fed my knowledge of how their respective libraries work. I surmised it was in my best interest to join committees; attend workshops, seminars, and conferences; and expose myself to the full library experience. Professional library and information organizations were also the catalyst to the employment positions I accepted. My interactions with other professionals who were advancing the role of librarianship in their respective institutions became an inspiration to me.

Looking back over my years of experience, I was fortunate to be employed and gain experience during the development of the modern day depositories and methods of delivery (i.e., the World Wide Web). Each opportunity I accepted gave me skills, leadership, and fortitude, which I use on a daily basis. I have learned to impress my customers, managers, and colleagues with courteous behavior and consequently quiet the naysayers. And when professional protocol is lacking or misused by others, I pepper my approach with firm dialogue.

I stand on the shoulders of my ancestors who were educated and articulate library professionals, and I often think of them when I find myself challenged. I think of how they would have handled the situation and that gives me pause to consider how I might handle my own circumstances. In addition to my ancestors, there are three outstanding African American women professional librarians who have been influences to me through their work: Nettie Seaberry, director of the Minority Business Information Center at the National Minority Supplier Development Council (NMSDC), New York, an active member of SLA, who spearheaded the Diversity Leadership Program for SLA from 1994 to 1996 and currently serves as the adviser to the New York chapter's Diversity Leadership Development Committee; Dr. Inez Brisfjord, a historian of the Rockland American Association of University Women and director of Special Projects of the John Ericsson Society, New York, and former assistant dean of the School of Information and Library Science of Pratt Institute, Brooklyn, New York; and Sandra Kitt, author and retired library manager of the Hayden Planetarium, Museum of Natural History, New York. These women have proven how to be an excellent information specialist and have shown me how to continue to develop in the profession.

If you display integrity and respect in your interactions with your clients and colleagues, you will be acknowledged for your excellence even as a person of color. Keep these principles in mind: learn your job, build your skills, become a valuable asset, be professional, and expand your knowledge of the subject matter and you will excel.

24

The Southern California Library: Opening the Doors to the Next Los Angeles

Michele Welsing

> The prevention of a free flow of information and the denial of access to information was one of the cornerstones of apartheid in South Africa. The lack of resource centers and community library centers in communities comprised of people who are black was an attempt to deny those communities information that could be used to better themselves socially, politically and economically.[1]

From the "Freedom Libraries" established during the 1964 Mississippi Freedom Summer to the emergence of information resource centers in apartheid South Africa, community libraries have long played a role in building and sustaining movements for justice. Founded almost 50 years ago, the Southern California Library (SCL) stands in this tradition, as an independent library and archive that documents and makes accessible histories of community-led struggles that challenge racism and other systems of oppression so we can all imagine and sustain possibilities for freedom.

However, for much of its existence, SCL has been underresourced and not very well known outside of small academic and activist circles. A few years ago, we began working to change that, to evolve from just "keeping the doors open" to opening the doors to the next Los Angeles and the complex issues it faces. We undertook the task of making the histories of resistance we hold more accessible and useful to those to those living and working in underserved, low-income communities of color, including South Los Angeles, where we are located.

The results have far exceeded our expectations. As just one example, school tours, artist workshops, and community meetings have jumped from a handful a year to almost 70 in 2010 alone. As we began offering dynamic, culturally relevant programming, we have reached many milestones we never thought possible. However, we have also faced challenges and hurdles that have taken a toll. This chapter offers a glimpse of our journey, both its peaks and its struggles.

WHERE WE CAME FROM

SCL was established in 1963 by members of the progressive, white community in Los Angeles who worked together politically and socially for decades, long before SCL was officially in existence. They founded SCL with a sense of urgency. In the aftermath of the McCarthy era, people were throwing out books and other materials in fear of government reprisals. SCL's founding director, Emil Freed, urged people to bring the materials to him so these histories wouldn't be lost. He and those working with him stored the materials in their own homes and garages, risking their reputations, livelihoods, even their freedom, because they believed that these materials and stories could change the world. Because SCL's founders were themselves activists, they knew and worked with a cross-section of others who were working for change. This is how SCL acquired rare collections like the papers of Charlotta Bass, an early civil rights activist, publisher of the *California Eagle* (one of the longest running black newspapers in the west), and a candidate for vice president of the United States in 1952.

However, it was hard to know at the time all the rare materials SCL housed. Photos from that period show a building with floor-to-ceiling boxes and file cabinets. It was mostly visited, and supported financially, by fellow travelers.

After the founder's death in the early 1980s, SCL entered a second era, with a more professionalized core staff who had backgrounds in history and librarianship and who, as middle-aged white women, reflected a demographic prevalent among librarians. As they brought greater organization to the collections, SCL began to acquire a reputation nationally and even internationally, especially in academic circles, as one of the most in-depth archives of Los Angeles' history of community change.

During these years, SCL's materials were primarily used by faculty and students from institutions of higher education, as well as by filmmakers and artists, who drew on its collections to produce hundreds of books, articles, films, and dissertations on Los Angeles's history, including the book *City of Quartz* by Mike Davis, the PBS documentary *Black Press: Soldiers without Swords*, and the play *Chavez Ravine*, by Culture Clash. SCL also initiated programming that put it on the map, such as a major panel on the Black Panther Party, mentioned in *Newsweek*; a conference exhibit on the 1965 Watts Rebellion; and a talk by Howard Zinn, author of the *People's History of the United States*.

By the early 2000s, SCL had a long history of accomplishment—but it was also at a crossroads. The second director was retiring, and most of the previous staff went with her. Always cash-strapped, SCL was out of money, low on staff, and, despite its years, weak in organizational infrastructure.

At this point, in November 2004—the day after George Bush reclaimed the White House—SCL gained its third director, Yusef Omowale, and entered into its next era.

OPENING THE DOORS

One of the immediate problems we tackled was enhancing and diversifying SCL programs to better respond to the educational, social, and political issues facing historically underserved, poor communities of color. This was not an abstract question. SCL is located in South Los Angeles, populated by primarily low-income black and Latino communities that had not always felt welcomed or found value in SCL in the past. Although most of the histories in SCL's collections are of marginalized communities—mothers on welfare fighting for basic rights for themselves and their children, immigrant street vendors facing crackdowns by police as they try to make a living, farmworkers struggling for decent working conditions and wages—for the most part members of marginalized communities were not accessing our resources. Believing that the histories we held were essential for understanding crucial issues facing Los Angeles and other major cities—including disparities in access to education and health care, poverty, unemployment, incarceration, and violence—we felt it was imperative to make our resources and services accessible and useful to the communities most impacted by these issues.

With this goal in mind, we shifted our focus to include members and staff of local community-based organizations that provide services in or organize marginalized populations, as well as local students, teachers, and community residents. As part of the shift, in 2006, we conducted a needs assessment. In a series of focus groups with organizers, teachers, youth organizers, and others, participants overwhelmingly told us they wanted to use our archives to conduct research to inform their organizing campaigns, to use our space as a place to connect, and to get online access to images and other primary source materials to create campaign and classroom materials.

Building on the information we gained, we began working toward a vision for SCL as a linchpin organization in Los Angeles, a vital intermediary space—one that both documents community history and dynamically engages organizations and people in strengthening their skills, analysis, and relationships through access to our collections. We centered our strategies to achieve this vision around a core principle—building relationships.

Although SCL has been in our South Los Angeles neighborhood for going on 40 years, at this point we were almost unknown to local residents, many of whom told us that they thought SCL was just for white people. We changed this message by literally opening our doors and introducing public computers and other technology accessible to the community. A video, *Recognitions of Place*, tells the story of this change.[2] We introduced culturally relevant programming and resources, creating a welcoming space for people and organizations of color, and ramped up the number of our events to bring people into SCL. We introduced sliding-scale memberships, including a "people's rate" of $10 per year—which made membership possible for residents of our local community who would not have been able to afford the previous $40 membership rate. We focused on building community partnerships, reaching out to community organizations not just to attend our events, but to work directly with us on developing and conducting programming.

RESPONSE

Our efforts met with an overwhelming response. From 2003 to 2005, we saw almost a 100% increase in new memberships from residents of South Los Angeles and other low-income communities. Visitors spiked from less than 200 in 2003 to *over 10,000 a year* by 2007. Research requests more than tripled, from 163 in 2003 to over 840 in 2008. Our active community partners jumped from 6 in 2003 to over 60 in 2008.

Beyond the numbers, we saw how people changed their relationships with one another, with SCL, and with the neighborhood, as they gained greater access to the histories of their communities through our programs, particularly those targeted at youth. By the simple act of offering culturally relevant spaces, information, and resources that speak to the lived realities of people's daily lives, SCL was becoming a transformative place in the community to remember freedom dreams of the past and to work toward new dreams for today.

CHALLENGES

We did not have a smooth path in getting to these milestones. Almost from the start, we ran into resistance—from within our own ranks. Especially as the staff and board became noticeably younger and primarily people of color, there was a sense of displacement among some of our traditional supporters, not all of whom understood or were comfortable with our diversifying direction. There were worried whispers that SCL was "in danger." Letters were sent and phone calls made accusing us of becoming a "community library" and not caring about history. A few longtime supporters told us to never ask them for money again. We were once even asked, "What were all these black children doing in the library?" The resistance became especially marked as we began focusing on state violence—including criminalization of youth, immigrants, queers, and other marginalized communities; police brutality; and mass incarceration—as one of our core issues.

STAYING THE COURSE

Despite the resistance, we have stayed the course because we believe that changing public discourse around issues such as state violence in Los Angeles can have a dramatic impact not only locally, but also regionally and nationally. Even as electoral gains are made in other parts of the state, all too often Los Angeles plays a determining role in blocking progressive action, such as in the fight to reform the Three Strikes Law. If we can effect change in Los Angeles, it can lead to change across the country. We believe SCL has a critical role to play as a place for research, reflection, and community dialogue, much as the Highlander Center had an impact on Rosa Parks, who, before she famously refused to give up her seat on the bus, attended a training session at this Tennessee labor and civil rights organizing school, where she met an older generation of civil rights activists and studied the history of previous challenges to segregation.

At the end of 2010, SCL dedicated its new mural "They Claim I'm a Criminal," which pays tribute to two Los Angeles organizations that fought against the discrimination of the poor in the criminal justice system: Mothers Reclaiming Our Children (Mothers ROC) and the Coalition against Police Abuse, both of whose historical documents are held at SCL. At the end of a long, hard year, where we have been struggling like many other nonprofits just to survive in the current economic climate, the dedication provided a moment of celebration, a reminder of community and solidarity that renewed our spirits for the year ahead. The description of (note: the description is not actually on the mural) the mural reads:

Because we are tired of living in the shadow
of violence

Because poverty is violence
And more police cars in the neighborhood
than parks is violence

Because we are weary
of seeing those we love locked in cages

Because we are not criminals

We offer this mural

Of people just like us:
tired and weary
angry and most of all
loving

People just like us
who came together
to fight back
defend build and transform the places we live in

We offer this mural

In this spirit, we offer SCL to the next Los Angeles.

NOTES

1. From "The status and role of resource centres in exHouse of Delegates schools under post apartheid," D. Govender, University of South Africa, 2006.
2. This video can be viewed at http://www.youtube.com/watch?v=O5XeI99Pwms&feature=youtu.be

25

The Dark *but Good* Side of Diversity in Corporate Libraries

Brendan Thompson

E. J. Josey led the way in identifying and enacting the changes that must occur for librarians, and specifically black librarians, to not only make a difference in our profession, but also in our homes, our community, our country. We as librarians have to recognize that although many parts of our profession have changed, we still have the same charge: to contribute to the betterment of the community, whatever community that may be, through the organization and dissemination of information.

Forty years after the first edition of Josey's *The Black Librarian in America* was published, diversification of the library profession has improved. There have been incredible developments in the country. We have a black president! What has not changed is the need to continue to increase the awareness of how a diverse workforce strengthens an institution, be it academic or, in my case, a small part of corporate America. There is also a need to broaden the perspective of what the idea of diversity includes. Black librarians continue to struggle to make their voices heard. This continuing struggle has expanded, however, to make necessary the addition of more men in the profession (especially black men) and the recognition of the gay experience. Both are still an underrepresented minority in the profession. Why haven't we overcome these boundaries? Why are we still actively recruiting for a diverse profession but failing to make the strides other professions have? The reason is because this discussion has occurred in larger parts of the profession, but desperately needs to occur in all parts of the profession.

One way we can cultivate a more diverse workforce is by identifying and expressing how diversity can increase business and encouraging it as a marketing strategy. Pivotal components in corporate marketing are racial relevance, regional diversity, and diversity of both sexual orientation and gender. These components will strengthen any organization. We as underrepresented parts of the community must embrace and convey this through our actions and our work. As our society continues to diversify, it's important that our companies do the same. Without this forward-thinking notion a company will quickly stagnate and, in the long run, fail. Massachusetts has had a recurring problem recruiting minorities, specifically in academia. Many of the colleges, even the Ivy Leaguers in Massachusetts, are experiencing problems recruiting a more diverse pool of candidates (Jan. 2010). Why? Because no one wants to be here alone. Why live or work in a place where there are no blacks? It is not encouraged to live or work in a place where there is an ill-proportioned balance of men and women. Why not expect the same related to race, gender, or sexual orientation? Forty years ago this might have been expected, even 20 years ago, but in 2011, a lack of diversity in a company, at a college, or in a neighborhood is not acceptable. This leads one to believe that the organization doesn't believe in the need for diversity and is now trying to catch up. Now, there's no problem in being a pioneer at a company, but one has to wonder why this didn't happen earlier. There isn't a lack of qualified candidates, so this is no longer an excuse. There has been a steady increase in graduation rates of minorities since the 1970s (Tierney, 1999). This increase in candidates more than provides a pool of both capable and qualified individuals.

In 2010 I interviewed 31 librarians regarding their job satisfaction. Questions addressed whether race, gender, or age played a part in their level of satisfaction. Of the 31 interviewed, only four respondents were African American. Five identified themselves as "nonwhite" (Thompson, 2010). Keep in mind this included two historically black colleges or universities. This sample of librarians focused on some of the largest library communities in North Carolina—Duke University, the University of North Carolina at Chapel Hill, and North Carolina Central University. Of the 31 respondents, many saw a need for an increase in diversity as playing a role in their job satisfaction. The lack of diverse representation is just one example of the need to remind our companies, our universities, our country that actively seeking diversity is still an important endeavor.

Being part of a small startup environmental engineering consulting firm has allowed me to play a role in several aspects of the company, which someone working for a larger company might not have the opportunity to do. I am a "special" librarian and for the first seven months I was a solo librarian setting up a brand new library. As a solo librarian I made all of the decisions related to the library and performed every role of a librarian: acquisitions, collection development, reference, and access services. Another role is taking part in the planning and implementation of marketing strategies, especially related to the library. I have the benefit of working with a company that not only recognizes the importance of an information specialist, but also recognizes the importance of diversity. Our company, comprising fewer than 50 employees nationwide, includes Hispanics, Asians, African Americans, a cornucopia of religious backgrounds, and a good mix of both men and women. This is especially apparent when you compare the ratio of nonwhite to white and men to women within our company compared to that within the profession, environmental engineering, which is mostly populated by white men. Sound familiar? It should, because the library profession has an unbalanced ratio of men to women and whites to other races and ethnicities. The director of the company actively sought a diverse workforce and didn't settle on race alone, but included other important traits such as experience and overall ability. The company is made up of individuals mostly with advanced Ivy League degrees from all over the country, adding to regional diversity and experience.

Something that allows our firm to stand out, aside from our excellent experience and unique skills, is its diversity. Because the company has acknowledged and embraced diversity, our clients are able to see that the company understands diversity's importance in allowing for strong and varied knowledge and ideas. A strong impact is made when one can see the diversity, not only because of skin color, but also through these ideas and knowledge. This is possibly the more powerful statement.

It is not only important to recognize and implement diversity within a company, but also within the library setting. One might say that a librarian is a librarian, regardless of his or her race, but I can say with certainty that diverse information specialists can contribute more in their research, their development of a collection, and their interaction with patrons and vendors. I have demonstrated this through my interaction with vendors, negotiating contracts. Patrons can also feel more comfortable when they recognize that you, their researcher, can relate to their experience both in their field and in life experiences. Although we still make up a small percentage of the profession, black librarians have a strong network. Through this network I've met and learned from some well-connected and intelligent people. If not for this connection, I might not have as wide an understanding of the profession as I do.

As we know, the word diversity isn't only about race, it also includes gender and sexual orientation. It's no secret that men are underrepresented in the library profession (Carmichael, 1994). Along with an underrepresentation of men is a lack of sexual diversity. Similar to the evolved notion that racial diversity adds to a company's strength, diversity in gender and sexual orientation does so as well. As a gay man, my life experiences help shape my view of the world, my ideas, and my unique vision, which can contribute to a marketing strategy for a company's growth. These life experiences also add to my knowledge of resources, and possibly most importantly related to marketing, my networks. One of the most important parts of marketing is the ability to connect to varying groups. If it were not for my diverse background, I would not have made the connections and necessary networks to improve my research capabilities. Use your diversity to your advantage.

As the library profession continues its struggle to diversify, we must continue to spread the word: not only are we adding to the company's marketing strength through our learned skills as information professionals, but we are also adding our experience and ability through our inherent nature as African Americans. Thinking outside the normal marketing box and identifying the power of including one's race, regional experience, gender, and even sexual orientation as an integral part of the company's profile will allow the company to stand out. It also allows the argument for more diversity to be heard more often and in a different venue. If we are to continue Josey's vision, we must allow that vision to evolve with the times.

REFERENCES

Carmichael, J. V. (1994). Gender issues in the workplace: Male librarians tell their side. *American Libraries*, *25*(3), 227–230.

Jan, T. (2010, February 16). Colleges lagging on faculty diversity: Number trail makeup of Hub's student bodies. *Boston Globe*. Retrieved from http://www.boston.com/news/education/higher/articles/2010/02/16/boston_area_short_on_black_hispanic_professors/

Thompson, B. (2010). Investigating job satisfaction with reference librarians (Master's Thesis). University of North Carolina–Chapel Hill.

Tierney, W. G. (1999). Models of minority college-going and retention: Cultural integrity versus cultural suicide. *Journal of Negro Education*, *68*(1), 80–91.

Part V

FROM THE STATE AND FEDERAL LIBRARIES

26

We Need Some Color Up Here: Educating and Recruiting Minority Librarians in Indiana

Deloice Holliday and Michele Fenton

What would it take to convince a person of color to become a librarian? And, once they've earned an MLS degree, what would it take to convince this same person to bring his or her skills and talents to Indiana, the "Heartland of the Midwest"? Also known as the "Hoosier State" and the "Crossroads of America," Indiana is famous for its Indy 500, its Indianapolis Colts, and of course, its cornfields. But did you know that Indiana also has 238 public libraries, 69 academic libraries, and 1,737 school libraries?[1] Sounds impressive! However, according to a 2006 survey of Indiana's libraries, of the 4,210 MLS degreed librarians, only 125 were African American, 18 were Asian, 14 were Hispanic, and none were Native American. In contrast, whites accounted for 94.9% of Indiana's librarians.[2] Not much diversity. More diversity is needed because according to the 2010 U.S. Census, Indiana's minority population as a whole has increased by 16.5%. Between 2000 and 2010 the Hispanic population increased by 82%![3] As Indiana's population continues to diversify, Indiana's libraries must also diversify to meet the challenges of serving a more racially and culturally diverse clientele. What efforts has Indiana put forth in bringing more minority librarians to its libraries? This chapter explores that issue.

In 2008, the Indiana State Library and the Indiana University School of Library and Information Science received a $1 million grant from the Institute of Museum and Library Services as part of the Laura Bush 21st-Century Librarian Program.[4] The grant's purpose was to fund a program to recruit and educate minorities into the library profession in Indiana. The program, Indiana Librarians Leading in Diversity (I-LLID), sought applicants in the fall of 2008. Requirements were:

1. Be a member of a minority group;
2. Have letters of recommendation;
3. Be accepted into the Indiana University School of Library and Information Science;
4. Work in Indiana libraries for two years after graduation.

The program recruited a total of 31 students representing a diversity of ethnic and racial backgrounds. Through support and partnerships with several organizations, including the Indiana Black Librarians Network, the I-LLID program has generated state and national interest in its efforts to increase minority representation in Indiana's libraries. However, this was not Indiana's first initiative to bring diversity to the profession.

In 1973, Indiana University received a $150,000 federal grant to train minorities in community college librarianship. The program, "Institute of Education for Librarianship in Urban Community Colleges," was funded by the U.S. Office of Education under Title II-B of the Higher Education Act of 1965 and was to last one year.[5] Requirements were:

1. Be a member of a minority group;
2. Have letters of recommendation;
3. Have a bachelor's degree.

Eighteen students were selected. The breakdowns of the students admitted to the program were: 13 African Americans and 5 Hispanics, comprising 7 men and 11 women.

Students received a one-year stipend of $2,400 plus $600 for dependents. Students were required to attend class regularly, complete assignments on time, do laboratory work, and complete a practicum. All students completed the program successfully but faced a tough job market. However, most found jobs, with some accepting positions at the Indiana University Black Culture Center Library, the Gary Public Library, the Indianapolis–Marion County Public Library, and DePauw University.

In contrast, the students of the Indiana Librarians Leading in Diversity Program received full tuition and a stipend with a maximum amount of $15,000. The students could take classes at the Bloomington or Indianapolis campus. Unlike the students in the Institute of Education for Librarianship in Urban Community Colleges Fellowship, the I-LLID students are required to work in Indiana for two years after graduation. The racial and gender breakdowns for the I-LLID program were 5 Asians, 23 African Americans, 1 Hispanic, and 2 Native Americans comprising 24 women and 7 men.

In addition, the I-LLID students were assigned mentors. Coincidentally, one of the graduates of the Institute of Education for Librarianship in Urban Community Colleges Fellowship is a mentor for the I-LLID program.

To help the I-LLID students get an idea of the types of libraries and librarian specialties available to them in Indiana, career expos were held. The first career expo was held on March 5, 2009, at the University Library on the campus of Indiana University–Purdue University at Indianapolis (IUPUI).[6] Representatives from several libraries across the state, various vendors, and library-related organizations were in attendance. Several information sessions dealing with academic, school, special, and public libraries were held. Some of the I-LLID students served as moderators. Lorelle Swader, director of the American Library Association's Office for Human Resource Development and Recruitment, was the keynote speaker.

Two months later, the I-LLID program held its first annual forum at the Indianapolis–Marion County Public Library. At the forum, each student gave a short talk on his or her experiences in the program and what each hoped to accomplish in the future. In addition, students participated in mock interviews, résumé reviews, and career counseling. Fanny Cox of the University of Louisville was the keynote speaker.

During the summer of 2009, a few students attended the American Library Association's Annual Conference and Exhibits in Chicago. Also that summer, an orientation session was held at the Indiana State Library to introduce the second cohort of I-LLID students. The second cohort began classes in the fall of 2009.

To help potential employers learn about the I-LLID program, the students gave their first (and only) presentation on October 18, 2009, at the 2009 Indiana Library Federation Annual Conference, held in Fort Wayne, Indiana, at the Grand Wayne Convention Center.[7] Unfortunately, attendee turnout for the presentation was low; however those who did attend were impressed by the program's efforts to bring diversity into the library profession in Indiana. In November 2009, an orientation session was held at the Indiana State Library to introduce the third cohort. These students began classes in January 2010.

The first nine I-LLID students graduated in May 2010. Like their predecessors in the Institute of Education for Librarianship in Urban Community Colleges Program, the I-LLID students faced a tough job market rich with graduates, poor in employment. The economic recession threw heavy punches at libraries all over the United States. However, some of the I-LLID graduates were able to secure positions.

After exposure at the local and state levels, it was time to take Indiana's latest initiative to the national level. During the Black Caucus of the American Library Association's seventh National Conference of African American Librarians, held August 4–8, 2010 in Birmingham, Alabama, a presentation was given on the history and success of the I-LLID program.[8] Deloice Holliday (Indiana University), Kirsten Weaver (I-LLID student), and Marcia Smith-Woodard (Indiana State Library) were the presenters. The presentation, "Indiana Librarians Are Leading in Diversity," was given on Friday, August 6. Dr. Ruth M. Jackson was the moderator. Audience members were very pleased with Indiana's initiative to draw minority librarians to its libraries.

In I-LLID's nearly three years of existence, the students continue to prove themselves as leaders in the library profession both behind the scenes and in the public eye, participating in various library organizations, projects, and activities. The second cohort graduated in December 2010. Students from the third and fourth cohorts graduated in the spring and summer of 2011. It's a bit early to tell how much of an impact the I-LLID program will have on the library profession in Indiana, but hopefully the impact will be a positive one.

NOTES

1. Indiana Division Reference Desk, Indiana State Library; Barbara Holton, Yupin Bae, Susan Baldridge, Michelle Brown, and Dan Heffron, *The status of public and private school library media centers in the United States: 1999–2000, NCES 2004–313*. Washington, DC: U.S. Department of Education, National Center for Education Statistics, 2004.
2. Marcia Smith Woodard, *2006 library diversity survey*. Indianapolis: Library Development Office, Indiana State Library, 2006.
3. U.S. Census Bureau, 2000 Census, retrieved from http://www.census.gov/main/www/cen2000.html; 2010 Census, retrieved from http://2010.census.gov/2010census/
4. Indiana State Library, I-LLID Project, retrieved from http://www.in.gov/library/3703.htm; "Indiana Receives $1 Million Grant for Library Diversity Initiative." *SLIS News*, June 20, 2008, retrieved from http://www.slis.indiana.edu/news/story.php?story_id=1794; "First Ten Fellows Named for Library Diversity Initiative." *SLIS News*, November 21, 2008, retrieved from http://www.slis.indiana.edu/news/story.php?story_id=1862
5. Charles Hale, *Narrative evaluation report of USOE Title II-B institute education for librarianship in urban community colleges*. Bloomington, IN: Graduate Library School, Indiana University, 1974; Charles Hale and Shirley Edsall, "The education of community college librarians," *Journal of Education for Librarianship*, *16*, no. 2 (1975): 75–85.
6. Kevin O'Neal, "Like libraries? They Might Like to Hire You." *Indianapolis Star*, March 6, 2009, p. A21; "Indiana State Library—Career Expo 2009," *SLIS News*, April 7, 2009, retrieved from http://www.slis.indiana.edu/news/story.php?story_id=1927
7. Marilyn Irwin, "Indiana's MLS Diversity Fellowship Project," presented at 2009 Indiana Library Federation Annual Conference, October 18–20, Grand Wayne Convention Center, Fort Wayne, Indiana.
8. Deloice Holliday, Kirsten T. Weaver, and Marcia Smith-Woodard, "Indiana's Librarians Are Leading in Diversity," presented at the Seventh National Conference of African American Librarians, Sheraton Conference Center, Birmingham, Alabama, August 4–8, 2010.

27

A Charge to Keep I Have

Steven D. Booth

During the late 1990s, library science schools and national library associations recognized the lack of diversity within the profession. This led to the establishment of several recruitment strategies targeting persons from racial and ethnic minority groups. Such organizations as the American Library Association (ALA), Andrew W. Mellon Foundation, and the Institute of Museum and Library Services have made strides toward resolving this predicament; and the results have proved to be inspiring. New, younger librarians of color are increasing ranks across the country thanks to the funding and support granted by these institutions. For most undergraduate students, librarianship is not an initial career choice. Those who choose it make the decision to do so on recommendation from people, previous work experience in a library, or the love of books. Through the financial support of institutes like ALA's Spectrum Scholarship Program, REACH 21, and the Mellon Librarian Recruitment Program, students of color gain exposure to the limitless opportunities the field has to offer. Participants are encouraged to enroll in accredited graduate programs, attend national and regional conferences, and join professional organizations—all of which expound upon their general knowledge. In addition, networking is promoted through collaborative projects and team-building exercises. During the institutes, the cohorts get to know one another by sharing their backgrounds, experiences, and opinions. This encourages conversation among them regarding the issues and concerns librarians face. Ultimately, these meetings build a sense of camaraderie in a field heavily dominated by white women, with minorities representing less than 13% of the profession (Davis & Hall, 2007). It is no secret that African Americans are the majority of the minority serving in information science–related positions. The same is true for the smaller archives community. The A*Census for the Society of American Archivists revealed 7% of archivists are racial and ethnic minorities, with African Americans leading at 3% (Banks, 2006). In regards to gender, black men represent less than 1% of all information science–related positions (Jefferson, 2008). This is a direct reflection of library science graduate programs.

Students face accomplishments and challenges while honing their craft in library science school. The joys of academic stimulation and professional development coincide with the uncertainties of potential employment and career advancement, not to mention life's unexpected circumstances. Although their achievements are based on individual experiences and aspirations, the aid of a mentor can make a difference. Responsibility for keeping graduate students and entry-level librarians of color in the profession must lie directly with mid-career and senior professionals. Having a supportive environment and network, where they can learn about the "do's and don'ts," increases students' chances for success. Mentorship helps bridge this gap, helping the inexperienced draw on the wisdom and knowledge not taught in the classroom. Mentees are capable of developing skill sets with this acquired information that will enhance their educational training, personal growth, and career advancement. The benefits of mentoring are countless not only for the mentee but also for the mentor. Mentors demonstrate their expertise, providing an understanding for the experiences of the apprentice, which improves interpersonal skills. Mentors typically function as a friend, information source, intellectual guide, or career guide. These relationships vary accordingly and are either formal or informal. Regardless of how the connection is made, both individuals must understand mentoring is a two-way street. Important factors to consider for a successful partnership are shared responsibility, regular communication (in person, by phone, or by e-mail), exchange of ideas, and mutual respect. To measure the relationship's effectiveness the mentor and mentee should address certain questions. Are expectations being met? Are there any problems or concerns? If so, are they being addressed and resolved? Is the mentee growing professionally? Based on answers from the assessment the efficiency of the affiliation can be evaluated. Those with positive experiences are likely to reciprocate and become mentors themselves, creating an evolving pattern of giving back to the village in which they were raised.

I chose to pursue a career in librarianship during my senior year at Morehouse College while majoring in music. Having no aspirations to become a starving artist and teach, I investigated a number of graduate programs within the arts and humanities. I began to explore disciplines with an emphasis in research, specifically library science, after a recommendation from my music professor and mentor David Morrow. Even with the experience I had from working at a public library in high school, being a library assistant for a performing arts camp, and serving as the librarian for the glee club, I never considered becoming a librarian. This could be attributed to the fact that I never saw a black male librarian or ever heard of a "Morehouse Man" choosing librarianship. As time progressed I would come to learn about several black male librarians who matriculated from the college dating back to the 1930s.

By happenstance, I saw a flyer advertising the Mellon librarian recruitment program hosted at the Atlanta University Center's Woodruff Library. Wanting to learn more about the profession before I committed myself to graduate school, I thought it would be in my best interest to apply. I was accepted, along with three individuals, into a six-week program led by the coordinator Warren Watson and Carolyn Hart, assistant director of planning and development. Staff members taught seminars about areas of librarianship ranging from cataloging to leadership. After hearing Karen Jefferson and Andrea Jackson of the Archives Department discuss their duties and the importance of collecting and preserving history, I was set on becoming an archivist. Shortly thereafter I met Meredith Evans-Raiford, who suggested I enroll in the archives management program at Simmons College in Boston. Her guidance helped narrow my choice on what school to attend. Upon arriving at Simmons College I was introduced to Assistant Professor Tywanna Whorley. Unbeknown to me I had been awarded a recruitment scholarship covering partial tuition and fees, books, and membership dues, as well as a paid internship at the college archives.

Under Dr. Whorley's tutelage I learned firsthand about access and ethics, the relationship between archives and social justice, and the practicality of archival theory. Beyond the classroom, however, she served in other capacities. Dr. Whorley made my success a priority, as I was the only black male in the graduate school. She required that I fully participate in professional organizations, which afforded me the chance to network with peers from other institutions and learn about the broad role of archives in society. To fulfill a class internship requirement I worked on the electronic finding aid project for Dr. Martin Luther King, Jr.'s papers, which are housed at the Boston University Howard Gotlieb Archival Research Center. Before the start of my second year, I was offered a full-time position thanks to Dr. Whorley's recommendation. Regardless of my needs, she listened, encouraged, and helped me develop greater self-awareness, providing both professional and personal support. Her knowledge and insight gave me an easy transition into the workforce after graduation. As an archivist for the federal government I have gained new mentors and with their aid I am obtaining essential information needed to fulfill my job duties and comprehend the bureaucracy of the agency.

The most important lesson I have learned from being mentored is the significance of helping others achieve their goals. When asked by Dr. Whorley to speak with prospective students about the archives program, I never hesitated, because it is an opportunity to share my knowledge. Unlike them, I did not have a peer to answer my questions, therefore, it is a priority of mine to be honest. The individuals I encounter leave with a better understanding about the formalities of graduate education, diversity of the school, and student living in Boston. From these conversations I have become a mentor for those who choose to enroll. This obligation requires that I remain active and informed during their matriculation and willing to provide assistance when needed. As a working professional, I offer advice relating to the courses and internships that will make them marketable after graduation. Although everyone's employment journey is different, my insight as a recent hire prepares them for the rigorous process of job searching, résumé editing, and interviewing. Being a mentor can be challenging at times, but knowing that I am making a contribution to their development is a reward in itself. I can only hope that one day they will also serve as a gateway.

Funding for education is imperative, but it is a small measure of graduate students' overall experience. More emphasis must be placed on their growth. In a society where self-gratification is becoming the norm, it is necessary for us find satisfaction in reaching back and helping one another. Our very existence in the profession depends on it. One person cannot effectively recruit and retain these up-and-coming professionals. As minorities, it is up to us to build our own community. If we fail to do so, we will only have ourselves to blame.

REFERENCES

Davis, D. M., & Hall, T. D. (2007). Diversity counts. American Library Association. Office of Research and Statistics. January 2007. Retrieved from http://www.ala.org/ala/aboutala/offices/diversity/diversitycounts/divcounts.cfm

Banks, B. (2006). A*Census: Report on diversity. *American Archivist, 69* (Fall), 369–406.

Jefferson, J. (2008). The black male librarian . . . An endangered species. Presented at the National Diversity in Libraries Conference in Louisville, Kentucky, in October.

28

Massachusetts Black Librarians Network, Inc.: Commitments and Challenges to Our 21st-Century Presence

Em Claire Knowles

Throughout the 30-plus years of existence of the Massachusetts Black Librarians Network, Inc. (MBLN), the organization has encountered peaks and lulls. In spite of challenges, the MBLN continues to maintain its position as a nonprofit organization committed to promoting library and information services within the African American community in Massachusetts. Its mission has grown as it has begun to reach out to provide information and communication within the context of global community.

Today, the network struggles to attract new members and retain current members who grow, gather, and wither at various times. This chapter looks at how the network has grown, considers its challenges, and suggests directions to continue to make the MBLN, and other local black librarians organizations, viable in the era of advanced technology and changing demographics.

HISTORICAL FRAMEWORK

The MBLN began in 1978 with the purpose of supporting African American librarians, who usually were solo African Americans in predominantly white institutions or who served predominately black clientele. The network became a force to interact with majority professional associations in the region, including intermittently holding affiliate status with the Massachusetts Library Association, the New England Library Association, and the Black Caucus of the American Library Association. Thus, the organization provided an opportunity and was a vehicle for professional networking at the local, regional, and national levels with the library and information studies community.

The organization also invited library and information studies students to participate as members. All members were engaged in encouraging and promoting scholarship opportunities to prospective students. Furthermore, the fundraising efforts consisted of black book fairs that were held for over a decade before the advent of the technological advances of Amazon, Barnes and Noble, and Borders online resources. There were also programs that brought the talents and accomplishments of authors, storytellers, academicians, and researchers of local and national prominence to the African American community. These funds would enhance the organization's coffers to support African American students pursuing their master's degree in the library and information studies field.

Over time and into the 21st century, the membership has shifted; as members are promoted, they may lose interest in the goals of the network or develop a focus in other directions, including home, church, or other professional directions. Other members are retiring, and although they may stay active for a while, they are less likely to take on active roles and the more intimate tasks of the network. Student membership is dependent on those students who are motivated to be involved with an organization that works in the community. Sometimes students are active for the year for which their membership covers, and then they disappear. Unfortunately, few become active with the network upon graduation. The major challenge is to find ways to keep membership strong and the directions relevant to keep the membership in the MBLN solvent and viable to the larger community.

This chapter addresses these challenges for the network because the same challenges are also found in other similar black librarians groups throughout the United States.

CHALLENGES FACING THE SURVIVAL OF THE NETWORK

Membership and Leadership

Challenges can also be viewed as opportunities. The challenges for the survival and growth of the MBLN come in many areas. The first area is membership and participation. The network has been in existence for over 30 years. The network is the oldest organization of its kind in the region. The other organizations include the Black Caucus of the American Library Association (Connecticut chapter) and Cornucopia, the multiracial librarians' organization in Rhode Island. The network holds its membership for the greater Boston area, and occasionally African American librarians from distances north and west join the network. There needs to be more ways to keep these long-distance members. At present, there are listserv postings and blog entries. All members need to be involved with the national Black Caucus of the American Library Association to obtain a broader access to relevant topics that can be also discussed on the local level. Thus, it would become more valuable to add themes for professional programs or programming that would attract members from the larger ethnic communities.

Although many professional, upwardly mobile librarians might not want to be involved with the details of planning events, they can be encouraged to contribute to fundraisers or assessments to support the black librarians group. For example, in the 2005, the ALA midwinter meeting was held in Boston, the first time in 40 years. The network devised a plan to assess current and past members $100 to raise funds needed to help with activities to encourage the black librarians to come to Boston for the midwinter meeting. The funds supported the organization for the activity, and the small leftover funds contributed to a scholarship.

An important component of membership is leadership. As members become nonworking members or retired, they are less likely to participate in leadership roles. The membership is small to begin with; as ranks continue to shrink, there are fewer members willing to take on leadership roles. There is a need to better prepare and support the leadership, so they do not feel as if they were doing everything on their own.

Programming

As technology has changed the profession, members in the network have not necessarily kept up with the changes. Thus, it is difficult to accommodate projects or programs that may be of interest or timeliness for new members or the community. For example, the network receives requests for help to organize and catalog materials, projects to digitize collections, and projects to help archive materials. The membership can pass these projects on, but it would be beneficial if members could take these projects on and complete them so we could share the final project on our website to show our visitors the capability of the organization. The more technological advancement of our finished products could also serve as a good promotion and programs for the community to observe what the network is about. Furthermore, the fruits of our labor could also bring more funding into the network. For example, the Northeast affiliates participated and sponsored events, such as a fundraiser for the Harlem Book Fair and volunteering at the Black Writer's Celebration and African American Children's Book Fair. By having events to participate in without meetings, some members think they are contributing by only attending the events. There may be a need to revisit the mission of the network and other organizations in order to focus on additional issues, including the marketing of the profession and issues of advocacy, employment, and networking to benefit library professionals and the community. We need to consider who can join the network, and we may need to broaden its membership to include nonpracticing library information science professionals as well as paraprofessionals who may consider entering the profession in order to strengthen the ranks of the black librarians' organization.

Funding

No organization can exist without the necessary funding to either sustain itself or to offer scholarships, which is a major thrust of the MBLN. The network has remained a viable organization over the years from its membership fees. During the 1990s, the network was very successful with its book fairs. The key factor was to find a niche to maintain fundraising efforts. Other black librarians' organizations, such as the New York Librarians Caucus, had held a successful annual jazz brunch. With increases in ranks, the membership can grow. There may be a need to increase the membership fees. It has been useful for the network to pursue and obtain nonprofit, 501(c)(3) status at the state and federal levels. This enables the organization to purchase items without paying sales tax; it also helps the organization to receive donations from members, interested persons, and corporations. Another recent avenue of interest for obtaining funds is from members who are looking for a nonprofit entity to leave bequests through their wills. This could become a dynamic way to enrich our coffers for scholarships for posterity. At the present time, with limited returns on bank investments, it is difficult for a small organization to maintain funding to conduct the work of the organization.

SUMMARY

The MBLN is a historical organization following in the footsteps of the national black librarians' organization, the Black Caucus of the American Library Association. However, the network has only a small number of active members to maintain its existence into the 21st century. The challenges facing active members, those who are willing to take leadership to develop a viable direction, raise membership, fundraise and develop programming, may lead the organization to a downward spiral out of existence. This chapter raises issues that need to be addressed in order for the network and other local black librarians organizations to move forward.

This type of organization will continue to be important as long as there is a need for black library professionals to have mentors, advocates, scholarships, and networking. The local African American library and information organization will be strengthened if these factors can be corrected for a positive advance into the 21st century.

Part VI

FROM THE LIBRARY AND INFORMATION SCHOOL

29

Going the Distance: Supporting African American Library and Information Science Students

Angel K. Washington Durr

The face of today's librarian is changing. Librarians are slowly becoming representative of the diverse patrons they serve. Nonetheless, white female librarians still make up the vast majority of library and information science students, as well as professionals. Universities and libraries across the country are actively seeking minority staff and students. However, African American students, and minorities in general, face a unique set of struggles while advancing their educations. These challenges lead many African Americans within the library profession to become and remain paraprofessionals within the library, instead of pursuing additional education and becoming library professionals. Therefore, what steps are universities taking to not only recruit African American library students, but also retain them and ensure employment upon graduation? Also, what steps are established professionals and professional organizations taking to encourage African Americans to pursue library and information science careers in order to ensure the rich legacy left by African American librarians like Dr. E. J. Josey is carried on for centuries to come? This chapter will explore these questions, and I will share some of my own personal experiences as a young African American library and information science student, as well as those of some of my peers, and compare them to previous and hopefully future generations.

Some would argue that the reason minorities are underrepresented in the library community, as well as in other professional communities, is due to the fact that they are underrepresented in society as well. However, minorities, immigrants, and women currently make up over 80% of the U.S. workforce. In fact, "by the year 2020, the number of U.S. residents who are Hispanic or non-white will have more than doubled to nearly 115 million" (Acree, 2001, p. 48). According to E. J. Josey, the late African American librarian:

> Since minorities will constitute a major segment of the workforce and will contribute substantially to the economic well-being of the nation, the United States government must be certain that its minority population receives a quality education and is guaranteed access to the library and information resources. Further, the minorities of this country must have the knowledge and skills to use the new technologies in the workplace as well as in every aspect of their lives. The nation cannot afford to ignore the education, training, and library needs of its minorities. (Josey, 1993, p. 302)

Josey, like many minority librarians of his time, realized the important role the library community as a whole plays in changing the current standard. Library schools began to take an active role in recruiting minorities by creating programs specifically aimed at helping minority students enter the library community.

The Association of College and Research Libraries (ACRL) published a study in 2002 titled "Achieving Racial and Ethnic Diversity among Academic and Research Librarians." This study presented new proposals on increasing racial and ethnic diversity. According to the paper, librarians need to do more to collaborate with other organizations in order to "eliminate duplication" (Pinkowski, 2007, p. 15). Also, librarians should focus on retention "by creating a welcoming and flexible environment that considers work culture issues, honors employee values and opinions, offers compensation and rewards, provides solid management, and recognizes the need for work-life balance" (p. 15). The paper states that minorities require special assistance with retention because they often lack the support system to do it on their own. Additionally, the report states that libraries need to "advance minority hires to management position, which includes providing opportunities for mentoring, shadowing leaders, soliciting nominations for awards and recognitions, rotating jobs, and fostering participation in fellowships and institutes" (p. 15). Professional organizations such as the American Library Association and the Association of Research Libraries have made diversity a commitment by offering opportunities for young professionals and students to grow within the library field. Yet more effort is still necessary and collaboration among organizations and institutions is going to have to be a real priority to encourage major changes.

As a first-generation college student as well as a first-generation graduate student, navigating the ins and outs of higher education was challenging to say the least. However, in my opinion, the hardest part of attending college and graduate school was and still is looking around my classes and noticing very few faces that resembled my own. Then, upon returning home, I began to look at my family and realized I was not only alienated within the four walls of my university but now in my own home as well. I discussed this issue with numerous minority classmates and realized that I was not alone in my struggles. Other minorities within my program discussed experiencing similar issues upon making the decision to further their educations.

A study from the *Review of Higher Education* conducted by Rachelle Winkle-Wagner (2009), titled "The Perpetual Homelessness of College Experiences: Tensions between Home and Campus for African American Women," describes similar situations. The author held discussions with 30 African American college-educated women, 24 of whom were also first-generation college students, to discuss the difficulties and hardships they experienced while attending college. Winkle-Wagner goes into detail about a common experience shared by the vast majority of the women she interviewed, an overwhelming feeling of "homelessness" due to loss of family ties and difficulty fitting into the college lifestyle. According to Winkle-Wagner, "The Black women in this study described their college experience as akin to being homeless, of 'not fitting.' All of the women, regardless of their parents' educational background, described feeling 'alienated' or 'isolated' in the predominantly White environment at some point" (p. 9). She continues: "While the women generally felt as if they did not belong on campus, they also described the sensation of no longer fitting at home. Some women described themselves as having had changed too much to still belong in their home or community environment" (p. 11).

If African Americans cannot turn to their families for guidance while they are attempting to obtain their degrees, who are they to turn to? The answer is simple—mentors. I, like so many other minority graduate students, have been able to find individuals along the way who have helped me through mentorship. Crawford and Smith (2005) suggested that the essence of mentoring is the development of individuals on both professional and personal levels. They defined a mentor as one who can "afford the protégé with opportunities to learn and practice and to reward him or her so that acquired knowledge, performance, and motivation can increase" (p. 64). However, often it can be difficult to find these individuals, so many students turn to faculty for mentorship.

According to the 2009 *Journal of Higher Education* article "My Sister's Keeper: A Qualitative Examination of Mentoring Experiences among African American Women in Graduate and Professional Schools," by Lori D. Patton, "mentoring can be very time-consuming for African American faculty, who are usually too few in number, to serve as mentors to every African American student who enters an academic program. African Americans, women in particular, tend to participate in activities such as mentoring at the risk of reducing their scholarly productivity and career advancement" (p. 513). Yet, according to several studies, Patton states, "Providing mentors to students of color plays a major role in diversifying university faculty" (p. 513). Therefore, universities can increase minority enrollment and retention simply by taking on additional minority staff and encouraging mentoring relationships.

Some people ask "Why diversity? If older white females want to be librarians, let them." However, diversity is a necessity of any profession that wants real growth or positive change. Diversity not only helps librarians serve their patrons effectively, but it also provides professionals with new and different perspectives that can help them implement the best service possible for their patrons. Providing excellent customer service, and ensuring our patron leaves satisfied, should always be the ultimate goal of any good librarian.

Those who have already established themselves within the library community need to make the effort to ensure that the rich legacy of information science professionals lasts for many generations to come. Therefore, rather than viewing the newer generations of library information science professionals as competition, we need to view them as new and vital blood that will ensure our profession continues to live on. New African American librarians and library information science students need to be nurtured and given opportunities to broaden and expand their professional expertise. I am so grateful for those individuals who have stepped forward and helped me along my journey to success. I have been lucky enough to meet people who truly want to see me succeed.

So I challenge all of you, young and old, student and professional, take charge and always be on the lookout for someone who you could potentially help along their own journey. In the words of the great Maya Angelou, "Each of us, famous or infamous, is a role model for somebody, and if we aren't, we should behave as though we are—cheerful, kind, loving, courteous. Because you can be sure someone is watching and taking deliberate and diligent notes" (African American Quotes, 2007).

REFERENCES

Acree, E. K. (2001). Using professional development as a retention tool for underrepresented academic librarians. *Journal of Library Administration, 33*, 45–62.

African American Quotes. (2007). Role Model. Retrieved January 6, 2010, from http://africanamericanquotes.org/role-model.html

Crawford, K., & Smith, D. (2005). The we and the us: Mentoring African-American women. *Journal of Black Studies, 36*, 52–67.

Josey, E. J. (1993). The challenges of cultural diversity in the recruitment of faculty and students from diverse backgrounds. *Journal of Education for Library and Information Science, 34*(4), 302–311.

Patton, L. D. (2009). My sister's keeper: A qualitative examination of mentoring experiences among African-American women in graduate and professional schools. *Journal of Higher Education, 80*, 510–537.

Pinkowski, J. (2007). Minority jobs at academic libraries. *Library Journal, 132*, 15.

Winkle-Wagner, R. (2009). The perpetual homelessness of college experiences: Tensions between home and campus for African American women. *Review of Higher Education, 33*, 1–36.

30

African American Faculty in Library and Information Science: Unresolved Issues in a New Era

Maurice B. Wheeler

Diversity and recruitment of students of color into library and information sciences (LIS) programs were fairly constant topics in the professional literature from the 1970s through the 1990s. However, there was little in the literature related to LIS African American or other faculty of color. The history of African American faculty in predominately white colleges and universities is fairly recent, dating to the turn of the 20th century. African Americans established a presence in library science education as a result of Edward Christopher Williams, who became the first African American to earn a degree in library science in 1900 (Josey, 1969). Williams, who later became the librarian of Hatch Library at Western Reserve University in 1894, also joined the library school faculty at Western Reserve in 1904. Despite Williams' achievements, subsequent contributions of African American library science educators were made primarily in historically black institutions because of the continuance of racially segregated practices in the United States. Although African American educators are included in the history of the profession, the discussion of their presence and contributions is primarily peripheral or separate, as is the case in Holley's (1976) 100-year glance into the past.

The first several decades of the 20th century saw very few African American faculty in white universities, and Weinberg (1977) asserted that although a significant number of African Americans had earned doctorates by the 1940s, the small percentage of the total employed by white universities was a clear reflection of discrimination at the point of hiring. Based on a 1961 study by Rose, the assumption could be made that 50% of all schools and colleges outside the South would consider the application of qualified "Negroes" on the same basis as all other applicants. Although, they further stated reluctance in hiring based on the absence of African Americans in the student body and surrounding community.

The *Brown v Board of Education* Supreme Court decision had a significant effect on admissions to doctoral programs in predominantly white universities and colleges. However, it wasn't until the period surrounding the initial establishment and enforcement of affirmative action programs that the greatest increase in admissions and hires was documented and subsequently reflected in research activity and professional literature.

AFFIRMATIVE ACTION IN HIGHER EDUCATION AND ITS IMPACT ON FACULTY RECRUITMENT

Affirmative action regulations were formally imposed in higher education in October 1972, when the director of the Office for Civil Rights, Stanley Pottinger, informed all colleges and universities that those with federal contracts had to comply with new hiring regulations. Goals were required for hiring more minority faculty and other employees in areas where they were considered underutilized or not employed in proportion to their availability. Thereafter, the enforcement and effectiveness of affirmative action regulations were uneven, largely reflecting the controlling political party's position at the time, both presidential and congressional.

Despite significant increases in the absolute number of degrees awarded to African Americans since the 1970s, the fundamental and most pressing problem has continued to be a shortage of African Americans in the academy who possess a Ph.D. In 1974, Garcia proposed that the problem lies with how African American candidates are treated in the hiring process. However, in one of the few explorations in library literature solely devoted to the topic of recruitment of African American faculty, Totten (1992) pointed to the need for a sincere commitment from administrators to implement a minority recruitment plan. William Moore (1987) presented a reminder that faculties are themselves primarily responsible for the search and selection process. Although a strong and committed administrative leadership can influence this process, the fact remains that, as a general rule, faculty control access to their ranks. In short, he suggested that they are the "gatekeepers." Affirmative action and other programs enlarged the pool of candidates, but it was not designed to nor did it ensure equity in the hiring and review process.

There was great opposition to affirmative action, and many of its opponents engaged in research and journalistic discussion in an effort to ensure that their voices were heard. Along with supply and demand issues, they argued that the U.S. government had no right to interfere in an institution's choice of its own faculty or to intervene in the normal practices of filling faculty positions, using procedures they believe have worked in the past to provide "qualified" candidates

(Sowell, 1975). Banks (1984) suggested that once the powerful white male establishment linked affirmative action to lowering standards, any and all women and minorities entering academia faced a dilemma. No matter how exemplary the training and credentials of individual faculty members, they were always vulnerable to insinuations that merit was not the main factor in their appointment. In response to the assertion of the added value of diverse perspectives, Bok argued that even the most avid proponent of diversity would be hard put to dispute that the special perspective of a minority scholar would contribute much to teaching and research in the "natural sciences or the classics, English literature, logic, or many other important fields of study" (1982). Sowell (1975) also concluded that if African Americans are concentrated in historically black colleges rather than at white colleges, it's because they prefer being where they are. As Exum (1983) pointed out, affirmative action addresses primarily who plays the game, rather than how the game is played. Because opponents of affirmative action presented their ideology as neutral and nondiscriminatory, their defense of the status quo based on "values" often allowed them to consider themselves liberal on race relations.

The existence of an expanded pool of potential candidates for doctoral degrees among African Americans with college degrees, combined with continued low enrollment, suggests that any number of barriers must be operating that prevent them from enrolling in doctoral degree programs. A research study conducted in 1993 revealed that 37 members (6.6%) of full-time LIS faculty were African American. However, that number is reduced by 23% if faculty at historically black colleges and universities are excluded (Wheeler, 1994). Ten years later, although the total number of faculty of color has increased, the number of African American faculty is not significantly greater, and the number of African American deans has dropped precipitously (Sineath, 2006).

RECRUITMENT AND RETENTION

The problem of faculty retention has become a nationally recognized problem and continues to grow in importance. In the 1980s, institutions of higher learning looked to the mentoring role to increase the productivity and scholarship of faculty and to socialize and mold graduate students into the mores and roles of the discipline (Lewis, 1980). Yet, Blackwell in 1983 reported that only one in eight African American doctoral recipients had the benefits of a true mentor during graduate school. It is likely that even fewer have the benefit of effective mentoring once joining the ranks of the professoriate.

A fundamental flaw in retention of faculty of color has been the lack of attention to the impact of culture and ethnicity or race on the mentor–mentee relationship. Ugrin, Odom, and Pearson (2008) reported the findings of an information systems study that explored how gender and ethnicity affect the strength of the social exchange between mentors and mentees. Pairing a mentee of color with a mentor of color may solve one set of problems while possibly exacerbating another. African American faculty in predominately white institutions are socially isolated from their white colleagues, and some may consider having a white mentor as a way to eliminate that isolation at some level. The greater challenge is to find senior African American faculty who have both the desire and time to devote to serious mentoring of junior faculty.

TENURE AND PRODUCTIVITY

The reason cited most frequently when African American faculty fail to attain tenure and are terminated is that of low productivity.

Publication for some is the game that must be mastered. However, the rules appear to be in constant transition. African American faculty are sometimes surprised by what they feel are unfair questions raised about the number of publications, the status of the journal in which they are published, or method or approach or the topic investigated. Higher education has and continues to be dominated by white males; consequently, their definitions of learning and of scholarship prevail. Charging that those definitions are incomplete, people of color sometimes offer their scholarship to compensate for what is missing. Although personally satisfying, this approach may be a hindrance in gaining tenure.

A successful review is likely to require recommendations from outside referees, and the old boys' network (fast becoming an old girls' network), important for hiring, is replaced at promotion and tenure time by an old referees' network. People of color are underrepresented in this group that comments on manuscripts and writes letters of recommendation. Thus, judgments may be influenced primarily by referees who are unfamiliar with or biased against the discourse of the candidate. In a study by Fox and Lefkowitz (1974) and supported by Sidanius (1989), there were indications that African American ratees receive significantly lower performance ratings than white ratees. Rafky (1972) also reported that untenured African American faculty who had been recruited by high-quality colleges and universities felt that they were intentionally hired only as a temporary measure, and that these schools did not intend to grant them or offer African Americans tenure.

There are many methods utilized to justify low performance evaluation ratings, and tenure is theoretically denied because of weakness in one of three areas: research, teaching, and service. Service, the criterion of lowest priority and recognition, seems to be where the strengths of many minority faculty members lie. The one constant theme in the discussion of productivity, evaluation, and tenure is the conflict of roles and competing demands that African American faculty experience. Whenever a person of color is hired in a faculty position, that person becomes a role model and is expected to be an adviser, a counselor, an advocate, and a sympathetic listener to all students of color. The dilemmas posed by competing demands and the sense of responsibility to students of color have placed a heavy burden on some African American faculty (Black, 1981). Most institutions, except the historically black institutions, hire African Americans in token numbers, and they are often drawn into activities that are quite unrelated to their areas of competence and interest. With very few exceptions, discussions have not acknowledged the supportive role of African American faculty for students of color, nor have they embraced the roles as worthy of recognition in the tenure and evaluation process.

Because the bulk of literature related to the topic was published prior to the 1990s, there may be an assumption that the issues have been resolved and that the playing field for African American faculty is now level. In contrast to the much written-about need for students of color in LIS programs, the vast majority of the professional literature does not address issues related to the need for diversity within the ranks of educators. The absence of these issues in the literature suggests either a discomfort or lack of interest that has prevented the discussion from extending beyond superficial statistical references. In a 1986 article that referenced African Americans in the academic pipeline, Scott Heller wrote, "if there were a time for colleges and universities to increase the numbers of minority-group members on their faculties, especially blacks, this is it." Despite the efforts of many within the profession to address the issue of diversity, there is no indication that such an edict has been fully taken to heart in LIS education.

REFERENCES

Banks, W. (1984). Afro-American scholars in the university. *American Behavioral Scientist, 27*(3), 325–338.

Black, A. (1981). Affirmative action and the black academic press. *Western Journal of Black Studies, 52*(2), 87–94.

Blackwell, J. E. (1983). *Networking and mentoring: A study of cross-generational experiences of blacks in graduate and professional schools.* Atlanta, GA: Southern Educational Foundation.

Bok, D. C. (1982). *Beyond the ivory tower: Social responsibilities of the modern university.* Cambridge, MA: Harvard University Press.

Exum, W. (1983). Climbing the crystal stair: Values, Affirmative Action and minority faculty. *Social Problems, 30*(4), 383–399.

Fox, H., & Lefkowitz, J. (1974). Differential validity: Ethnic group as moderator in predicting job performance. *Personnel Psychology, 27*, 209–223.

Garcia, R. L. (1974). Affirmative action hiring: Some perceptions. *Journal of Higher Education, 45* (April), 268–270.

Heller, S. (1986). Women flock to graduate schools in record numbers, but fewer blacks entering the academic pipeline. *Chronicle of Higher Education, 33*(2), 1, 24.

Holley, E. G. (1976). Librarians, 1876–1976. *Library Trends* (July), 177–207.

Josey, E. J. (1969). Edward Christopher Williams: A librarian's librarian. *Journal of Library History, 4*, 106–107.

Lewis, L. S. (1980). Academic tenure: Its recipients and its effects. *Annals of the American Academy of Political and Social Sciences, 448*, 86–101.

Moore, W. (1987). Black faculty in white colleges: A dream deferred. *Educational Record, 68*(4), 116–121.

Rafky, D. M. (1972). The black scholar in the academic marketplace. *Teachers College Record, 74*, 225–260.

Rose, H. M. (1961). The market for Negro educators in colleges and universities outside the south. *Journal of Negro Education, 30*(4), 432–435.

Sidanius, J. (1989). Racial discrimination and job evaluation: The case of university faculty. *National Journal of Sociology* (Fall), 223–256.

Sineath, T. W. (2006). Faculty. In E. Daniel & J. D. Saye (Eds.), *Library and information science statistical report 2005* (pp. 1–50). Raleigh, NC: Association of Library and Information Science Education.

Sowell, T. (1975). *Affirmative Action reconsidered: Was it necessary in academia?* Washington, DC: American Enterprise Institute for Public Policy Research.

Totten, H. L. (1992). Perspectives on minority of faculty for schools of library and information science. *Journal of Education for Library and Information Science, 33*(1), 46–54.

Weinberg, M. (1977). *Minority students: A research appraisal.* Washington, DC: U.S. Department of Health, Education and Welfare.

Wheeler, M. B. (1994). African American faculty perceptions of recruitment, retention and tenure processes and practices in U.S. ALA accredited library and information science programs: A descriptive study. Ph.D. diss., University of Pittsburgh.

Ugrin, J. C., Odom, M., & Pearson, J. M. (2008). The importance of mentoring for new scholars: A social exchange perspective. *Journal of Information Systems Education, 19*(3), 343–350.

Part VII

FROM LIBRARY TECHNOLOGY

31

Technology Skills for the 21st-Century Librarian

Fantasia Thorne

So, which are you? *Mac* or *PC*? Do you remember when you thought the most challenging aspect of being a librarian was learning how to use the ever elusive and confusing Mac computer? Today, librarians are faced with myriad technological challenges. Some include deciding which tablet PC to purchase for patron use, selecting the best technology to outfit the latest "smart" classroom, or how to implement QR (Quick Response) codes in the library. As librarians, it is beneficial to keep abreast of emergent technologies that may become important to our field. Informed librarians contribute to the selection, purchase, and implementation of technologies that improve library service and the overall perception of librarians.

There are a number of ways librarians stay well informed of new technologies. Monitoring websites, RSS (Really Simple Syndication) feeds, and attending conferences and webinars are just a few of them. Weekly reading of technology columns in the *New York Times* and other national newspapers is a quick and reliable way to increase aware of emergent technologies.

It is important to be open to new technologies. As librarians we never know when we will be confronted with some new form of technology in the library. Soon after joining the staff at Syracuse University, I found that the Learning Commons Department wanted to experiment with an alternate methods of reference service called roving reference. So I became a roving reference librarian with a tiny netbook. I have to say initially using a PC that small was a challenge while trying to walk around! Currently, I carry my iPad around the library in case I'm stopped and asked for help. It's proven to be an invaluable tool.

With the invention and success of the iPad and other tablet PCs, librarians oftentimes find themselves adopting some duties that have been traditionally assigned to information technology (IT) professionals. More than ever, librarians are expected to know enough about new information technology to determine the best way to utilize it in the library. For instance, I am the Facebook coordinator and facilitator of the Learning Commons Flickr account. Recently, I was charged with creating a library guide for staff and patrons with instructions and recommendations for QR code usage. I could not have imagined while in library science school that I would someday have such unusual responsibilities. I love being able to say that managing the department's Facebook page is actually a part of my job!

If you are a new librarian or have been assigned new duties related to technology, it is wise to tap into the expertise of co-workers and those with related skills. Join a group or team that will enable you to meet others with similar responsibilities and more experience and skill. If you don't have much background in technology, seek out information by reading about technology librarians or information professionals with similar responsibilities or perhaps directing questions to knowledgeable colleagues.

At Syracuse, I became a member of the Learning Commons Technology Team. We met periodically with the User Technology Services to discuss the new technologies under consideration for adoption by the library. As a team member, I was exposed to in-depth discussion, questions, and the entire critical review process employed by librarians and library administrators to evaluate new technologies before they are used in library service.

Librarians of the new millennium must attend classes, webinars, and workshops to keep abreast of new technology in the field. On most campuses, free classes are offered to staff members for professional development purposes. Seek out lunchtime discussion groups or demonstrations using tools or technologies unfamiliar to you. In addition to learning about emergent technologies, these are great opportunities to network. I attended a workshop facilitated by a staff member of the campus Online Learning Services (OLS) department on a presentation tool called Prezi, which is an engaging alternative to Microsoft's PowerPoint. I now incorporate this tool into my presentations.

It is beneficial to both you and your organization when you attend professional development seminars offered face to face or online. Facilitators of these seminars and workshops are typically available for further discussion afterward. I spoke with the presenter, Samantha Duncan (the OLS online learning analyst, who is also a librarian), about how she keeps abreast of new technology. Duncan subscribes to various social media sites, RSS feeds, blogs, and online technology magazines, as well as attends conferences and seminars. She takes time to read each new issue and often incorporates new knowledge into presentations as appropriate.

You may find that taking just a bit of time each day to read about or learn a new technology will be a great way for you to not only take a break from your regular routine, but to also keep abreast of the latest news and trends in technology. An article titled "Bridging the Gap: Self-Directed Staff Technology Training," by

Quinney, Smith, and Galbraith (2010), describes the "Technology Challenge," wherein staff and faculty at the Harold B. Lee Library (HBLL) of Brigham Young University were given the opportunity to spend 15 minutes of their workday to learn or read about new technologies. Those who participated found it to be a very useful activity, enabling HBLL librarians, staff, and students to discuss the advantages and disadvantages of emerging technologies. Participants in the activity stated they would participate in another technology challenge.

Receiving RSS feeds from technological websites has proven to be a useful tool for monitoring new developments. Personally, I enjoy monitoring a website called Engadget. This website keeps me abreast of the latest technology news and features new gadgets tested and reviewed by staff members. Google Reader is also a useful tool that manages RSS feeds.

Donna R. Berryman (2010), a medical librarian, suggested a number of sites for use by librarians to monitor technology news and provided tips to create a technology awareness plan.

Whether you've got it or not, as a librarian, you should still be in the know! So you may say to yourself, "I'm monitoring sites, diving head first into emerging technologies and more, but is this really going to help me get a job or assist me in my present position?" I'd say yes! You can certainly make a name for yourself if your employer knows she can count on you to tackle new technology without reservation. Today's librarians are expected to possess basic technical skills such as creating and posting to a blog and, most importantly, being able to talk about emerging technologies with a sense of familiarity and a curiosity that allows them to pick up a new device and figure out how to use it.

The Library and Information Technology Association (LITA), a division of the American Library Association (ALA), is an excellent resource for tips and updates on emerging library technology. New technology is rolled out each year at ALA conferences, providing additional opportunities to keep up with technological developments. Even if your library has no immediate plans to purchase new technology, ALA Technology Roll-out is an awesome event.

Library demographics influence the type of technology a library employs and offers to its patrons. Many urban public libraries may find there isn't enough money in their budgets to focus on the latest technology when putting books on the shelf is a difficult feat in itself. However, increasingly, patrons come to the library to use computers because they don't have computers in their homes. Additionally, patrons want to download e-books or access a database from their mobile device. In such cases, librarians should be aware of these technologies and be prepared to discuss the possibilities of such services.

Until I met Samantha Duncan, I held the assumption that the majority of African American librarians work in departments with specialized libraries such as African American studies! Surprisingly, black librarians work in all aspects of academic libraries, including library technology, information management, and computer labs, as well as have traditional public service responsibilities in reference, instruction, and collection management. Growing up, students may or may not have had a computer in their homes; however, today we expect every college student to be proficient and comfortable with technology. If not, instruction librarians are quick to work with students to build their technology and information literacy skills.

Although it is impractical for libraries to secure every new technology available, librarians in the 21st century should know where to find reliable information and reviews on emerging technology to make informed decisions about its usefulness to library patrons. Additionally, librarians should keep an open mind and read widely regarding new technologies. Even if the technology is quickly replaced, patrons appreciate libraries that are willing to experiment with new technological services, and, more importantly, patrons respect librarians who are in the know!

REFERENCES

Berryman, D. R. (2010). Learning to drive: Developing a workable awareness plan for monitoring new technology. *Medical Reference Services Quarterly*, *29*(2), 166–174.

Quinney, K. L., Smith, S. D., & Galbraith, Q. (2010). Bridging the gap: Self-directed staff technology training. *Information Technology and Libraries*, *29*(4), 205–213.

32

Advancing Digital Resources from the Black Musical Experience: An Archival and Digital Challenge at Hampton University

Gladys Smiley Bell and Harvey J. Stokes

Music in its varied types—Christian, classical, blues, jazz, rap/hip hop, or R&B—penetrates almost every aspect of life today. Its assimilation into even the most limited activities in education, commerce, entertainment, and artistic or traditional cultural expression marks it as a particularly serious form of expression for academic scrutiny, discovery, research, and interpretation. This chapter addresses the challenges of archiving, preserving, and streaming audio of existing music collections in historically black colleges and universities (HBCUs) libraries using the Indiana University Digital Library Program (2009) open-source software system called Variation 3.

The operation of such an archive for African American music in general and specifically its preservation project will enhance the scholarship in HBCU institutions and throughout the academic community at large in many ways. Music recordings represent a significant cultural contribution to the historic traditions of African American music performance, as well as a legacy of the HBCU experience.

The Hampton University's Harvey Library and the Music Department ventured into a partnership and cooperative initiative that involved the digitization of musical recordings and other related material that will improve access, preservation, and the virtue of the musical cultural materials. Partnering allowed the two academic areas to collectively contribute their music collections to be streamed via the online catalog using the Indiana University Variations 3 product managed by one entity and to be more easily managed under an element of control at Hampton University's Harvey Library. The software is customized to allow access to be authenticated and accessed only via the HUWebCat or Harvey Library online catalog (OPAC).

The ability to deliver the medium and preserve the musical cultural expression is applicable by the use of this new technology, and its products create a turnkey digital musical library system at Hampton University. The manner in which the sound of music is disseminated or delivered to the campus community highly impacts the ability of the library to preserve and provide access to music for lifelong research and instruction. Hampton University's initiative to create an African Diaspora archive of digital black music is only the beginning of a shared cooperative with other HBCUs that will aid scholars in their awareness of scores, speeches, and readings of all kinds, as well as record albums and recordings previously inaccessible or unknown.

BACKGROUND

Hampton University is one of 105 HBCUs in the United States. Founded in 1868 to help former slaves achieve self-sufficiency, Hampton University is a comprehensive institution of higher education, dedicated to the promotion of learning, building character, and preparing students for positions of leadership and service.

Within the William R. and Norma B. Harvey Library is the George Foster Peabody Collection, a historical literature and turn-of-the-century (1900) African American history depository of rare books and other ethereal material. The emergence of a music collection began in the 1950s, with the library's acquisition of musical recordings, housed in the Peabody Collection.

The music tradition at Hampton University actually began in 1868, when the school first opened its doors as Hampton Normal and Agricultural Institute. Founded by R. Nathaniel Dett, the department is of course an integral part of the Hampton University academic and cultural life. Dett was a nationally noted composer, conductor, pianist, poet, and faculty member. Throughout the years, the department has not only sustained excellence in choral, marching band, and symphonic wind traditions, but it has also established an outstanding record in educating and training music educators, music engineers, and performers. Among Hampton's famous music graduates are Dorothy Maynor, Charles Flax, Chauncey Scott Northern, Rudolph Von Charlton, Georgia Ryder, Willia Daughtry, Nathan Carter, Roland Carter, Marilyn Thompson, D'Walla Simmons-Burke, Bob Ransom, Harold Summey, Theodore Burgh, and Derrick Gardner.

Since early in their formative years, HBCUs collected materials that documented the historical and cultural experience of people of African descent, because it was the one place in America that the subject of black heritage could or should be constructively established. R. Nathaniel Dett was the arranger, composer, director, and father of the Hampton Institute choirs from 1913 until 1932; he set the standard for educational institutions nationwide and realized the importance of a commitment to and support of preserving the legacy of musical cultural expression by HBCUs:

> Negro music, even now, is in danger of running on the rocks. Here is where the Negro educational institution has its great opportunity. It is in the Negro school for the most part that the songs of the race have been most carefully preserved. It is in the Negro school that these folk songs, especially the "spirituals" have been used to create and intensify the atmosphere of religion, which is, as their name implies, their best and most natural office. It is in the Negro school that music directors have led Negro songs with no idea other than to produce the effect of beauty and naturalness; so it is that now only in the Negro school is the ideal presentation of Negro music to be found. (Dett, 1927, pp. 304–305)

Indiana University's Digital Library Program has developed the Variations 3 system, and this technology gives libraries a tool that will stream audio and scan score images through their library catalogs. The history and successfulness of Variations 3 was proven initially in the Cook Music Library at Indiana University, and subsequently it has been adopted by more than six large library systems at research universities across the nation.

The project enhances library catalog performance and is a forward-thinking collaboration and technological effort for all HBCUs and other institutions to prevent the lost of at-risk music and music collections.

Black music at Hampton University will grandly contribute to the knowledge, location, and accessibility of musical cultural expressions in digital format for national and international research and discovery.

CHALLENGES

Preservation

Primary resource materials used included reel-to-reel stereo and mono tapes, cassette tapes, 78 and 33 1/3 rpm recordings, and original scores of music by HBCU choirs, bands, and orchestras. Primary source music material is also included, for example, the *Joe Jordan Ragtime Manuscript Collection* at Hampton University, which includes original scores, analog sound storage mediums (ASSM), photographs, and other source documents by the famous ragtime composer and entrepreneur.

Those of us engaged in the preservation of collections in academic libraries at HBCU institutions know that our source materials are deteriorating rapidly. It is evident that these rich resources will not last for future generations of students without intervention. Although we can record and store audio to CD format, this musical storage medium becomes endangered within a decade. We are interested in collectively preserving a variety of music formats so that they will be available to generations of users far into the future via an archival digitization process. Consequently, we must provide access to music stored in both old and new technologies. Our preservation decisions anticipate the many ways in which future audiences will use the music materials.

The dynamic nature of musical resources presents preservation challenges. It is essential to preserve the musical data and the way the musical data interacts. So, to protect and maintain the physical record (vinyl) in our library collections is only one piece of the preservation program. Today, it is Hampton University's charge to break through into the cutting-edge technologies for conservation and preservation with digital media and provide access to our music scholars and, at the same time, provide the best practices for the archival storage of the original object. With cooperation, the project will establish a streaming archive of African American music and other African American recordings, such as oral histories, audio artifacts, and other sound collections. The project will move digitalization forward by taking advantage of products for streaming audio—all through established library online catalogs.

Technology

Preparing a server with the Variations 3 software requires experience with the LINUX operating system. This requires the knowledge for configuring or branding Variations 3 server or client software from the Indiana University Library environment to the Harvey Library workroom server or client environment and getting it to work with the Hampton University musical collection.

Sustainability

The vision for the future lies in the commitments of a firm or institutional budget to support staffing on all levels: cataloging, musical editing, preservation, and information technology. The result will be a project capable of ascertaining the rich and viable black musical collections housed in every HBCU library or campus for posterity.

Music education in this context can offer and deliver education in a way most relevant and useful to the future success of its graduates. The principles of scholarship—discovery, integration, application, and teaching—allow musical disciplines to be progressively responsive to changes in the educational and social context of higher education. As we look at higher education today, it is clear that we must adapt to new trends and directions; new media make it possible, but a challenge.

REFERENCES

Dett, R. N. (1927, July). As the Negro school sings. *Southern Workman*, *56*, 304–305.

Indiana Digital Library Program. (2009, February). Variations 3: An integrated digital library and learning system for the musical community. Retrieved from http://www.dlib.indiana.edu/variations/

33

Web 2.0 in Libraries

Jennifer W. Baxmeyer

Just as the face of librarianship has changed dramatically since the 1994 publication of E. J. Josey's *The Black Librarian in America Revisited*, library services have also changed, due in part to the proliferation of resources available electronically and on the World Wide Web and the evolution of Web 2.0 technologies. It is difficult to find a concrete definition of "Web 2.0," a term attributed first to Dale Dougherty of O'Reilly Media,[1] but Web 2.0 applications can all be characterized as being interactive and user-oriented. Although many Web 2.0 applications are simply newer versions of technologies that, as of this writing, have been around for several years, they have evolved into useful tools for delivering services and information to librarians and the users they serve. It is also difficult to discuss in depth all of the technological developments that have occurred since 1994.

Libraries have been moving away from collecting print journals in favor of electronic journals (e-journals) for many years, often as a way to compensate for rising journal costs and shrinking budgets. A 2007 study of Association of Research Libraries (ARL) university libraries found that over the four-year period from 2002 to 2006, the number of print journals being subscribed to by ARL university libraries decreased steadily at a rate of about 17%, while subscriptions to electronic journals increased by the same amount.[2] In addition to adding more e-journals, libraries have made more electronic books (e-books) available to their users. Further, as the extent of reliable information available on the World Wide Web has increased, many libraries are including records for librarian-evaluated web resources in their online public access catalogs (OPACs) as a way to facilitate user discovery. Libraries are also digitizing materials from their special collections to make them available to remote users. The James B. Duke

Memorial Library at Johnson C. Smith University in Charlotte, North Carolina, for example, has a digital archive of scanned images of photographs and historical documents related to the history of the university.[3] Online access to scanned photographs and posters, radio interviews, and other material related to the career of radio pioneer Felix Grant is available on the website for the Felix E. Grant Collection at the University of the District of Columbia.[4] Streaming video and audio services that deliver content over the Internet to play on a remote computer have also become popular offerings in libraries. The Black Oral History collection from Washington State University offers users the ability to listen to interviews of African American pioneers and their descendants in the Pacific Northwest.[5] Another streaming audio collection from Washington State is the Civil Rights Oral History Interviews collection, which consists of recorded interviews of several individuals involved with the Civil Rights Movement within the state of Washington.[6] The availability of more digital and electronic content over the Internet has made information much more accessible to people than it has ever been, and libraries offer free access to computers that allow virtually anyone to use these resources.

With digital archives and other electronic resources being added to library collections at an increasingly rapid pace, libraries have had to devise new ways for users to discover these resources easily. Bibliographic information about these resources is often located in different places on the library's website—the library's online catalog for some materials, an A–Z list for electronic journals, multiple databases for journal and newspaper articles, and a separate webpage for digital archives—making it difficult for users to find the resources. In fact, it was found in a 2005 study that most users find the search tools available on library websites difficult to use and prefer beginning their searches with a search engine like Google.[7] In order to facilitate easier and more intuitive searching of all resources, libraries have begun experimenting with and implementing next-generation catalogs and web-scale discovery services. Next-generation catalogs can be thought of as the successor to traditional library OPACs in that they employ federated searching, which allows the user to search individual library resources simultaneously and gather the results in one place. Web-scale discovery systems work in a similar fashion, but instead of broadcasting a search across multiple resources, a web-scale discovery system allows the user to search preharvested content that has been collected in one single index. The advantage of this is that the single index of a web-scale discovery service allows for faster, more accurate search results than does federated searching.[8] Howard University's Sterling Library uses a web-scale discovery service that gives its users the ability to search multiple resources from one search box on its home page, much like Google has just one search box.[9] The Jefferson County (Missouri) Public Library offers a similar service.[10]

The increase in number of available electronic resources and the introduction of improved searching capabilities have also resulted in a change in the day-to-day work of many librarians. In my work as a cataloging librarian, the impact of trying to provide access to greater numbers of electronic resources became noticeable in the late 1990s. The number of print journals that came across my desk for cataloging began to decrease steadily while the number of e-journals, e-books, and websites needing cataloging increased. In order to keep up with the workload, I began using technology to streamline and expedite the cataloging. Although some e-book providers supply bibliographic records for their e-books, in many cases these records need to be edited in order for them to comply with established cataloging rules and practices before they can be loaded into the OPAC. Instead of editing records one by one, I use a small, open-source program called MarcEdit[11] to edit batches of records. For example, some e-books require a unique identifier for the institution to be included in the URL that links to the book online, and I use MarcEdit's global "find and replace" feature to make changes to the URLs in a quick and accurate manner. Then I use a macro, a small computer script that can automate sequences of keystrokes and mouse actions,[12] to add the records to the library's catalog while I work on other projects.

Another project that has benefited from technology is keeping track of the library's e-resource purchases and making sure bibliographic records for the packages are added to the catalog in a timely manner. To assist with the tracking, I designed a database for recording information about the e-resource packages. I create a record for each package, and each record has fields for the various data I need to track, including the name of the e-resource provider, where to get bibliographic records for the titles, what modifications need to made to the records before they can be added to the library's catalog, how often new titles are added to the collections, and by what method I find out about new additions. Some e-resource providers have an e-mail alert service that notifies customers when new titles and records are available, but many do not, and the frequency of updates varies by provider. To keep track of the packages for which there are no e-mail notifications, I use a Visual Basic program created by a student worker to automatically send me reminders when it is time for me to review a package. The program simply looks at the last date a package was reviewed and calculates a new review date. Two weeks before the new review date, the program generates a task in Microsoft Outlook and sends me an e-mail reminder. As a result, I no longer have to remember to visit the websites of the providers to check for new titles and records.

My increased workload has resulted in less time to keep up with news and developments in the field of cataloging. To help myself and other catalogers with this issue, a colleague and I created a website called Planet Cataloging, which is an aggregation of blogs related to cataloging and metadata.[13] The website is updated automatically every hour by a script that harvests cataloging-related posts from a selected list of blogs on the web and combines the posts into a single dynamic webpage. A blog is a type of online journal or diary that contains brief entries called posts. Some blogs are maintained by one person, while others are collaborative endeavors, and the posts are arranged chronologically from newest to oldest. What distinguishes most blogs from regular websites is that they are interactive and allow readers to post feedback as well as communicate with other readers.[14] Some librarians have personal blogs in which they share everything from day-to-day thoughts and opinions to useful information related to a particular topic or their area of expertise. Many libraries use blogs to share news and updates about new materials, as well as offering subject-specific blogs that highlight resources on a given topic. For example, the Charles W. Chesnutt Library at Fayetteville State University maintains a blog that is "designed to promptly and efficiently provide timely news, inform of library events, books, databases and more for our students, staff and faculty."[15] The InfoBlog from East Baton Rouge Parish Library provides "interesting and useful websites, online resources, and search hints" to its patrons.[16]

In addition to providing library news on its blog, the Chesnutt Library includes a scrolling RSS (Really Simple Syndication) feed of blog topics on its home page. RSS is a web-feed format used to publish frequently updated works, such as blogs, in a standardized format.[17] Users can subscribe to RSS feeds using a software application called an RSS reader, feed reader, or aggregator, which can be web-based, desktop-based, or mobile-device–based. Once a user subscribes, the software retrieves information about changes to a website, new blog posts, or recent news stories and delivers them to the user in a single interface. Many libraries make RSS feeds available for users, allowing them to be notified about changes in hours, programs and events, as well as new materials, all without the user having to visit the library's website.

Another technology that makes it easier for users to communicate with librarians and get assistance with research is instant messaging. Instant messaging is a form of real-time, text-based communication between two or more people using personal computers or other devices.[18] The Robert W. Woodruff Library in Atlanta offers a virtual reference service using an instant messaging service on its home page[19] that allows patrons to ask reference questions through the library's website. A status bar at the top of the chat window alerts users when a librarian is available. This instant messaging virtual reference service allows Woodruff Library to provide a service that "meets its users where they are, both technologically and geographically."[20]

Social networking services offer another way for libraries and librarians to communicate remotely. Social networking services are usually web-based applications that provide a way for users to share information, ideas, activities, and interests with one another over the Internet.[21] Some of the more popular services being used today include Ning, Facebook, and Twitter, and many libraries have found these services useful for reaching patrons. Ning is a web service that allows its users with shared interests to create customized, social websites.[22] Ning was used by librarian Marcellaus Joiner to create the Black Librarian Nation, a website for African American librarians to network and share experiences.[23]

Facebook, a social networking site that allows users to connect with friends, co-workers, and businesses by creating a profile page and connecting that page with others' pages, is used by the Downs Jones Library at Huston-Tillotson University in Austin, Texas, to inform faculty and students about upcoming events and other library news.[24] Twitter, a real-time information network, allows subscribers to post short messages called tweets.[25] One innovative way Twitter is being used by librarians is for reporting conference news. Library conferences organizers are beginning to promote the use of Twitter as a way to reach librarians who are unable to attend conferences in person. A designated hashtag, a special keyword preceded by a pound sign inserted into the body of the tweet, is used by conference attendees to identify posts related to the conference. As attendees post, people can follow along with sessions or view an archive of all of the tweets posted during the conference. The Jacksonville (Florida) Public Library uses Twitter to send short news items to its followers.[26] Another benefit of using Twitter and other social networking services is that these services allow users to keep track of conversations and other information without relying on e-mail, and because the services are web-based, the information can be accessed from any computer.

The ability to access information from any computer has improved greatly with the introduction of Web 2.0 technologies, and these technologies have also broken down geographic barriers. Webinars, web-based seminars or presentations transmitted over the web,[27] are being used more frequently by libraries and librarians in place of face-to-face meetings and workshops. Podcasting, a form of broadcasting over the Internet, allows users to listen to an audio file on a computer or portable media player. Podcasts, which are usually parts of a series and are distributed via individual episodes, can be subscribed to using an RSS feed so that podcasts are downloaded automatically when new episodes are available. The Denver Public Library offers podcasts for children on its website that include nursery rhymes and fairy tales.[28] The list of creative ways libraries and librarians are using technology today to connect with one another and users goes on and on, and examples could fill an entire volume. It is my hope that this chapter has highlighted some of the current uses of technology and will inspire others to find new ways to use technology in their libraries to better serve users.

NOTES

1. J. Musser, T. O'Reilly, & the O'Reilly Radar Team, "Web 2.0: Principles and best practices." 2006. Retrieved from http://www.oreilly.com/catalog/web2report/chapter/web20_report_excerpt.pdf

2. C. Prabha, "Shifting from print to electronic journals in ARL university libraries." *Serials Review*, *33* (2007), 4–13.

3. "Down through the years: The heritage of Johnson C. Smith University." 2010. Retrieved from http://archives.jcsu.edu/echo/

4. Felix E. Grant Jazz Archives. Retrieved from http://lrdudc.wrlc.org/jazz/felix.php.

5. Black Oral History Collection. Retrieved from http://content.wsulibs.wsu.edu/cdm-5985/

6. Civil Rights Oral History Interviews. Retrieved from http://content.wsulibs.wsu.edu/cdm-cvoralhist/

7. C. De Rosa, "Perceptions of libraries and information resources: a report to the OCLC membership." 2005. Retrieved from http://www.oclc.org/reports/2005perceptions.htm

8. D. Way, "The impact of web-scale discovery on the use of a library collection." *Serials Review*, *36* (2010), 214–220.

9. Howard University Library website. http://www.howard.edu/library/

10. Jefferson County Public Library website. http://www.jefferson.lib.co.us/

11. MarcEdit website. http://people.oregonstate.edu/~reeset/marcedit/html/index.php

12. "Macro (computer science)" (2011, April 4). Wikipedia, The Free Encyclopedia. Retrieved from http://en.wikipedia.org/w/index.php?title=Macro_(computer_science)&oldid=422302235

13. J. Baxmeyer & K. Clarke. Planet Cataloging website. http://planetcataloging.org/

14. "Blog." (2011, April 6). In Wikipedia, The Free Encyclopedia. Retrieved from http://en.wikipedia.org/w/index.php?title=Blog&oldid=422700890

15. Chesnutt Library Reference Department (2006, September 14). Chesnutt Library Blog. Retrieved from http://chesnuttlibrary.blogspot.com/

16. East Baton Rouge Parish Library. InfoBlog. Retrieved from http://ebrpl.wordpress.com/

17. Dan Libby, RSS 0.91 Spec, revision 3. Retrieved from http://web.archive.org/web/20001204093600/my.netscape.com/publish/formats/rss-spec-0.91.html

18. "RSS." (2007, December 12). In Wikipedia, The Free Encyclopedia. Retrieved from http://en.wikipedia.org/w/index.php?title=Rss&oldid=177488969

19. Robert W. Woodruff Library, Atlanta University Center. http://www.auctr.edu/

20. S. Lihitkar, "Establishing a virtual reference service." *DESIDOC Journal of Library and Information Technology*, *31*(2011), 31–34.

21. "Social networking service" (2011, April 21). In Wikipedia, The Free Encyclopedia. Retrieved from http://en.wikipedia.org/w/index.php?title=Social_networking_service&oldid=425164724

22. Ning website. http://www.ning.com/

23. Black Librarian Nation website. http://blacklibrariannation.ning.com/

24. Downs-Jones Library. Huston-Tillotson University. http://aa.htu.edu/Library.aspx

25. Twitter website. http://twitter.com/about

26. Jacksonville Public Library's Twitter page. Retrieved from http://twitter.com/#!/jaxlibrary

27. "Webinar." In Webopedia. Retrieved from http://www.webopedia.com/TERM/W/Webinar.html

28. Denver Public Library Podcasts website. http://podcast.denverlibrary.org/

34

From MARC to Mars: The Impact of Technology on Librarianship

Allene Hayes Farmer

One could say that my career in librarianship started as a work-study student at Robert W. Woodruff Library, Clark College, in Atlanta, Georgia. An English major, my choice to work in the library was a no-brainer. I knew the library inside out, and the hours provided many options. It was open seven days a week and located just across the street from Morehouse College—many options indeed!

Looking for a job after graduating from college during the Ronald Reagan years was tough, but I was offered a position at the Library of Congress (LC) with my first application and interview. I started at LC as a preliminary cataloger of Spanish and Portuguese books. This is where I first learned about MARC. Developed at LC, MARC is an acronym for *Ma*chine-*R*eadable *C*ataloging. MARC automated the cataloging process and serves as the foundation for today's online cataloging system.[1]

Working at LC made me realize that I needed to attend library school. Fortunately, at that time, LC sponsored graduate school tuition for library science students. I attended the University of Maryland's Library School and concentrated on automation and library administration. I also took computer programming classes and volunteered at LC for automation-related projects. I remember working with huge mainframes and computer cards and hanging out in the computer labs while completing homework assignments and reading computer dumps to help an LC programmer find programming errors.

I received my MLS degree in 1986 and soon thereafter things got very exciting on the technical horizon. Personal computers (PC) were introduced to the workforce, the card catalogs became obsolete, we started to communicate on the Internet via e-mail and Gopher, and now with the World Wide Web one can search and learn about anything from MARC to Mars.

For clarification, the Internet is the network infrastructure that allows computers to communicate with one another globally as long as the computer is connected to the Internet. Very simply speaking, the World Wide Web (WWW) is one of the ways in which information is distributed over the Internet so that the information can be read by humans. The computers can communicate with one another, but it is difficult for humans to read computer code. Gopher was one of the first ways that we communicated across the Internet and is still in use, but the WWW has become the most popular medium. We communicate on the WWW via browsers such as Internet Explorer and Firefox, which utilize search engines such as Google. Google continues to expand with various tools of the digital information trade even as I write this.

As a profession, librarians first feared Google. We thought it was trying to take over our business. But, being the dynamic and affluent institution that it is, Google romanced libraries, donated a lot of time and money to libraries, and now Google is so popular that its name has become a verb. Love or hate it, I believe that all librarians use Google. As technology continues to advance, libraries and librarianship has had to evolve with it.

There are so many ways in which computers have impacted librarianship. Since the printed book, published works have morphed into so many information formats from microforms, video disks, floppy discs, to CD-ROMs, e-books, and e-journals. And now, anything available on the Internet is considered "published."

The impact of digital resources has had a major impact on authors and publishers due to the changing formats, preservation, and copyright issues. There is much to be said about copyright in the digital age. The copyright laws have not kept up with technology, but the U.S. Copyright Office is working on it. Among other things, the Copyright Office formed the Section 108 Study Group, which was charged "to conduct a reexamination of the exceptions and limitations applicable to libraries and archives under the Copyright Act, specifically in light of the changes wrought by digital media." The group studied "how Section 108 of the Copyright Act may need to be amended to address the relevant issues and concerns of libraries and archives, as well as creators and other copyright holders."[2]

As stated in the executive summary of The Section 108 Study Group Report:

> Rapidly evolving digital technologies have transformed the way that works of authorship are created, disseminated, stored, preserved, accessed, and experienced for scholarly, entertainment, or other purposes. Rights holders—including authors, musicians, artists, publishers, photographers, computer programmers, record companies, and motion picture studios—are now creating and distributing works in digital formats, and as a result their practices have undergone significant changes. Libraries, archives, and museums, in keeping with their missions to collect, preserve, and make available the cultural heritage on behalf of the American people, have likewise altered many of their traditional procedures and practices and have started to collect new materials. Increased use of digital technologies has prompted a corresponding

> increase in the public's expectations regarding access to content. Users have begun to expect trustworthy, immediate desktop access to digital materials from all sources, whether local or remote.
>
> Copyright law structures many of the relationships among users, creators, and distributors of copyrighted content. Due to the rapid pace of technological and social change, the law embodies some now-outmoded assumptions about technology, behavior, professional practices, and business models. For instance, Section 108 of the Copyright Act of 1976, which provides libraries and archives with specific exceptions to the exclusive rights of copyright owners, was enacted in the pre-digital era. At that time, works were created and distributed primarily in analog format and library and archives copying consisted of photo-duplication and microform. Much has changed since then. The Digital Millennium Copyright Act (DMCA), enacted in 1998, amended portions of Section 108, but its provisions only began to address the preservation practices of libraries and archives in the digital environment and did not attempt to be a comprehensive revision of that section.[3]

Librarians are quite comfortable with the traditional library; brick and mortar buildings with books and information items of various formats. But, what are our thoughts concerning digital libraries or as some may say electronic libraries or virtual libraries? What is a digital library? Wikipedia defines it as "A library in which collections are stored in digital formats and accessed by computers. The digital content may be stored locally, or accessed remotely via computer networks." Or "A type of information retrieval system."[4]

When I was first employed at LC, it was considered the library of last resort. There were so many patrons who came from all over America and from around the world to use LC's unique and unparalleled collections that LC recommended that patrons use their local libraries first and come to LC if they could not find what they needed. Now, the objective is for LC to go where the people are; be it Second Life, Facebook, YouTube, or Twitter. LC is even "pushing" its digital resources out to mobile devices: cell phones, PDAs, and such. Students and researchers no longer want to go to the library. They want to be able to do all their research online from the comfort of their homes, dorms, or local coffee shops. With the onslaught of digital information and computer access, patron traffic in most libraries has dwindled.

In 2007, I worked on the Library Services Strategic Planning Discussion Document, which recommended that LC "employ new technologies, including Webcasts and podcasts, to deliver collections to users; determine user interest in new delivery methods and determine feasibility of those delivery methods."[5]

Our report explored RSS (Really Simple Syndication) feeds, webcasting, podcasting, vodcasting, blogs, wikis, instant messaging, Internet 2, videoconferencing, web-conferencing, institutional repository software, virtual worlds (e.g., Second Life), social networking technologies (e.g., MySpace, Facebook, YouTube, etc.), including the delivery of standalone material to mobile devices and PCs. I am very proud to say that LC is now using them all!

Today, some of my digital projects include web archiving, which is the process of collecting a website and preserving it as if taking a picture of the entire website and maintaining it before it changes. I have been serving as the lead on metadata issues for LC Web Archives since 1999.[6]

I serve as the project manager for the Electronic Resources Management System (ERMS) pilot project. I conceptualized the ERMS team structure, recommended the team leader, and the division. This project team acquires and processes monographs, serials, and integrating resources in electronic format to make them available to the public.[7]

The Electronic Resources Stakeholder's Group (ERSG) comprised 21 staff from all units at LC. We were charged to address and make recommendations to resolve issues for managing and sustaining the ERMS implementation. The group had to consider issues related to electronic resources workflow (including subscriptions, e-deposits, and freely available web resources); ongoing maintenance of the ERMS OPAC (online public access catalog); and resolution of metadata and technical support needs. I served as co-chair. We have since formed a smaller permanent electronic resource management team. This team is the decision-making group that responds to issues associated with the acquisition, description, technical maintenance, and access of electronic resources available from LC.

For the World Digital Library (WDL),[8] I served as the coordinator for metadata. I worked with the WDL directors and catalogers throughout LC to ensure that all WDL metadata needs were met, and I continue to serve as a member of the International Federation of Library Associations and Institutions (IFLA) WDL working group.

My work has rewarded me with invitations to train or speak at various institutions across the United States and around the world. I have traveled to the Netherlands, India, Germany, South Africa, Sweden, Canada, Cameroon, and Jamaica to discuss metadata and the work that I do on digital initiatives. I've met with librarians, students, professors, civil society leaders, dignitaries, and library patrons of all ages.

In summary, MARC is a term to which all librarians should be able to relate. It is an icon of the beginning of digital libraries. Some librarians say that MARC is dead. Some may say that MARC is not yet dead, but dying a slow death. I think that like technology, MARC cataloging has evolved into metadata creation, which shows that libraries and librarianship is evolving, but more drastic measures must take place.

It doesn't matter if one is with a public, private, academic, special, or a government institution, librarians of the future must keep pace with the tools of the trade. It would be nice if technology would slow down a bit so that we could catch up, but our competitive society keeps things motivated. Skill sets for librarians have changed. Librarians today should be encouraged to experiment with the new technology, and the librarian of tomorrow must have strong technical skills.

Embracing technology has provided me the opportunity to work my way up from a technician position, to the position of a chief, which is rather rare for African Americans at LC. I have had the opportunity to attend the conferences of American Library Association (ALA), Black Caucus of the ALA (BCALA), IFLA, Online Computer Library Center (OCLC), and other library-related organizations. I have met and continue to work with librarians around the world. Ironically, the very conferences and meetings that brought me and other writers of this book together are now being streamed online.[9] Had we attended those same meetings and conferences online, our paths may have never crossed. The world is now "computing in the cloud,"[10] but it has yet to be resolved if that is a pro or a con.

NOTES

1. http://www.loc.gov/marc
2. http://www.section108.gov
3. http://www.section108.gov
4. http://en.wikipedia.org/wiki/Digital_library
5. Hayes, Allene F. (Coordinator). "Performance Goal 2.B.4: Employ new technologies, including Web-casts and Podcasts to deliver collections to users." *Library Services Strategic Plan 2008–2012*, 94 p., 2007.
6. http://loc.gov/minerva
7. http://eresources.loc.gov
8. http://www.wdl.org/en
9. http://en.wikipedia.org/wiki/Streaming_media
10. http://en.wikipedia.org/wiki/Cloud_computing

35

Historically Black Colleges and University Library Alliance: Preserving Our Culture

Ira Revels

In October 2002, members of SOLINET (Southeastern Library Network) recognized a lack of representation specifically for historically black college and university (HBCU) library issues within the organization. As a result, members who were directors at HBCU libraries worked with SOLINET to issue a call to all HBCUs to meet. The invitations resulted in a gathering of professionals representing 100 of the 105 White House–designated HBCU libraries. This unprecedented meeting laid the foundation for the HBCU Library Alliance (HBCU LA) membership organization. The mission statement of the HBCU LA is to support the collaboration of institutions dedicated to providing resources designed to strengthen the libraries of HBCUs and their constituents.

During the meeting, HBCU library leaders explored the role of libraries in supporting the unique educational and research roles of their institutions. By the meeting's end, participants had reached the consensus that cooperation between HBCUs would significantly strengthen the role of libraries on campus and expand access to information and cultural resources.[1] Participants formed five working groups whose purpose was to explore top priorities and report their findings. These groups were:

- Preservation and Digitization for Cultural Materials
- Information and Advocacy A Information Collection and Analysis
- Information and Advocacy B Advocacy and Communication
- Human Resources: Shared Expertise, Recruitment, and Staff Development
- Better Access to Collections/Facilities

Participants in the Preservation and Digitization of Cultural Materials working group noted that HBCUs hold a wide range of cultural materials. They recognized that there is significant interest among HBCU library leaders in providing access to and preserving the unique materials held in their institutions. These materials include printed text, manuscripts, photographic images, memorabilia, and electronic records. They agreed that a collaborative effort among the members in digital collection building would:

- Promote the mission of each university
- Preserve the history and culture of the institution and community
- Provide access to valuable collections held by HBCU libraries and archives
- Promote networking, collaboration, and sharing among HBCUs.

A primary focus of the group became exploring funding opportunities for training and implementation in digital collection building and preservation.[2] This focus is what led Cornell University Library to partner with the HBCU LA to develop a project that would provide staff training and support for digital collection building. The goal of the HBCU LA is to link digitized special collections at all HBCUs through a portal designed specifically by its members to advance the use of these materials and preserve their cultural integrity.

CORNELL UNIVERSITY LIBRARY

Concurrently, Cornell University Library (CUL) was investigating creating a digital library curriculum with an accredited School of Library and Information Studies. In 2003, The Andrew W. Mellon Foundation awarded CUL a yearlong planning grant to investigate the development of a collaborative digital librarianship program for the HBCU Clark Atlanta University (CAU) and its School of Library and Information Studies. Shortly afterward, the CAU board of trustees announced the plan to close the School of Library and Information Studies by May 2005. At the time there were two accredited library schools at historically black colleges: Clark Atlanta University and North Carolina Central University.

The result of the planning grant helped lay the foundation for a meeting with representatives of the HBCU LA board of directors and CUL project staff members Ira Revels, Peter Hirtle, and Anne Kenney. These meetings resulted in the project Building Collections, Building Services, and Building Sustainability: A Collaborative Model for the HBCU Library Alliance. The overarching goal of the HBCU LA–CUL Digital Initiative, as it came to be called, was the development of a shared HBCU digital library.

CUL entered into collaboration with the HBCU LA because it has a long commitment to sharing its expertise in preservation, digital imaging, digital technologies, and program management. Anne R. Kenney, who co-authored *Moving Theory into Practice: Digital Imaging for Libraries and Archives* with Oya Y. Rieger,[3] has been leading CUL's efforts at providing continuing education training for over 20 years to library professionals and staff. Kenney is currently the Cornell University Carl A. Kroch University librarian.

CUL has trained librarians at the Library of Congress and in Cuba, China, South Africa, Thailand, and Vietnam to use best practices in digital preservation and imaging. CUL created tools and workshops for the Research Libraries Group and still edits under contract with RLG DigiNews. The library has programs to bring Southeast Asian and Native American librarians to Ithaca, New York, for training in preservation, and it has developed online preservation training programs for librarians in Southeast Asia and the Middle East. The library views education of other librarians as part of its mission.

The Andrew W. Mellon Foundation funded a series of three 18-month grant projects for the CUL and the HBCU LA. The overarching result that the HBCU LA hopes to achieve is a sustainable digital library program that will enable all HBCU libraries to participate in the shared digital library. The third and final project phase is set to end in the fall 2011. Each phase has four components: intensive training on digital imaging; the construction of digitized collections at each of the participating institutions; analysis to determine the pros and cons of a common portal of digitized resources; and planning on how to address the governance, financial, intellectual property, metadata, and sustainability issues associated with building a shared digital collection.

The first phase of the training and digital image production initiative began in the summer of 2005. A grant from The Andrew W. Mellon Foundation made it possible for CUL to partner with the HBCU LA, the SOLINET (now LYRASIS), and the Atlanta University Center Robert W. Woodruff Library of Georgia (AUC RWWL) to undertake a collaborative effort involving HBCUs. The HBCU LA–CUL Digitization Initiative was the first effort of its kind to involve 10 HBCU libraries and the project partners. As a result of phase one, within 18 months, the HBCUs' library staffs developed a digital collection of 2,000 historic and founding documents that celebrate the rich cultural heritage found in their institutions.[4]

The second project phase, which began in 2007, was designed to increase the number of HBCU library partners in the project. Unlike in the first project where a select group of 10 HBCU libraries participated, all members of the HBCU LA were invited to submit an application to participate in the digital initiative. The HBCU LA selected all 10 applicants that applied, and the project was under way. Additionally, two new partner libraries came on board: Meharry Medical College of Tennessee and Lincoln University of Pennsylvania. As a testament to the success of the collaborative model, the Meharry Medical College archivist utilized project equipment at Fisk University Library and worked with the project liaison there to digitize archival records at Meharry and then contribute them to the HBCU digital collection from the archives department. By the end of phase two, partners had developed an online collection of more than 10,000 digital objects.

This project had four objectives. The first was to train at least 10 HBCU library staff in digital imaging. At least 14 staff members were trained. Two were trained at the expense of their own institutions. Another objective of phase two was to develop guidance on how to participate in the digital initiative for libraries that were not chosen as one of the first 20 partners. A variety of resources to help new partners contribute digital collections were developed. Guidance to new partners includes:

- Recommendations concerning the selection of archival materials
- Informational videos on material selection and information technology requirements
- A budget spreadsheet to list the estimated costs for hardware, software, materials, supplies and training.

The third objective of phase two was to explore digital service centers at a few of the most productive HBCU partner libraries. The HBCU LA Committee on Digitization identified at least four issues that must be resolved before libraries could feel comfortable going to their campus administrators with this request:

- How to gain buy-in from HBCU libraries on developing digitization services for other HBCUs
- How to gain support for digitization centers at the highest levels of campus administration
- Understanding the legal issues involved in cooperative agreements with the HBCU LA and any other entity for library digitization centers
- Understanding the staffing and other resource requirements for digitization centers.

Although the partners were unable to resolve these issues fully during the second phase of the project, during the third project phase, the digital service centers worked toward a common service delivery model.

Finally, the third phase of the project began in 2009. During phase three, partners explored an economic model that would enable a sustainable HBCU LA digital collection. The goal of the project, therefore, is to develop a sustainable business and economic model for HBCU digital collections. Its objectives are twofold: (1) to develop a business plan and (2) to develop digital service centers that will support the program that will begin once the HBCU LA–CUL Digital Initiative ended in June 2011. The third phase had accomplished the overall goals of increasing HBCU library contributions and becoming sustainable.

The HBCU LA–CUL Digital Initiative provided a platform for the CUL to share its award-winning tutorial *Moving Theory into Practice: Digital Imaging for Libraries and Archives* into a classroom environment with numerous HBCU librarians and information technology professionals.[5] Over 18 months, the workshop participants successfully applied their training toward building the collaborative digital library. In support of their efforts, CUL staff visited each institution and offered scanning and metadata workflow consultation and advice. CUL and HBCU LA staff developed a website containing written technical guidelines that participants used to accomplish scanning and metadata creation. SOLINET,[6] the HBCU LA, and the AUC RWWL assisted throughout the project by providing administrative, logistical, and database support for the 10 partner institutions.

NOTES

1. HBCU Library Alliance, "A call for cooperation among HBCU libraries." *HBCU Library Alliance*. 2006. Retrieved from http://hbculibraries.org/html/cooperation.html
2. HBCU Library Alliance, "Organizational meeting." *HBCU Library Alliance*. 2006. Retrieved from http://hbculibraries.org/html/meeting.html
3. Anne R. Kenney and Oya Y. Rieger, *Moving theory into practice: Digital imaging for libraries and archives.* Mountain View, CA: Research Libraries Group, 2000.
4. The digital collection can be viewed online at http://hbcudigitallibrary.auctr.edu
5. Information on the workshop Moving Theory into Practice: Digital Imaging for Libraries and Archives can be found at http://www.library.cornell.edu/preservation/workshop/
6. http://www.solinet.com/

Part VIII

ISSUES AND PROFILES

36

The Black Body at the Reference Desk: Critical Race Theory and Black Librarianship

Tracie D. Hall

Socially the natural body is coded as a fleshy field of dreams—a projected and imagined representation of identity formations that reinvests the political and cultural objectives of the dominant power structure . . . the cultural and theoretical essence of America's developing discourse on "difference," shape the racial imaginings of our culture, and as such provide a segue into implicit and explicit historical and social development of American identity particularly as it relates to the "black" body (Henderson, 2009, p. 14).

An object that absorbs all the radiation incident upon it is called a blackbody. A blackbody is a perfect observer and also an ideal radiator (Luna, n.d.).

From segregated libraries and the first efforts to integrate the library profession to current efforts to recruit a library workforce representative of the constituencies served, libraries have often operated in environments critically informed by race. Indeed it can be argued that the African American experience in and of the library, from segregation to the beginning of the 21st century, has socially informed, politically shaped, and given professional urgency to the notion of black librarianship.

Despite the nostalgic and widely popular narrative that posits libraries—public libraries as altruistic, motive neutral, Ellis Islands of race and culture neutrality and academic libraries as autonomous, color-blind havens of academic goodwill and playing-field leveling—there is a simultaneous, if suppressed, counter-narrative that calls out libraries as deeply racialized spaces where race-conscious motives, practices, and policies are inevitably enacted.

That library and information science and practice in this country are deeply infused, indeed "colored" (pun intended), by racism, given the larger social context in which libraries operate and (un)intentionally propagate, is hardly surprising. What is unsettling, however, to the point of frustration is the unwillingness of the profession to deeply engage in an open discussion of race, racism, and the accompanying acts of personal discrimination and structural exclusion that often result without seeking to sublimate that critical conversation to one that ends in cosmetic attempts at diversity. To be sure, diversity—in its quest to achieve equitable representation and participation—is a fundamental goal; but it is a concept that has been increasingly co-opted by systems that use it as a smoke screen for disingenuous efforts that serve to reify racism.

In his lamentation on the entrenchment of "educational apartheid" in the United States, journalist Jonathan Kozol (2005) wrote that rather than naming racism or racial segregation, "linguistic sweeteners, semantic somersaults and surrogate vocabularies" are increasingly being employed to deflect any meaningful criticism or taking-to-task. Chief among these semantic devices is the word "diverse," which Kozol argues elsewhere has come to signify its opposite and "which is not an accurate adjective but a mere euphemism for a plainer word that has apparently become unspeakable."

If the education system has been reticent in its discussion of racism, the library and information science field has seemingly slapped itself with a gag order. While the discussion of diversity in libraries has proliferated over the past few decades, meaningful dialogue around race has been eviscerated or altogether evaded. In his important treatise, "Trippin' Over the Color Line: The Invisibility of Race in Library and Information Studies," Todd Honma asked "Why is it that scholars and students do not talk openly and honestly about issues of race and LIS? Why does the field have a tendency to tiptoe around discussing race and racism, and instead limit the discourse by using words such as 'multiculturalism' and 'diversity'? Why is the field so glaringly white yet no one wants to talk about whiteness and white privilege?" (2005, p. 1).

Though the exploration of critical race theory and whiteness in librarianship has grown since Honma's writing, the documented professional underrepresentation of and inequitable provision of services to people of color in libraries necessitates the continued mining of critical race theory as a means of linking individual anecdotes of racialized, personal experiences to a larger structural and systemic phenomenology of racism as a (sub)consciously, sociopolitical device in libraries as in the larger sociopolitical arena's in which they operate.

History attests that the black body has posed a particular "problem" in libraries in the same way that it has proved a quandary for formal educational environments. As writer and politician William Cabell Bruce asserted in 1891, "it should be borne in mind that the Negro Problem is a race problem," (p. 4) the construction and propagation of race in this country has symbiotically relied on a racial caste system that has centered and privileged whiteness and white cultural expression as exemplary and normative while exoticizing (at best), marginalizing, and penalizing racial "others." That this caste system has been undergirded and cyclically compounded by educational and economic discrimination has meant that attempts at equalizing access to these resources and say over their dissemination—even and especially in libraries—has confronted contestation either in design or delivery. As British librarian and activist Shiraz Durrani noted, despite industrial progress, Western and Eurocentric machinations have resulted in a

> divided society with millions who are excluded from the benefits that advanced technologies make possible. The ranks of the "excluded" include working people, Black communities, disabled people, lesbians, bisexuals, gay men and transgendered people as well as other communities. . . . There is an urgent need for a change in thinking on the part of those who hold power in libraries and local authorities. The first step is to admit that all is not well in the library world. (2008, p. 96)

That the notions of racial superiority and inferiority have symbiotically propagated and relied on racialized constructions of intellectual superiority and inferiority is perhaps as evident as water is to fish for those of us who operate in education and information environments—in that it is and it is not—depending on one's positionality and how long one can stay under without the need for air. To be certain the library is one of many stages in the larger racial theater. It is a place where socially subjective ideas of how information should be collected, organized, and disseminated by and for whom are played out and inevitably influenced by the hyperracial discourse being played out in this and many other countries. For Durrani, it is the responsibility of "black" library workers (and his definition of "blackness" is both culturally expansive and politically identified) to lead the vanguard in destabilizing racism in libraries. Silence and avoidance are acts of complicity.

Though librarianship as a "calling" has traditionally been characterized by a profound service ethic that at the turn of the 20th century in the United States found most libraries championing the delivery of services to the poor and new immigrants, distinguished researcher Clara Chu noted that even this beyond-the-call service was racially imbued. "Public library history shows that services have not been equally provided to all residents of the United States . . . for example, during the early part of this century services to immigrants and African Americans were differentiated." Chu continues, "Librarians set policies to encourage basic educational opportunities for immigrants and discourage the availability of such opportunities for Blacks" (1999, p. 2).

This distinction, this purposeful exclusion of blacks and black bodies from altruistic, bootstrap-offering services, did not originate in libraries, but has characterized the very foundation of literacy in this country and has been and arguably continues to be fundamentally, if not always intentionally, propagated by libraries. As Honma astutely observed, "by examining the sociopolitical histories of libraries, in particular public libraries in the United States, we can get a better understanding of the library's formation—the ontology, if you will—as one that is both racial and racist" (2005, p. 4). To examine the histories of libraries and literacy in this country is to understand that the very act of reading to acquire or disseminate knowledge by blacks has been considered a subversive act.

In 1818, the city of Savannah passed the following ordinance:

> Any person that teaches any person of color, slave or free, to read or write, or causes such persons to be so taught, is subjected to a fine of thirty dollars for each offense; and every person of color who shall keep a school to teach reading or writing is subject to a fine of thirty dollars, or to be imprisoned ten days, and whipped thirty-nine lashes! (Goodell, 1853)

An 1831 Slave Code Law enacted in 1831 warned:

> In North Carolina, to teach a slave to read or write, or sell or give him any book [Bible not excepted] or pamphlet, is punished with thirty-nine lashes, or imprisonment, if the offender be a free negro; but if a white, then with a fine of $200. The reason for this law, assigned in its preamble, is that teaching slaves to read and write tends to dissatisfaction in their minds, and to produce insurrection and rebellion. (Goodell, 1853)

As Gil Kujovich (1994), higher education researcher attests, "For nearly a century after freedom from enslavement and enforced illiteracy, the nation's answer to black Americans' desire and enthusiasm for learning was consistent and pervasive discrimination." This de jure and de facto segregation carried over into libraries. As black code laws segued into Jim Crow legislation in the 1930s through the 1960s, public education facilities—including schools and libraries—were segregated throughout the South. In communities where separate not only meant unequal, but often nonexistent, blacks were banned from using the libraries. That some of the first antidiscrimination sit-ins in the South would take place not at lunch counters but at libraries is testament to how fundamental blacks viewed library access and services.

> In 1939, just before World War II broke out, five young men staged a civil protest to open the Alexandria, Virginia public library to African Americans. One by one they walked into the library and asked for library cards. When they were refused, each sat down at a separate table with a book quietly reading. A library clerk who saw them panicked, yelling, "There are colored people all over the library." The police were summoned and the men were arrested. (Spangler & Becker, 2000)

In the 1960s sit-ins would be staged at libraries across the South. Indeed, the first sit-in in the state of Mississippi was a protest at the Jackson Public Library in 1961. Efforts to integrate libraries were met with the same brutal resistance experienced elsewhere in the Civil Rights Movement. In cases where legal concessions were offered, they were often demoralizing. In one response to a judgment in favor of library desegregation, all chairs and tables were removed from the library buildings. Meanwhile, in Birmingham, Alabama, policy was augmented to dictate that if a book was transferred by request from the white Central Library to the black branch it was to be replaced, not returned (Spangler & Becker, 2000).

If the very presence of black bodies in the library has proved problematic and potentially disruptive to the centering of white privilege, what has occurred when blacks have progressively—though slowly—moved around to the other side of the reference desk as information guides and gate openers? Librarian and theorist Isabel Espinal (2004), who as a Latina characterizes her examination of whiteness in librarianship as "reverse anthropology," suggested that efforts to diversify the profession are equally fraught with contention and divisiveness and may pose a problem, "which at times can evoke reactive agencies of whiteness in defense of white privilege."

Though the library profession has for the past two decades increasingly focused on diversifying the profession in the effort to better reflect and respond to an increasingly heterogeneous user and potential-user demographic, we must come to the realization that both sides of the reference desk are equally racially loaded and sometimes for different reasons.

To occupy or observe the reference desk in today's libraries is to note that race consciousness is alive and well. That librarians may, often unconsciously, give differing levels of services to some users while library users may similarly read one librarian as more desirable or competent an information navigator than another are decisions as informed by race (and the attending inference of intellectual ability) as they are by gender, perceived class, or other forms of difference. When as a new librarian, a white patron felt compelled to slowly spell out "Plato. Peee-Elll-Ayyy-Teee-Ohhh" for me, I knew that my own black body on the imparting side of the reference desk marked me as conspicuous and suspect. Though I have found myself at a few decision-making tables since those early days as a librarian, this assigned "outsider" status, compounded as it has been by race, has remained. And beyond my own lived experiences, I have confirmed in the experience of other librarians of color that to be a black or brown body in the library is to be perpetually problematic. That this, borrowing from physics theory "blackbody problem," in libraries—this quality of being simultaneous absorbers, observers, radiators, and even disrupters of race—has informed and must continue to shape the trajectory of black librarianship (as both a professional and political agency) in the fight for human equity, and social justice is an assertion worthy of greater depth and dissection than can be accomplished here.

Based on own my experience as speaker on a panel some years ago in South Africa, I would assert that this is an issue, a question, that transcends race, ethnicity, any broad or limiting categorization and unites all librarians who identify or are identified as different. Looking out on an audience of librarians working to redefine library service in the wake of apartheid, I broke away from my prepared remarks and opined that to assert one's black body at the reference desk is in itself a political act. The rest of what I had to say was lost as the crowd stood up even as the words were leaving my mouth. I remember stepping from that podium into a sea of black librarians (black reading broadly) who had heard me name something that they knew, that I knew, but that I had never named for myself before.

If, as Carol Henderson surmised, "the social pathology of cultural and critical discourses makes the black body an interlocking contradiction of various possibilities" (2009, p. 14), it is time that we more intentionally mine and theorize the histories of race and resistance in libraries and the promise of black librarianship in the fight for racial equity and social justice.

REFERENCES

Bruce, W. C. (1891). The Negro Problem. Retrieved from http://www.archive.org/details/negroproblem00bruc

Chu, C. M. (1999). Uniting multicultural voices in libraries. *EMIE Bulletin, 17*(1), 2–4, 17.

Durrani, S. (2008). *Information and liberation: Writings on the politics of information and librarianship.* Duluth, MN: Library Juice Press.

Espinal, I. (2004). Whiteness at work: Latina librarian ethnography in a white female profession. Prospectus for the Magical Mask of Whiteness: Disguising Racism and Doing Whiteness Studies under the Second Bush Reich panel for the 2004 American Anthropological Association. San Francisco, November 17–21. Retrieved from http://people.umass.edu/hepage/pdf_files/MagicWhiteMask.pdf

Goodell, T. (1853). *The American Slave Code in theory and practice: Its distinctive features shown by its statutes, judicial decisions and illustrative facts.* New York: American and Foreign Anti-Slavery Society.

Henderson, C. E. (Ed.). (2009). *America and the black body: Identity politics in print and visual culture.* Madison, NJ: Fairleigh Dickinson University Press.

Honma, T. (2005). Trippin' over the color line: The invisibility of race in library and information studies. *InterActions: UCLA Journal of Education and Information Studies, 1*(2), 2005, 1–26.

Kozol, J. (2005, September 1). America's educational apartheid. *Harper's Magazine,* 311 (1864). Retrieved from http://www.mindfully.org/Reform/2005/American-Apartheid-Education1sep05.htm

Kujovich, G. (1994). Public black colleges: The long history of unequal instruction. *Journal of Blacks in Higher Education, 3,* 65–76.

Luna, E. (n.d.). The blackbody problem. Quantum Theory Paper. Retrieved from http://facultyfiles.deanza.edu/gems/lunaeduardo/QuantumTheoryofLight.pdf

Spangler, M., & Becker, E. (2000). *Out of obscurity: The struggle to desegregate America's libraries.* Video River Road Productions. Distributed by California Newsreel.

37

Diversity in Librarianship: Is There a Color Line?

Cheryl L. Branche

> Why is it that scholars and students do not talk openly and honestly about issues of race and LIS? Why does the field have a tendency to tiptoe around discussing race and racism, and instead limit the discourses by using words like "multiculturalism" and "diversity"? Why is the field so glaringly white yet no one wants to talk about whiteness and white privilege?"
>
> —Honma, 2005, p. 1

At the beginning of the 20th century, W. E. B. DuBois wrote that "the problem of the twentieth century is the problem of the color line" (1903, p. xi). A century later, race relations in the United States remain as crucial an issue as ever.

From 1990 to 2000, the number of African American librarians dropped 4.4%, while the numbers of white librarians increased 23.6% and the numbers of Native American librarians increased 140% (ALA, 2007, p. 6). It is well known that the library profession has historically been a predominantly white female profession (Yeo & Jacobs, 2006, p. 5). Although African Americans represent 12.9% of the U.S. population, they only represent 6.2% of public librarians. In contrast, whites represent 65.1% of the U.S. population and 86.6% of public librarians. Hispanics represent 15.8% of the U.S. population and 3.0% of public librarians (Jaeger & Franklin, 2007, p. 21).

DIVERSITY AND MULTICULTURALISM

Cultural diversity and multiculturalism are buzzwords in the library profession. Stent, Hazard, and Rivlin (1973), in their book *Cultural Pluralism in Education: A Mandate for Change*, describe cultural diversity as

> a state of equal co-existence in a mutually supportive relationship within the boundaries or framework of one nation or people of diverse cultures with significantly different patterns of belief, behavior, color, and in many cases, with different languages. Each person must be aware of and secure in his own identity and be willing to extend to others the same respect and rights that he expects to enjoy himself. (cited in Clay, 2006, pp. 2–3)

"Prior research has posited that diversity, as a term and a concept, is essentially a euphemism, designed to avoid the complexity and emotion laden natures of terms, such as race, racism, sex and sexism" (Winston, 2007, p. 131). Diversity and multiculturalism suggest inclusiveness of diverse and many cultures; the obverse racism and race consciousness are rarely used, acknowledged, or studied. The need for diversity cannot be investigated effectively without addressing the origins of the diversity deficit. The social reasons, cultural beliefs, and racial attitudes that account for the relative absence of people of color should be examined.

U.S. LIBRARIES IN CONTEXT

U.S. libraries were originally set up to promote the white, American culture and Eurocentrism. Unlike immigrants, blacks, as slaves and former slaves, were not eligible to benefit from the services offered in the early libraries. Early collections were designed to help new immigrants navigate the new American bureaucracy on the way to citizenship (Clay, 2006, p. 1). This lack of emphasis on the black American may be one reason why we don't see such titles such as "How to Handle Racism" or "Racism in the Workplace." Understanding the historical context puts diversity into a better, more appropriate perspective. Having libraries remain Eurocentric and white normative means that other cultures and races are institutionally marginalized. As long as other cultures and races are described as "other," libraries are not compelled to include books about these cultures and races. As long as collections are Eurocentric, and not Afro-centric or America-centric (think South and Central America), then the tacit control that libraries have over the knowledge-based function and perspectives is retained and the white normative perspective will prevail.

BRIEF REVIEWS OF THREE ARTICLES

Much has been written on diversity and multiculturalism, but little research has been done within the past five years on race, racial attitudes, and librarianship.

In "Are Virtual Reference Services Color Blind?" Shachaf and Horowitz showed that virtual reference services are not color blind. In this study names represented ethnic groups. Latoya for African American, Rosa for Hispanic, Chang for Asian, Mary for white and Christian, Ahmed for Muslim, and Moshe for Jewish. Latoya and Ahmed were discriminated against the most compared to the level of services Moshe and Mary received. Wait times for answers were longer for Mary and Ahmed (2006, p. 15).

Honma (2005), in "Trippin' over the Color Line," stated that race, racism, and racial attitudes and issues must be addressed if one is to effectively address diversity. The concept of whiteness must be relieved of its honorific perception. At first glance, U.S. libraries are largely staffed by white people. The whole issue of race and color line is left out of the discussion. Not only is race as it relates to the relationships between librarians left out of the discussion, but so too is race, as it informs the behaviors white librarians have toward the minority patrons.

> Library and information science needs to embrace this spirit of social justice if it is to truly engage in meaningful discussions about race. . . . In a world of neoclassical capitalist accumulation and the continued spread of imperialist violence and global racism, now more than ever there is an urgent need for the field of library and information science to articulate a renewed commitment to anti-racism and social justice. (Honma, 2005, pp. 19–20)

In Yeo and Jacobs' "Diversity Matters," libraries have evolved along the same contexts as U.S. history; it is not surprising that genocide, slavery, segregation, Jim Crow laws, white supremacy, and oppression of minorities have had effects on the way librarians and libraries as institutions treat their patrons (Yeo & Jacobs, 2006, p. 1). U.S. libraries have set up systems of knowledge organization that are imperialistic (Yeo & Jacobs, 2006, p. 1) and oppressive to many minorities.

> Rather than stressing the importance of diversity and inclusion, as do most multiculturalists, I think that significantly more emphasis should be placed on the social and political construction of white supremacy and the dispensation of white hegemony. The reality-distortion field known as "Whiteness" needs to be identified as a cultural disposition and ideology linked to specific political, social and historical arrangements. (Yeo & Jacobs, 2006, p. 1)

I agree with this. Today the U.S. library represents democracy and intellectual freedom (Yeo & Jacobs, 2006, p. 1). It does not represent equal opportunity.

Diversity and multiculturalism are not terms that can be effectively used unless our own racist and bigoted behaviors are exposed and addressed. I contend that there are two color lines: white privilege and racism/bigotry and discrimination. The deficit of black librarians is no accident. There is a need to keep librarianship white to support the societal construct of Euro-centricity and white normatively. The study of diversity must include the study of the subconsciously unresolved racial issues and cultural beliefs about race, white superiority, and privilege that librarians carry. Whiteness and white normativity are embedded in U.S. library culture. As long as white normativity is tacit, there will be little room for Afro-centric or "other"-centric perspectives. As long as whites perceive one another as a force of expectancy and satisfaction (called "white privilege") and view non-whites, in the absence of expectation and satisfaction, through a veil that results in racism and bigotry, U.S. libraries will fail to reflect the diverse and multicultural facets of our world. The second color line, called discrimination/racism and bigotry, occurs when otherness is marginalized and underestimated.

> Unfortunately, despite the strides that the profession has made, librarians across America still struggle each day with such obstacles as equal access, as insufficient resources, low staffing, negligible political power, institutional and individual racism and bigotry, and many other factors that seem to block the most reasonable of requests and expectations. Equal library service for all people still eludes the profession. (Wheeler & Johnson-Houston, 2004, p. 45)

Until we can address our own racist biases, diversity efforts will be futile.

REFERENCES

American Library Association. Office for Research and Statistics. Office for Diversity. (2007). *Diversity counts report*. Retrieved from http://www.ala.org/ala/aboutala/offices/diversity/diversitycounts/diversitycounts_rev0.pdf

Clay, III, E. S. (2006). They don't look like me. *Library and Multicultural Awareness and Issues*, *52* (October–December). Retrieved from http://scholar.lib.vt.edu/ejournals/VALib/v52_n4/clay.html

Du Bois, W. E. B. (1982). *The souls of black folk*. New York: Penguin (Original work published 1903).

Honma, T. (2005). Trippin' over the color line: The invisibility of race in library and information studies. *InterActions: UCLA Journal of Education and Information Studies*, 1–26. Retrieved from http://escholarship.org/uc/item/4nj0w1mp

Jaeger, P. T., & Franklin, R. E. (2007). The virtuous circle: Increasing diversity in LIS faculties to create more inclusive library services and outreach. *Education Libraries*, *30* (Summer), 20–26.

Shachaf, P., & Horowitz, S. (2006). Are virtual reference services color blind? *Library and Information Science Research*, *28*, 501–520.

Stent, M. D., Hazard, W. R., & Rivlin, H. N. (1973). *Cultural pluralism in education: A mandate for change*. New York: Appleton-Century-Crofts.

Wheeler, M., & Johnson-Houston, D. (2004). A brief history of library service to African Americans. *American Libraries*, *35* (February), 42–45.

Winston, M. (2007). Diversity: The research and the lack of progress. *New Library World*, *109*(3/4), 130–149. Retrieved from http://www.emeraldinsight.com/journals.htm?articleid=1714535

Yeo, S., & Jacobs, J. R. (2006). Diversity matters? Rethinking diversity in libraries. *Counterpoise*, *9* (Spring). Retrieved from freegovinfo.info/files/freegovinfo.info/diversity_counterpoise.pdf

38

Beyond the Spectrum: Examining Library Recruitment of Blacks in the New Millennium

RaShauna Brannon and Jahala Simuel

In the 1994 *Black Librarian in America Revisited*, Carla D. Hayden issued a twofold prophetic call to action regarding black recruitment efforts in librarianship, calling for an increased consciousness to improve employment opportunities for African American in libraries and emphasizing the necessity of committing substantial fiscal support toward recruitment efforts of this demographic. In the years to follow, the response would be the creation of several diversity initiatives in order to recruit and educate prospective librarians from traditionally underrepresented populations, including black Americans. Although there has been significant progress in black recruitment efforts, we face a similar set of challenges 17 years later. In spite of these challenges, there have been meaningful, successful efforts to recruit black librarians across the nation, due in large part to the advocacy, scholarship, and support of librarians, researchers, and organizations devoted to fostering greater diversity in libraries.

The economic recession, which began in 2008 and continues to affect the nation as this chapter was written, adversely affected state revenue and endowments for institutions of higher education. During this time period, there was a dramatic increase in the number of students enrolled at all levels in postsecondary institutions, with a 15% increase between the fall of 2005 and fall of 2009. At the graduate level for this same period of time, there was a 23% increase in enrolled students (Knapp et al., 2007, 2011; State Higher Education, 2010). From 1997 to 2007, the number of master's degrees earned by black students increased nearly 50%, rising from 28,500 to 57,433 (Ryu, 2010). The field of library and information science saw an overall 11% increase in enrollment from the fall of 2003 to the fall of 2009, with an increase of 16% in the number of black students enrolled. Even with the increasing number of students enrolled in higher education institutions overall, there continues to be an underrepresentation of black students enrolled in master's programs for library and information sciences (LIS). Of the 25,586 students documented in the fall of 2009, black students numbered 1,388, representing 5% of students enrolled in LIS master's programs (ALISE Library and Information Science Education Statistics Committee, 2005, 2010).

With the publication of Dr. E. J. Josey's *The Black Librarian in America Revisited* and other scholarship devoted to the climate of the library profession, coupled with the collaborative efforts of library trailblazers, the dialogue morphed into action with the creation and support devoted to several diversity initiatives. Betty J. Turock, past president (1995) of the American Library Association (ALA), along with former ALA executive director Elizabeth Martinez embarked on a mission to create the Spectrum Scholarship Initiative. The path to the creation of this and other diversity initiatives has certainly not been a clear and easy one. Proponents of such programs have faced the opposition of detractors at many levels who may become threatened by the notion of diversity and perceptions of exclusivity (Cooke & Edwards, 2010). The notion of a diverse workforce lends itself to breaking down barriers and bridging cultures together to serve the information needs of all people.

The Spectrum Initiative, established in 1997 to address the issue of underrepresentation of librarians of color and to bring diversity issues to the limelight, has supported well over 650 students from underrepresented populations as of January 2011 (American Library Association, 2011b). It is financially supported by the ALA, along with the benevolence of organizations and individuals. These organizations include library schools and professional organizations that provide matching funds when affiliated students are chosen. The Institute for Museum and Library Services (IMLS) has continuously provided support for the Spectrum Initiative and also sponsors several other diversity and recruitment initiatives.

The awardees of funds from IMLS include North Carolina Central University (NCCU), University of North Carolina at Greensboro (UNCG), and the Association of Research Libraries (ARL). Under the umbrella of the Laura Bush 21st Century Librarian Program, NCCU found support for four cohorts of diversity scholars beginning in 2006. In 2009, UNCG implemented the Academic and Cultural Enrichment Scholars Program. ARL has sponsored the Initiative to Recruit a Diverse Workforce since 2002, which is designed to support students from diverse backgrounds to careers in academic research libraries. All of these programs were designed to recruit and prepare students from ethnically diverse backgrounds to serve as librarians while allowing opportunities for internships, research, financial support, and mentorship as they completed their studies (Institute of Museum and Library Services, 2011).

To address the need of recruitment efforts specifically for high school and college students from ethnically diverse backgrounds, ALA developed a project in 2010 with the support of IMLS titled "Discovering Librarianship: The Future Is Overdue." Currently in its developmental stages, it is designed to support 35 early career librarians from diverse backgrounds to serve as field recruiters to expose this demographic of students to careers in librarianship (American Library Association, 2011a).

For a new approach to black recruitment efforts, it would be interesting to examine the efficacy of using social networks and online resources to further promote careers in librarianship to diverse populations. In 2008, Marcellaus Joiner created the social network Black Librarian Nation on the Ning platform, "created to give African American Librarians a place to network, and share their experiences in the field." Joiner's original intent for this network was for it to reach a broader audience in efforts to recruit prospective librarians (personal correspondence, April 1, 2011). However, the populace of the social network largely remains a place for current practitioners. Another model for recruitment may be found in the development of a website specifically for the recruitment of students from diverse background. This website was developed for the recruitment of nursing students of color, which also serves as a career and education resource for nursing students, professionals, and faculty (Alloy Education, 2011). A similar resource for the library world could expose a larger audience to librarianship as a profession with proper advertising and outreach. These innovations could serve as prototypes of a resource designed specifically to recruit and promote the next generation of black librarians, as well as those from other diverse backgrounds.

Library schools must continue to recruit students from diverse backgrounds and also expose prospective students to the professional world of librarianship and the opportunities that exist therein. It is imperative for alliances to be maintained between library schools, professional organizations, and libraries of all types in order for students to get the support and exposure they need once they enter the workforce. Transcending beyond black recruitment, LIS faculty of the future must continue to reflect the multicultural makeup of society in order for all students enrolled in LIS programs to be exposed to issues of multiculturalism and diversity.

The words and scholarship of Dr. E. J. Josey and many other pioneers in black librarianship continue to resonate loudly within the field. Although significant strides have been made in black recruitment efforts to librarianship since Hayden's 1994 research, we must continue to advocate for and sustain efforts to recruit and support black librarians. Our commitment to financial support and sustained dialogue will ensure that our efforts will not be in vain, and that we will be able to pass the torch along to many future generations of black librarians.

REFERENCES

ALISE Library and Information Science Education Statistics Committee and the Association for Library and Information Science Education (2005, 2010). *Library and information science report*. State College, PA: Association for Library and Information Science Education.

Alloy Education (2010). Welcome to MinorityNurse.com. Retrieved from http://www.minoritynurse.com/

American Library Association (2011a). Discovering librarianship: The future is overdue. Retrieved from http://www.ala.org/ala/aboutala/offices/diversity/imls/index.cfm

American Library Association (2011b). Spectrum scholarship program. Retrieved from http://www.ala.org/ala/aboutala/offices/diversity/spectrum/index.cfm

Black Librarian Nation. http://blacklibrariannation.ning.com/

Cooke, N. A., & Edwards, S. (2010). The Spectrum doctoral fellowship program: The future is overdue. *Journal of Education for Library and Information Science, 51*(3). Retrieved from http://jelis.org/featured/the-spectrum-doctoral-fellowship-program-the-future-is-overdue-by-nicole-a-cooke-and-sheri-edwards/

Hayden, C. D. (1994). New approaches to black recruitment. In E. J. Josey (Ed.), *The black librarian in America revisited* (pp. 55–64). Metuchen, NJ: Scarecrow Press.

Institute of Museum and Library Services (2011). Laura Bush 21st Century Librarian Program. Retrieved from http://www.imls.gov/applicants/grants/21centuryLibrarian.shtm

Knapp, L. G., Kelly-Reid, J. E., Ginder, S. A., & the National Center for Education Statistics (2011). *Enrollment in postsecondary institutions, fall 2009; graduation rates, 2003 and 2006 cohorts; and financial statistics, fiscal year 2009: First look.* Washington, DC: National Center for Education Statistics, Institute of Education Sciences. Available from http://nces.ed.gov/pubs2011/2011230.pdf

Knapp, L. G., Kelly-Reid, J. E., Whitmore, R. W., & the National Center for Education Statistics (2007). *Enrollment in postsecondary institutions, fall 2005; graduation rates, 1999 and 2002 cohorts; and financial statistics, fiscal year 2005: First look.* Washington, DC: National Center for Education Statistics, Institute of Education Sciences. Retrieved from http://purl.access.gpo.gov/GPO/LPS82752

Ryu, M., American Council on Education, & American Council on Education (2010). *Minorities in higher education: Twenty-fourth annual status report: with a special essay on the U.S. Hispanic population.* Washington, DC: American Council on Education.

State Higher Education Executive Officers (U.S.) (2010). *State higher education finance FY*2010. Denver, CO: State Higher Education Executive Officers. Retrieved from http://www.sheeo.org/finance/shef/SHEF_FY10.pdf

39

Exploring the Generational Transfer of Tacit Knowledge in a Two-Generation Librarian Dyad

Valeda Dent Goodman and Johnnie O. Dent

Dr. E. J. Josey's work (1970, 1994) in charting the historical development of black librarianship in America continues to offer numerous insights into the ways in which the major cultural challenges in America—racism, sexism, workplace inequity, to name a few—impact the profession today. The challenges that black librarianship faces for the 21st century are extraordinarily complex and are now being impacted by such phenomenon as the rapid digitization of resources, increasingly user-driven technologies, and the access to large quantities of information without boundaries. Attracting new librarians to the profession has long been a struggle, and library and information science programs continue to explore ways to enhance the diversity of their student bodies and thereby the profession. A number of scholars have examined the reasons why librarianship faces such challenges in terms of diversification. Perhaps one area that has been overlooked in terms of drawing new librarians into the fold is that of generational influence and familial mentorship. It is not uncommon to find strong generational alliances within professions such as accounting, medicine, and law enforcement. Sons and daughters follow in the footsteps of their parents for a variety of reasons, and often, a single profession helps to define the identity of the family through the generations. The brief case study presented in this chapter examines tacit and experiential knowledge transfer between two generations of librarians, a mother and a daughter—one from a public library background and the other from an academic library background—and explores the ways that this transfer of knowledge through the years supported and influenced the career choice of a second-generation librarian. The work of various scholars is used to support and frame the discussion. A broader question is also asked: How can this type of knowledge transfer, which is rich and informal in nature, be generalized so that greater numbers of sons and daughters, nieces and nephews, grandsons and granddaughters of librarians, or those who have close-knit community ties with librarians, might enter the profession?

A BRIEF OVERVIEW OF TACIT KNOWLEDGE

Smith (2001) suggested that tacit knowledge is a key component in the shaping of the workplace. Smith (2001, p. 313) provides this definition of tacit knowledge: "practical, action-oriented knowledge or 'know-how' based on practice, acquired by personal experience, seldom expressed openly, often resembles intuition." Employees utilize both tacit and explicit knowledge, and both types are important in the growth and sustenance of any business. "Knowledge plays a key role in the information revolution. Major challenges are to select the 'right' information from numerous sources and transform it into useful knowledge. Tacit knowledge based on common sense, and explicit knowledge based on academic accomplishment are both underutilized" (Smith, 2001, p. 311). Tacit knowledge is the type of information that is hard to quantify and may not necessarily be transferred to another by some formal means (writing and speaking). Each of us relies on what may be described as "common sense" or "intuition" (Smith, 2001, p. 311) to accomplish goals, to understand tasks that need to be completed in the workplace, and to be productive. "Many companies are using tacit knowledge to augment a person's academic learning and experience" (Smith, 2001, p. 311). In addition, some scholars feel that acquiring and using this type of knowledge is critical to the success of those in managerial positions (Wagner & Sternberg, 1987). "Opportunities to use tacit knowledge are prime factors in attracting and maintaining a talented, loyal, productive workforce" (Smith, 2001, p. 314). On the other hand, explicit knowledge is very formal and easily recognized. Information contained in a book of mathematical formulas is explicit knowledge, as is information in an owner's manual for a new digital camera. Smith (2001, p. 314) described explicit knowledge as "academic knowledge or 'know-what' that is described in formal language, print or electronic media, often based on established work processes, use people-to-documents approach."

In the case of familial transfer of knowledge related to work, much of this may be tacit in nature. It is not uncommon to hear second-generation craftspeople, for instance, say that they "learned the trade" from their father or grandfather, when in reality, little formal instruction or teaching was ever done. The value of this type of knowledge transfer is easily overlooked in an environment where explicit knowledge is seen as the main vehicle for bringing new recruits into a field. As Smith suggested:

> the value of tacit knowledge, like customer good will, is often underrated and underutilized in the workplace. Nearly two-thirds of work-related information that is

> gradually transformed into tacit knowledge comes from face-to-face contacts, like casual conversations, stories, mentoring, internships and apprenticeships. One-of-a-kind, spontaneous, creative conversations often occur when people exchange ideas and practicalities in a free and open environment. (2001, p. 314)

Ambrosini and Bowman (2002) suggested that in order to be useful, tacit knowledge must be operationalized. In this case, tacit knowledge transferred from mother to daughter over the course of a number of years formed the basis for a later career choice. The knowledge was further operationalized as the daughter transitioned into a professional role as a librarian. Tacit knowledge can take many different forms. Eraut (2000, p. 113) articulated three different types of tacit knowledge: "tacit understanding of people and situations, routinized actions and the tacit rules that underpin intuitive decision-making." In this brief case study, the first type—an understanding of people and situations—is perhaps most relevant.

Linde (2001, p. 160) suggested that narrative is also a key element in the transmission and expression of tacit knowledge. Stories and the retelling of events within communities are types of social knowledge, and certainly stories told within families about the workday, the work environment, and so on can transfer information and knowledge in an informal way. Although the focus in the literature tends to be on tacit knowledge and its role in business and management, those are not the only domains where tacit knowledge is relevant. Some of the most important tacit knowledge—whether about childrearing or riding a bicycle—is conveyed within the context of the family.

Bourne and Özbilgin (2008, p. 322) stated that one of the key factors in terms of career choice selection has to do with "promoting exposure to varied experiences and contexts." This case study will approach the role of tacit knowledge with this in mind.

LIBRARIANSHIP AS A FAMILY PRACTICE

Dr. E. J. Josey once wrote, "a library workforce that represents many nationalities, cultures, and languages bring with it special sensitivities that give a powerful edge in our ability to serve our customers. The library and information profession must reflect the communities that our libraries serve" (Josey & Abdullahi, 2002, p. 15). Darden and Turock (2005) suggested that mentorship is key in terms of factors that influence the career choices of librarians of color. Families also play a role in career choice. Whiston and Keller (2004) stated:

> across the lifespan, both family structure variables (e.g., parents' occupations) and family process variables (e.g., warmth, support, attachment, autonomy) were found to influence a host of career constructs; however, the process by which families influence career development is complex and is affected by many contextual factors such as race, gender, and age (p. 493)

Bardick, Bernes, Magnusson, and Witko (2004) also found that parents have a great deal of influence over the career choices of their children.

In what practical ways might tacit information and knowledge—conveyed within the framework of the familial environment—have informed the career choice of a second-generation librarian? A brief case study is presented below.

The first-generation librarian (the mother) in this case study has worked for the Queens Borough Public Library in Queens, New York, for more than 37 years. Her daughter is also a librarian, currently serving as the dean of the University Libraries at Long Island University in New York. The daughter—who never formally aspired to "follow in her mother's footsteps" or declared she was going to be a librarian when she grew up—was nonetheless heavily influenced as a child and young adult by her mother's work. Unconsciously, the daughter integrated the nature of and exposure to her mother's work into her own identity, where it eventually helped to shape her own career choice. Interestingly, the daughter also attended the same library school her mother had attended some 30 years prior. What types of tacit exposure and experiences were exchanged between mother and child that may have influenced a later career choice?

There are several domains where a diverse level of exposure to experiences and activities closely associated with "librarianship" and "the library" existed:

1. Community outreach and activism: The mother was actively involved in several community-based activities during the daughter's early and later childhood. This included parent–teacher associations, community boards, and church-related work. Within the family household, this type of engagement was commonplace. In many ways, these activities were linked to the library—either by way of personal or by professional connections fostered by the mother in her role as "community librarian." The tacit information might have included the importance of community engagement and the importance of caring for the community as a whole.
2. Communication, public speaking, and social skills: These skills were perhaps the most prevalent of the tacitly conveyed knowledge, as the daughter frequently observed her mother in public and interactional settings, connecting with a wide variety of people from diverse backgrounds and speaking publically.
3. Library-specific work: This was mainly through exposure to library settings, other librarians, and library procedures in areas such as collection development and acquisitions. The daughter frequently spent time at the library where her mother worked, and she was allowed to explore and engage in a broad range of activities, including helping to process books, being exposed to new library material as it was added to the collection, and being exposed to programming for the community. The tacit knowledge here included some of the basic elements of the traditional library world, such

as book handling and collection development. Perhaps the most important element was exposure to other librarians, who each had very different roles within the library. The diversity of work and the fact that librarians could actually be engaged in creative, innovative work was a part of the tacit message that was conveyed.

4. Literacy and reading practices in the home: Reading was an important activity in the family household growing up. There was a constant stream of reading materials made available from the library. The tacit information supported the fact that access to reading materials was very important. Managing tasks associated with checking books out and returning them in a timely fashion also conveyed an important sense of responsibility and independence.
5. Personal exposure to local and community writers, poets, and performers: The community libraries where the mother worked had as a unique feature culturally rich programming for library users and community members of all ages. Local and nonlocal talent were featured, and all of the arts were represented. The daughter was exposed to plays, concerts, poetry readings, dance, and many other types of cultural performances. Libraries were not only places to read and find books, but also places to go and be exposed to art, music, and literature. The library was a place to develop an appreciation for culture. Interestingly, it was through this exposure that the daughter eventually developed a love for writing, which supported her later career as a faculty member and library scholar.

CONCLUSION

When all of these elements are combined, the level of exposure and varied experiences as articulated by Bourne and Özbilgin (2008, p. 322) are clear. The role and meaning of the "library" in the case study household, and in particular the tacit information that was conveyed, is highly illustrative of an immersive, engaged experience that was framed by culture, learning, outreach, and activism. The library and the mother's role as librarian were both highly symbolic of these ideas. The daughter saw her mother as not just a librarian, but as someone who was articulate, passionate, dedicated, and people-oriented. The concept that librarians are held in high regard in the community, and do important work outside of the library, was tacitly conveyed. The mother's work also allowed her to connect with and develop relationships with a wide variety of people from all walks of life, and this diversity of interaction tacitly conveyed to the daughter that librarians are also socially engaging and communicative.

This chapter has highlighted a few of the areas where tacit knowledge and information may have played a role in the career choice of a second-generation librarian. Informal transmission of certain types of information through exposure to a wide range of experiences, people, and activities is an undeniably important element in this case. The role of mentorship and similar exchange of tacit knowledge and information is important if the profession of librarianship is to be better aligned with the demographic and population changes currently happening at both the local and national levels.

> Greater diversity has become more than a social and moral issue. Increasing diversity will not only capture unique leadership talents, it will also yield benefits in innovation and creativity that arise as a result of seldom tapped perspectives being brought to problems from different backgrounds and life experiences. (Turock, 2001, p. 116)

Librarians should constantly seek to expose younger generations to the work they do, always being conscious of the fact that their actions leave an impression on those around them. Librarians can take the opportunity to talk about their work in informal ways, on a daily basis, with the students, children, and young family members they come into contact with. There is no stronger influence on a child than a mother, father, grandparent, or older sibling. Librarians in these roles should also take the opportunity to expose younger family members to what they do in informal but engaging ways. The impact of doing so may be surprisingly rewarding to the library and information profession.

REFERENCES

Ambrosini, V., & Bowman, C. (2001). Tacit knowledge: Some suggestions for operationalization. *Journal of Management Studies, 38*, 811–829.

Bardick, A. D., Bernes, K. B., Magnusson, K. C., & Witko, K. D. (2004). Junior high career planning: What students want. *Canadian Journal of Counselling, 38*, 104–117.

Bourne, D., & Özbilgin, M. (2008). Strategies for combating gendered perceptions of careers. *Career Development International, 13*, 320–332.

Darden, B., & Turock, B. (2005). Career patterns of African American women academic library administrators. In J. Nyce, E. Garten, & D. Williams (Eds.), *Advances in library administration and organization* (Vol. 22, pp. 315–360). Bingley, UK: Emerald Group Publishing.

Eraut, M. (2000). Non-formal learning and tacit knowledge in professional work. *British Journal of Educational Psychology, 70*, 113–136.

Josey, E. J. (1994). *The black librarian in America revisited.* Lanham, MD: Scarecrow Press.

Josey, E. J. (1970). *The black librarian in America.* Lanham, MD: Scarecrow Press.

Josey, E. J., & Abdullahi, I. (2002). Why diversity in American libraries. *Library Management*, 23(1/2), 10–16.

Linde, C. (2001). Narrative and social tacit knowledge. *Journal of Knowledge Management, 5*, 160–171.

Smith, E. (2001). The role of tacit and explicit knowledge in the workplace. *Journal of Knowledge Management, 5*, 311–321.

Turock, B. J. (2001). Women and leadership. *Library Administration*, 32(3/4), 115–137.

Wagner, R. K., & Sternberg, R. J. (1987). Tacit knowledge in managerial success. *Journal of Business and Psychology*, 303–312.

Whiston, S., & Keller, B. (2004). The influences of the family of origin on career development. *Counseling Psychologist, 32*(4), 493–568.

40

The World Outside Your Library: My Alternative Career Experience

Carol Nurse

Librarianship was not my first profession; prior to receiving my MLS degree, I worked in a variety of social service settings, including an agency that served pregnant teens and teenage parents. Although this position convinced me that social work could not be a lifelong career for me, I didn't realize that my experience co-presenting workshops and making home visits was the beginning of acquiring marketing and customer service skills needed to sell to an often reluctant clientele.

Although I have worked in public, special, academic, and nonlibrary settings, my first post-MLS position was in the public library. I felt like I had come full circle from the day when my mother took me to my local public library in Harlem, and although too young to actually have a signature, I made my mark to get my first library card. After working in the branches of the Brooklyn Public Library, I was transferred to the Central Library, where I worked in the Education and Job Information Center. For those who know me now, it may be hard to believe that I was somewhat shy and reserved and was very anxious when I was asked to present workshops, by myself, such as "Resume Writing" and "Introduction to the Internet." However, it was like releasing the genie from a bottle; once I started, I loved it! The more workshops I did, my confidence increased exponentially, and eventually I decided to make the move to working as a vendor representative.

In hindsight, my move to library vendor work was pretty brave. During the 1980s, most African American librarians worked in public, academic, or school libraries, with a few in special libraries. African Americans were almost nonexistent in the vendor field. At conferences, I would search the exhibit halls for a face that looked like mine, but there were none. Finally, I would see African

Americans when the exhibits opened and librarians rushed into the hall. This experience increased my respect for pioneers like E. J. Josey, who often stood alone in a sea of white librarians.

The company I worked for was just beginning to use field representatives, so my colleagues and I did it all, customer service, marketing, and training. I served as tech support manning a toll-free helpline, traveled to sites to install hardware and software, and even helped to troubleshoot billing issues. This experience was similar to military basic training in that it prepared me in many areas, and for any possibility.

At one event in Canada, with an audience of 500 librarians, the equipment decided it would die. This didn't faze my co-worker and me at all. We knew from past experiences to always have handy the telephone number of a local computer equipment store. And of course, we ordered more food, and the audience was kept content while the technical issues were resolved. Working as a vendor representative enabled me to see much of the United States and Canada. I traveled to academic, public, medical, and school libraries to train librarians on our products and computer systems. Not surprisingly, I encountered racial prejudice at many U.S. sites; fortunately, I had a supportive supervisor who would back me up when necessary. At one site training in Florida, my supervisor was contacted while I was still presenting and told that my presentation was "not up to their usual standard of what they expected from vendor training." Even my supervisor, who was white and had received glowing reviews from training sites about me, knew the meaning of this coded statement.

On the contrary, Canadian librarians loved me, so I was lucky to be able to traverse the country from coast to coast and met many African Canadian librarians who encouraged me to move to Canada. I thought this experience must be similar to the welcome reception African American writers and artists received when they moved to Paris, when they couldn't "get love" or acceptance in their own country. I made a lot of contacts in Canada, many I still have today.

The disadvantage of working for a library vendor or publishing company is the same as the advantage: the travel. Although it may sound glamorous, constantly living out of a suitcase can become tiring. "Living on the road" involves careful planning, making sure all of my bills at the home base are paid. Additionally, it is difficult to have any kind of social life.

My experiences precede modern telecommuting and the strict airport security measures of today. The reality of post-9/11 travel restrictions probably make it more difficult and costly to catch a last minute flight back home if you finish your business earlier than expected. While I don't regret the experience working as a vendor representative, I am glad that I was younger and more able to run through the airport with a garment bag on my shoulder like a professional football player! After about four years, it was time for me to come home.

My next position as a consultant with a multitype library organization was a good transition from constant travel to occasional travel. In this new job, I made local field visits to medical library members. I trained the librarians how to use a variety of software and databases used in medical librarianship, and in some cases, helped them set up a computer that had been sitting in a box in the closet for months. I had some initial problems with librarians in suburban hospitals, who would cancel even grant-mandated visits. Finally, their resistance was broken through my patience and the provision of good service.

Since many of the libraries I serviced were run by solo librarians, they were happy to see a friendly librarian face! Under constant pressure to prove their worth in an institution filled with health care professionals, medical librarians were anxious to enhance their computer skills, thereby making me very valuable to them.

A more interesting challenge of the multitype library organization was the absence of African American librarians, yet the support staff was overwhelmingly African American. In addition, there was a very strict distinction between librarians and support staff that was never to be crossed. I dared to have conversations with support staff and was promptly told by management that "I socialized too much with support staff." I found it ironic that management was fairly clueless about culturally based communication styles. They just couldn't figure out why "those people" needed to be so loud!

In spite of management's issues with me and my natural inclination to communicate with others like me, they couldn't deny that the member libraries really liked me. Routinely, libraries praised my performance with positive comments through letters and phone calls. As in most positions, particularly in nontraditional library positions, if management will not make a place for you, then you must make a place for yourself. I enjoyed my interactions with member libraries and continued to mentor African American librarians I met through professional associations. At the same time I encouraged the support staff at my workplace to continue their education and not to get stuck "on the plantation."

Eventually, I made my way back to a traditional library setting, this time academic, but I wouldn't trade my nonlibrary experiences for anything. It has been 20 years since my first foray into alternative careers, but I question whether the library field has seen the "aggressive affirmative action" that Vivian Davidson Hewitt called for in her essay in this book's predecessor, *The Black Librarian in America Revisited* (1994). In Dr. Josey's introduction to that book, he welcomed the 1990s as a positive period and the inauguration of Bill Clinton as a "ray of hope."

We are now in the 21st century, with an African American president, and indeed the number of African American librarians has increased tremendously. This is due to scholarships awarded by the American Library Association's Spectrum program, the Association of Research Libraries (ARL) career training and mentoring initiatives, and other successful minority recruiting efforts within librarianship. As a library school student, I benefited from Title IIB funds, but can an influx of money solve the continuing problems of institutional and societal racism?

Will African American librarians become more prevalent in careers that are "outside the library box"? Perhaps the most significant barrier is not racism anymore, as the current economic crisis has led to some very tough decision making. With funding to nonprofits drying up and businesses that serve libraries merging to stay afloat, will they need, or be able to continue, the practice of "tokenism"? Using the unscientific technique of observation, I still see very few African Americans vendor representatives in the exhibit halls. It is my hope that the next edition of this book will highlight a positive change within librarianship and related businesses to reflect the true nature of our multicultural world.

REFERENCES

Josey, E. J. (1994). *The black librarian in America revisited.* Metuchen, NJ: Scarecrow Press.

McKee, A. E., Geer, B., Markwith, M., Oberg, S., Schatz, B., Stamison, C., & Langendorfer, J. M. (2008, May). Hitting the trifecta: Alternative career paths for those with an MLS. *Serials Librarian, 54* (1–2), 179–192.

Tenopir, C. (2005). Working for a vendor. *Library Journal, 130* (12), 29.

41

The 21st-Century Black Librarian: Renewing Our Commitment to Liberation and Cultural Activism

Taneya D. Gethers

In 1970, fueled by the momentum and self-determination of the Civil Rights and black power movements, black librarians from different parts of the nation mobilized to form the Black Caucus of the American Library Association (BCALA). Their first public act of solidarity was confronting the governing body of the American Library Association with a record that addressed systematic racism embedded within the profession and greater social landscape:

> On Wednesday night, January 21, 1970, 98 percent of the black librarians in attendance at the Midwinter Meeting of the American Library Association convened in a black caucus for the expressed purpose of addressing themselves to many of the pressing problems and issues facing this country, in general, and the American Library Association, in particular. Black librarians are especially concerned about the effects of institutional racism, poverty, the continued lack of educational, employment and promotional opportunities for blacks and other minorities. Although these socio-economic ills have been condemned by the Kerner Commission, the Commission on Violence, and many other studies, the library profession has been slow in responding to these problems.
>
> As black librarians we are intensely interested in the development of our professional association and our profession; therefore, a committee of the Black Librarian's Caucus has been charged with the responsibility of preparing a program of action. The Black Caucus will continue to meet at American Library Association conferences for the purpose of evaluating progress being made by the Association in fulfilling its social and professional responsibilities to minority groups in this profession and the nation. (Josey, 2000, pp. 86–87)

Under the title "Black Librarians: A Statement of Concern," this statement openly identified the injustices perpetrated against black librarians and African

American communities. Intertwined with the denouncement of societal and professional racism by the largest professional organization of libraries and librarians was a charge to black library professionals to unite as a vigilant, activist collective.

Recounting BCALA's early history, founder and first president Dr. E. J. Josey asserted:

> if black people were to have an impact on their professions and their professional development, it was necessary for them to band together, in a black caucus or all-black organization, in order to ensure their contributions to the liberation of black people . . . and the liberation of themselves as professionals. (2000, p. 83)

The professional duty of black librarians is not separate from our cultural responsibility as people of African descent. An essential part of our mission is to help empower black people throughout the African Diaspora, and this undertaking is critical to our mission today.

"A LUTA CONTINUA" (THE STRUGGLE CONTINUES)—MOZAMBIQUE

> Race and racism are not figments of demented imaginations, but are central to the economics, politics and culture of this nation.
>
> —Robert Blauner[1]

In an examination of the core factors that impact social mobility and quality of life, the lived reality for black Americans from BCALA's founding to the present is dismally the same. For most of the 1970s, the African American unemployment rate more than doubled that of white Americans (Pinkney, 1984), and this trend continues. In May 2011, black unemployment rates had reached 16.2%—more than twice the 8% white unemployment rate (U.S. Department of Labor, 2011). Similarly, there was a gap in educational attainment, with 4.4% of black Americans holding a college degree or higher in 1970 compared to 11.3% of whites (U.S. Census Bureau, 2011a). Today, the gap is even greater, with 19.3% of African Americans earning a college degree compared to 29.9% of whites (U.S. Census Bureau, 2011a).

Disparities also persist between the life expectancy rates for white and black Americans. In 1970, the life expectancy for whites was 71.7 compared to 64.1 for blacks (U.S. Census Bureau, 2011b). Four decades later, the life expectancy rate for white Americans, 78.9 years, is still higher than the life expectancy for blacks, 73.8 years (U.S. Census Bureau, 2011b). These multiple disparities demonstrate that race and racism continue to be pervasive factors in American life.

Following the 1964 Civil Rights Act, conservative theorists argued race was no longer a major factor impeding social mobility (Pinkney, 1984). In 2008, this idea reemerged as talk of a "post-racial society" entered mainstream discourse following the election of 44th U.S. President Barack Obama, the first African American to hold this post. Yet, U.S. statistical data illustrate that the collective black experience in the United States is still one of struggle. The struggle is deceptively masked by individual African American achievement, or as sociologist Alphonso Pinkney (1984) characterized, "the myth of black progress." More than ever, 21st-century black librarians are needed to mobilize against social injustice like their 20th-century counterparts.

"THE BEGINNING OF WISDOM IS KNOWLEDGE OF SELF"—KEMET

The role of the black librarian as cultural activist is part of our tradition, predating the founding of BCALA. Our activist roots stretch back to Timbuktu, Mali, West Africa, where during the Moroccan invasion in 1591 and French colonization in the 1880s, librarians, or "culture keepers" (Huffman, 2006), buried sacred manuscripts in the sand to protect the history and culture of the region. Our activism is rooted in ancient Egypt (Kemet), birthplace of the book, the written word, and librarianship. In Egypt, librarians were not only regarded as keepers of culture, but as librarian-priests responsible for the spiritual well-being of the people. "Custodians of the Unlimited Knowledge," "Scribe of the House of Sacred Writings," "Scribes of the Hieroglyphics," and "Keeper of the Scrolls" are just a few of the names bestowed upon the librarians of ancient Kemet (Zulu, 1993). The black librarian is also an "African teacher," who has a calling, a "constant journey towards mastery, a scientific activity, a matter of community membership, an aspect of a learning community, a process of 'becoming a library,' a matter of care and custody for our culture and traditions" (Hilliard, n.d.).

LIBERATION THROUGH CULTURALLY RELEVANT LIBRARY SERVICE

Knowledge of our rich past clarifies our role in the present and our collective work and responsibility in safeguarding the future. In addition to being a cultural activist and bridge to information, the advancement of liberation necessitates gaining full social and economic opportunities, not simply for individuals, but for entire communities. For the disenfranchised, historically and disproportionately people of African descent, the library is a vital tool in the quest for self-determination. Public libraries, in particular, with their free and open access to life-changing resources, are essential to developing a progressive society. Public libraries support social and economic parity and foster a "critical consciousness" (Hilliard, n.d.) that arms one to take positive action in the world.

As the custodians of these institutions, black librarians are responsible for creating meaningful library experiences that incorporate our history and cultural knowledge to intellectually, socially, emotionally, and politically empower our communities. Every facet of the library, from collection development to book merchandising, programming, and recommendation of resources during reference help, should reflect a culturally responsive paradigm. Community members should see themselves and feel a cultural pride when they walk in and out of library doors.

The advancement of liberation is also invested in recommitment to one of the fundamentals of our work: literacy. Literacy, under a culturally responsive model, is the "ability to think critically as well as creatively about the reality of the world through one's culture, history and language" (Peavy, 1993, p. 213). Building on this foundation, "information literacy"—identifying, comprehension, analysis, application—provides our communities with the necessary skill set to make learning transformative and liberating.

"THE FIERCE URGENCY OF NOW"

> This is no time to engage in the luxury of cooling off or to take the tranquilizing drug of gradualism.
>
> —Dr. Martin Luther King, Jr.[2]

Presently, we are living in an increasingly challenging time, in which political, economic, and educational disparities are ever widening, and institutional racism, while still pervasive, is viewed as a social ill of the past. While corporations are profiting from federal financial aid and never-before-seen amounts of money are being invested into mass incarceration and the military industrial complex, the number of U.S. citizens living in poverty is swelling, reaching 43.6 million in 2009 (U.S. Census Bureau, 2010)—the largest count on record.[3] African Americans comprise the largest segment of this population and the second highest year-over-year percentage increase of any racial group. We are rapidly multiplying as members of the excluded underclass, and tremendous resistance is needed to launch a new course.

Now, at this very moment, we as librarians of African descent must rise and renew our commitment to cultural activism and liberation. We cannot wait for permission or for worsening library budgets to get better. We cannot perform at the status quo, or worse, sit and do nothing at all. In the spirit of the trailblazers who in 1970 launched a courageous campaign for social and professional freedom, we must rededicate our work to unlocking the chains that hold our communities in bondage.

NOTES

1. As cited in *The Myth of Black Progress* (Pinkney, 1984, p. 59).
2. Section header and quotation from M. L. King, Jr. (1963). "I Have a Dream" speech.
3. Between 2008 and 2009, the poverty rate increased for whites from 8.6% to 9.4%; blacks 24.7% to 25.8%; and Hispanics 23.2% to 25.3%. The 2008 and 2009 poverty rates for Asians, 12.5%, remained statistically the same (U.S. Census Bureau, 2010).

REFERENCES

Josey, E. J. (2000). Black Caucus of the American Library Association: The early years. In E. J. Josey& M. DeLoach (Eds.), *Handbook of black librarianship* (2nd ed., pp. 83–98). Lanham, MD: Scarecrow Press.

Hilliard, A. G. (n.d.). To be an African teacher. Retrieved from http://nuatc.org/consultant/retreat/retreat2006/hilliard/to_be_an_african_teacher.pdf

Huffman, A. (2006, Winter). Unburied treasure. *American Legacy,* 12–17.

Peavy, L. (1993). Promoting liberation literacy: A grassroots solution. In S. Biddle & Members of BCALA NCAAL Conference Proceedings Committee (Eds.), *Culture keepers: Enlightening and empowering our communities. Proceedings of the First National Conference of African American Librarians* (pp. 212–215). Westwood, MA: Faxon Company.

Pinkney, A. (1984). *The myth of black progress.* New York: Cambridge University Press.

U.S. Census Bureau. (2010). *Income, poverty and health insurance in the United States: 2009—Highlights.* Retrieved from http://www.census.gov/hhes/www/poverty/data/incpovhlth/2009/highlights.html

U.S. Census Bureau. (2011a). Table 225. Educational attainment by race and Hispanic origin: 1970 to 2009. *U.S. Census Bureau, statistical abstract of the United States: 2011.* Retrieved from http://www.census.gov/compendia/statab/2011/tables/11s0225.pdf

U.S. Census Bureau. (2011b). Table 102. Expectation of life at birth, 1970 to 2007, and projections 2010 to 2020. *U.S. Census Bureau, statistical abstract of the United States: 2011.* Retrieved from http://www.census.gov/compendia/statab/2011/tables/11s0103.pdf

U.S. Department of Labor, Bureau of Labor Statistics. (2011). *The employment situation—May 2011.* Retrieved from http://www.bls.gov/news.release/pdf/empsit.pdf

Zulu, I. M. (1993). The ancient Kemetic roots of library and information science. In S. Biddle & Members of BCALA NCAAL Conference Proceedings Committee (Eds.), *Culture keepers: Enlightening and empowering our communities. Proceedings of the First National Conference of African American Librarians* (pp. 246–266). Westwood, MA: Faxon Company.

42

Dismiss the Stereotype! Combating Racism and Continuing Our Progress

Margaret J. Gibson

W. E. B. Dubois stated in *The Souls of Black Folk*, "The problem of the twentieth century is the problem of the color-line" (Dubois, 1989, p. 13). It is 11 years into the 21st century and there is still evidence of discrimination against some librarians because of their race. As a public librarian examining librarianship, a percentage of white counterparts have yet to accept a black librarian. Contrary to the stereotypes that librarians are "old white ladies with their hair pulled back in a bun asking people to shush," to date, we can be seen behind reference desks in public libraries. To maintain a visible presence, it is our responsibility to support one another and prepare the younger generation in an increasingly global society. This chapter evaluates personal experiences and observations related to racism and stereotypes because of skin color. Additionally, it will explain why it is necessary to prepare and educate young African Americans and continue our progress in librarianship.

RACISM AND STEREOTYPES

Transitioning to a librarian position after being a clerk for over nine years, I finally became conscious of racism in the world of librarianship. Observing the disparities that exist between white and nonwhite librarians, I considered it an ethnic disconnect that needs mending. In *Effects of Diversity on Black Librarianship: Is Diversity Divergent?*, Teresa Y. Neely stated: "The November 1, 1997 *Library Journal* cover story on racism in the profession reveals evidence that racism is still alive and thriving in the library profession, and not just an artifact left over from the past" (2000, p. 134). While evaluating librarianship with a small group of black librarians, it was unanimous that racism still exists among library professionals. Participants included general librarians and branch and senior managers.

The questions were not restricted to racism and stereotype, but included preparing young African Americans for the field of librarianship. Their years of experience range from four years to over 20 years. Everyone clearly described personal experiences of racism or observations of discrimination being directed at others.

Some of the librarians revealed that some minority employees are required to provide coverage in certain community libraries that are considered undesirable, while white employees are never sent to those locations. Black librarians questioned the reasoning that white counterparts immediately assume black librarians are clerks when they arrive at another agency to provide coverage. It is important to know our position in the profession and avoid relying on others to define us. There were sentiments that on average when black employees are rightfully promoted there is always a need to question the person's abilities and qualifications. Disappointment was clearly directed toward predominately minority communities, because they were found to be equally guilty as whites. They have the same preconception that only a white employee can be the manager, disregarding the black librarian. I believe a segment of the black community continues to be deceived, based on negative connotations deriving from history.

Maurice B. Wheeler is of the opinion that "Neither personal nor organizational change can take place without the commitment of effort" (2000, p. 171). We need to be united in our efforts to work on eradicating racism from within the profession. One suggestion that I know is not unique is to work on increasing the number of black librarians. Narrowing the gap between whites and nonwhites will most likely alleviate some of the issues. In March 2011, during an annual librarians' reception in New York City, vice president of the New York Black Librarians' Caucus recalled what he believes to be a form of racism.

> Today I attended a reception for librarians and I was the sole black man in a room with 65 other librarians. I reached out to shake another male librarian's hand during a meet and greet, and he offered me his empty cup and a used napkin. I asked "What is this?" He responded, "Oh, I thought you worked here." Later when I was introduced as the vice president of the New York Black Librarians' Caucus, he looked stunned. I later addressed the gathering of librarians and explained why there is a need for a greater presence of African American librarians, especially males. I am certain this type of racism is not an isolated incident. I am new to the professional side of librarianship but not to racism. This is just another hurdle we as people have to counter in our quest for equality in work and social settings. (personal communication, Richard Ashby, April 2, 2011)

Neely noted, "over the years, and currently as we approach the beginning of a new century, the primary concerns of black librarians have remained constant" (2000, p. 131). It is the 21st century, and we as a nation need to have minds of progression instead of digression. As professionals, it is pertinent to think beyond skin color and refrain from judging others because of ethnicity.

PREPARING THE NEXT GENERATION OF LIBRARIANS

Thirteen years ago Queens Library started a program called Page Fellows. The program accepted part timers who were employed for six months or more with Queens Library. Each person was paired with a librarian and met two hours weekly for 15 weeks. I am fortunate to have worked with a few of the program's graduates after they completed their MLS degrees. The librarians possess a high level of competence and knowledge. Without statistics to accurately evaluate the overall success of the program, my assessment is based on observation. A mentorship program similar to the Page Fellows can be embraced to prepare our youth for a career in librarianship.

Youth service librarians can utilize community outreach to educate youth about the benefits and personal satisfaction of being a librarian. It is surprising every time I have the opportunity to speak at a Career Day or college fairs, both youth and adults, especially blacks, display a limited knowledge of library information science. Too many are misinformed that librarians are found only in public libraries and schools. After hearing I am a librarian, some students appear surprised to learn it is a chosen career path for many blacks. I strongly believe it is our responsibility to clearly communicate the requirements and specialized areas of librarianship. Library organizations that have an interest in the progress of African American librarians can unite and establish an ongoing career development program for prospective minority librarians. It is necessary to facilitate some type of support group that can effectively prepare the next generation of black librarians.

According to the American Library Association's (ALA) Office for Research and Statistics (2006), African Americans represent 4% of librarians in public libraries, placing them second in line to white librarians, who are a disproportionate 89%. Clearly, whites dominate the field of librarianship. The report divulged that African Americans are exiting the profession for promotional opportunities and management positions. Additionally there are concerns because the average librarian leaving the profession is under 40 years of age, with a 4.4% decline of African American librarians. In "Averting a Crisis," Wheeler stated that "Librarians career development requires a strong and nurturing support system" (2000, p. 181). With limited staff and finances, library schools and institutions must consider a model that will adequately motivate the younger generation of minorities to pursue a career in librarianship. I suggest library management to network with high schools and organize an internship program for nonwhite high school seniors. Give students the opportunity to gain hands-on experience, with the hope of having an influence in their decision to become a librarian. We must take action before our faces vanish from among the library profession.

CONTINUING OUR PROGRESS

In "Averting a Crisis," Wheeler stated that "Black librarians and the caucus must take the first step and invest in ourselves" (2000, p. 176). In order to continue our progress, it will take action. Conduct a self-evaluation to determine long- and short-term goals that are intended for success in the profession. Consider standards to follow and remain focused while being receptive to constructive criticism. It is necessary to acquire an experienced mentor who is not egocentric and is willing to assess any progress. As Wheeler indicated, "An equally important part of the success equation is the support and guidance of a mentor" (2000, p. 180). I am a product of being mentored, and I agree with Wheeler. Being mentored is a vital part of growth and success. In addition to a professor's suggestion, Andrew Jackson from Queens Library encouraged me to attend library school. He continues to encourage and support my development as a librarian. Take the initiative and become active in library organizations; there you will find potential mentors and librarians with a wealth of knowledge and experience. I am thankful to Linda Bannerman-Martin from Queens Library for introducing me to the New York Black Librarians' Caucus (NYBLC). I was one of the 2005 scholarship recipients and the current president of that caucus. The NYBLC is where I met another mentor, Professor Madeline Forde. Since then she has been unwavering with her support throughout my professional development.

Dismiss racism and stereotypes and rise beyond expectations; there should be simply no distractions from our progress. As a result of innovation and constant change in library trends, we must take advantage of continuing educational programs. Being current with best practices supports opportunities to grow and also allows us to become competitive among other librarians.

> Knowledge is freedom and ignorance is slavery, and I just couldn't . . . be that close to freedom and not take advantage of it.
>
> —Miles Davis, jazz musician

REFERENCES

American Library Association. Diversity Counts. (2006). Retrieved http://www.ala.org/ala/aboutala/offices/diversity/diversitycounts/diversitycounts_rev0.pdf

Dubois, W. E. B. (1989). *The souls of black folk.* New York: Penguin.

Neely, T. Y. (2000). Effects of diversity on black librarianship: Is diversity divergent? In M. L. DeLoach & E. J. Josey (Eds.), *Handbook of black librarianship* (2nd ed., pp. 131–134). Lanham, MD: Scarecrow Press.

Wheeler, B. M. (2000). Averting a crisis: Developing African American librarians as leaders. In M. L. DeLoach & E. J. Josey (Eds.), *Handbook of black librarianship* (2nd ed., pp. 171, 176–177, 180). Lanham, MD: Scarecrow Press.

43

❖ ❖

Walking in the Footsteps of Giants: My Journey in the Chicago Public Library

Emily R. Guss

The Chicago Public Library (CPL), where I spent the bulk of my career, helped shape me professionally. It was there that I benefited from the nurturing and guidance of African American librarians, who gave me a strong work ethic, involved me in professional activities early on, and encouraged me to attend local and national conferences.

When I attended my first Black Caucus of the American Library Association (BCALA) meeting in 1977, the caucus was embroiled in a heated debate over *The Speaker*, a movie commissioned by ALA to celebrate its centennial. Though the intent of the film was to highlight the First Amendment, the subject was presented with a speaker who talked about genetic and racial inferiority being invited to a high school. It was in this arena that I witnessed activism, up close and personal, among African American librarians. African American librarians continue to fight for our communities, to increase our ranks in the profession, and to hold leadership roles in professional organizations and libraries. Despite some progress, the struggle continues. The hope is that a new generation of African American librarians will pick up the mantel.

Following various stints as a library helper in grammar and high school, I worked in the library while attending Rosary College (now Dominican University). It was there one librarian in particular stood out. She was perky, friendly, walked to the shelves with patrons, and made you feel at ease with your questions. When she gave me assignments, usually a card catalog drawer and catalog cards to put in order and file, I finished them quickly. She would compliment my work and then tell me I should think about going to library school. I'd smile politely, but I had a totally different career path in mind.

Kathleen Heim, now Kathleen de la Pena McCook, distinguished university professor at the School of Library and Information Sciences, University of South Florida, was that "perky" librarian whose message to go to library school slowly crept into my psyche.

After graduating from Rosary in May 1975, armed with a degree in psychology, I'd planned to pursue an advance degree in the field. As chance would have it, I landed a job at the CPL George Cleveland Hall Library after my summer job ended. Hall was the branch I had attended as a child and where I received my first library card. This would be the place that would be the turning point in my decision to pursue librarianship as a career.

The George Cleveland Hall Library, which opened in 1932, had a rich history as the first CPL branch built to serve a bustling African American community. Vivian Harsh's appointment as branch manager at Hall made her the first African American in CPL to hold that title.

Charlemae Hill Rollins was assigned to Hall as the children's library the same day and remained there for 31 years. Both women made significant contributions to the community and the profession.

At Hall I was assigned to the children's department. This proved to be a great time of learning for me. The branch manager, Eileen Lawrence, was full of stories about difficult days for blacks working at the library. She told of how her work schedule would be changed in the middle of the semester while attending college, or being assigned to work in the stacks on days she was scheduled for class. She shared many stories about working on Chicago's West side, a community just now recovering from the riots following Dr. Martin Luther King Jr.'s death in 1968. She also told me it took her three days to reach her Southside home from her branch on the West side during Chicago's crippling 1967 snow storm. I found these stories fascinating as well as a lesson in perseverance.

I was also fortunate to have three children's librarians—Annie Lee Carroll, Dorothy Evans, and Shirley Gaines—take me under their wings. These women took me to local conferences and meetings and provided a solid standard of service and participation in local professional organizations.

A co-worker took me to a meeting of the Chicago chapter of the Black Caucus of Librarians. Avery Williams, librarian at Roosevelt University, was president at the time. I was surprised to know there was such a group and at the level of activism exerted to tackle some of the problems black librarians faced in the workplace and the profession.

After this close-up and personal view of libraries and librarians in action, I set my sights on going to library school. The ALA midwinter meeting was in Chicago, and while attending a reception for BCALA at Woodson Library I met a librarian who encouraged me to apply to Michigan. By the fall of 1976, I was on my way.

My leaving for library school after working only a year was bittersweet for Mrs. Lawrence. She lamented about getting the young people trained only to have them go off and do their own thing. The staff at Hall gave me a nice party and a beautiful blanket as a gift, which Mrs. Lawrence fondly referred to as my "security blanket." And indeed it was.

My areas of concentration at Michigan were medical and public librarianship. It was in the medical library track that I had the opportunity to be taught by Dr. Gwendolyn Cruzat. I was gratified and proud to see an African American at the helm of the medical library program. Her presence alone provided additional motivation to make it successfully through the coursework and to get certification.

After graduation I returned to CPL and became the children's librarian at Sherman Park branch and later the branch manager. The branch served a community that was 99% African American. The library was assigned to 18 elementary and four high schools, and the staff worked hard to visit all 22 schools once a year. Having had wonderful role models during my previous entrance into the library, I was prepared to give the best service possible to my community.

One of the highlights of my return to the CPL was to witness Amanda Rudd's appointment to commissioner in 1982. She is to date the only African American to hold the title of commissioner at CPL. Her tenure as commissioner came at a time when economic and social ills, such as high unemployment, gangs, and poor quality schools, were on the increase. Libraries in African American communities were greatly impacted by these problems and as a result library usage began to decrease.

Faced with the growing sentiment among the board of directors that funding should be reduced in branches with low circulation, Rudd set out to demonstrate that with an adequate materials budget and staff, branches in African American communities could have high circulations. Her test case was the Whitney Young Branch, which served a middle-class African American community. Whitney Young Branch was a huge success as the circulation began to match or exceed that of branches serving comparable white communities.

The impact of this bold move helped stem the tide of budget reductions in African American communities and brought attention to outside factors that contributed to library usage. She understood the value of libraries and fought to make sure none of the libraries and their communities were disenfranchised. She was a risk taker and willing to try new initiatives.

Rudd also provided encouragement and opportunities for advancement for African American librarians within the CPL and in the profession.

I was appointed to director of the Carter G. Woodson Regional Library in November 1991. The Woodson Library was held in high esteem by the community and staff. Woodson was a large and busy 61,000-square-foot building with a collection that ranged from preschool to community college in scope. It was also the new home of the Vivian G. Harsh Research Collection of Afro-American History and Literature, which was moved from the Hall Branch Library when Woodson opened. I was preceded in the job by two African American librarians I held in high esteem: Dr. Alice Scott and Mrs. Hattie Power. I knew the energy and zeal each had put into making Woodson regional a premier addition to the CPL as well as their challenges, and sought to maintain that standard.

I retired from the CPL on February 29, 2004. I've had time to look back at the lessons learned in those 27 years and have fond memories of the African American librarians who took me under their wings as a children's librarian, as well as those who were unknowingly role models for my career. I especially enjoyed being able to attend Mrs. Lawrence retirement party to thank her and to be one of her "success" stories.

My retirement was short lived. In August 2004, I embarked on a new adventure as assistant professor and head of the Access and Technical Service Department at the University of Illinois–Chicago's Library of the Health Sciences. In many ways the transition from a public to an academic library was like starting over as a new librarian, but soon many of the "transferable skills" began to materialize. This time around, I'm the "seasoned" librarian, but it has been an exciting exchange of ideals, skills, and interaction with a new generation of librarians. These librarians, who have helped me learn and keep pace with the new technology, enabled me to give that sage advice on how to navigate through their professional careers.

I look forward to continued exchanges with the new generation of librarians and hope the profession will be as good to them as it has been to me.

44

In Retrospect and Beyond: Issues Facing Black Librarians

Binnie Tate Wilkin

Dr. E. J. Josey was a learned man who experienced racism at its worst but determined to give back his best. Accolades have rightfully been bestowed on this leader, professional advocate, civil rights activist, mentor of students and professionals, and more. His enduring, lifelong battle for cultural equity was most admirable. While promoting the advancement of African American librarians, he challenged his profession to advance toward its potential. Josey's collections of writings by African American librarians informed the library world and others. The writings of a few librarians illuminated the work of many. Josey's contributions to the American Library Association will be lasting and his personal grace and concern for humanity will long be remembered.

THE PAST REVISITED

In the introduction to *The Black Librarian in America Revisited* published in 1994, E. J. Josey previewed essays by the various contributors and acknowledged that 20 years after his earlier publication in 1970, racism was still alive and well in this country, but, "African American librarians are committed to the complete eradication of racism in our time" (Josey, 1994a, p. 15). Essays in Josey's *The Black Librarian in America* (1970), produced just after many of the nation's civil rights revolts and during continuing sporadic uprisings, strongly referenced issues of race. Writers spoke frankly about indignities with the hope that major changes would come, improving the information and educational gaps facing minority communities and the poor. The following selected comments are from that edition of *The Black Librarian in America*:

> Most of the books which included black characters represented them as shiftless, happy, grinning, dialect-speaking menials. (Baker, p. 118)
>
> There will never really be a free library as long as many who work there are not themselves truly free. (Tate, p. 129)
>
> Traditionally, the black librarian has encountered problems much like those of black people in other fields, problems essentially imposed by America's rigid social structures. (Alford, p. 130)
>
> The obsolete designs some institutions have used to discourage minorities from seeking professional library training should be discredited and discontinued. (Moses, pp. 140–141)
>
> Participation by blacks in the progress of the American Library Association was minimal before the 1940s. Even under the humiliating conditions of segregated accommodations, a few made it a practice to attend as regularly as possible. (Marshall, p. 178)
>
> One white patron, anti-black to the point of psychosis, was compelled by his own bias to wait until my lunch hours or coffee breaks for fulfillment of his library needs. (Mapp, p. 185)
>
> At meetings with southern whites it is common for me and other black people to be totally ignored. (Smith, p. 200)
>
> Black schools were without adequate books, libraries or trained library personnel for reading guidance and instruction in library usage. (Allen Shockley, p. 229)
>
> My earliest recollection of racial terror was when I was four years old. The Ku Klux Klan marched right by our house and burned a cross on the hill at the end of our street. (Davidson Hewitt, p. 255)
>
> And a dear school librarian, with tears in her eyes and a tremor in her voice, expressed willingness to have black librarians attend the convention, provided they used the freight elevator and refrained from attending the dinner meeting. (Robinson, p. 282)
>
> The dominant white society has been so obsessed with its own survival that it is completely oblivious to the presence, needs and hopes of any other group. (Cunningham, p. 286)
>
> Over the years, my affiliation with ALA has given me an opportunity to show the profession that, given a chance, the black librarian can be an asset to the organization, and at the same time, can make a contribution to the profession. (Josey, p. 317)

Many writers for the first edition actively worked in community and higher education programs, commonly called "outreach" and "experimental education." Questions of discrimination were openly discussed. Too often, such programs were token and temporary, considered corrective for the moment and soon dismantled or dismissed.

As the past informed the future, racial issues became the backdrop, again, for many essays in *The Black Librarian Revisited.* Major Owens, in his article titled "The Specter of Racism in an Age of Cultural Diversity" wrote eloquently:

> We cannot escape a legacy of racism which has to be confronted. We are so steeped in that racism until very reasonable and scholarly people find themselves defining "truths" which have very little supporting evidence or facts. On the other hand, we have certain groups inventing new "truths" that have no evidence to support them either. (Owens, 1994, p. 288)

He further suggests that "we [librarians] are the keepers and managers of information and knowledge. We should look to our particular role and see how it can be done better" (p. 291). Owens finally insists that "Librarians must be highly visible drum majors for intergroup tolerance, understanding and appreciation" (p. 297).

FORWARD TO THE FUTURE

Overarching concerns about racism continue as we consider questions about the future of the library profession, support for libraries, and support for education as we know it. James F. Williams II (1994) in his essay on research librarianship wrote about technology's helpfulness to researchers and scholars. However, he did not foresee the demise of library professions and he emphasized the need for research specialists in the near future.

Rapidly, the public has become enthralled with the technological prowess of the Internet and other swiftly developing communication devices. Will new gadgets be exciting and useful tools of the future, or will vendors of these wares control all thought? While supporting and utilizing new developments, it seems imperative that professionals and leaders focus simultaneously on the "human good." Librarians in particular can present questions to those in power, such as: Can developing systems of democracy, around the world, secure lasting social and political strategies based on unconfirmed, unsubstantiated bits and bytes of information? The political world is becoming one of global information sharing and cooperation. Will it not be necessary to utilize institutions such as libraries to broaden social, political, and religious thought and lessen destructive conflicts?

In spite of technological advances, many populations remain severely undereducated. There is speculation that computers will eventually command many educational functions. Will libraries figure in this picture? Children must still learn to communicate and to read in order to advance and prepare for leadership in future political systems. Probably, in the immediate future, public and school libraries will figure prominently in any new developments. Black librarians will need to continue advocacy for children of color. However, competition for funding will demand creativity. While focusing concern on those with the most deficits (children of color and the poor), broader perspectives will be required for success. Perhaps equity will arrive in a future where every individual child can access education through small affordable or free handheld devices devised for that purpose.

Although there is no way to view or predict future developments, human progress has always been built on the knowledge of the past while circumstance and invention drive the present. Those contributing to this volume and past editions of *The Black Librarian in America* are trailblazers, doing exactly what is necessary for advancement. Facts and opinions shared will inform future conversations and decision making. To affect change, all black librarians must examine their own strengths and carefully choose appropriate roles in professional organizations, on the job, in the community, and in social and personal relationships.

Expanded global information sharing will produce information overload, forcing black librarians and others to think within the backdrop of encompassing international realities. Minority concerns may be lost in the fray. Separate entities such as the Black Caucus of the American Library Association (BCALA) may be *more* needed, locally and nationally, to isolate those areas of major concern to one cultural group. But, it also become imperative for stronger liaisons to be established with other ethnic and power groups. Perhaps such functions as the Joint Conference of Librarians of Color need more emphasis, with national meetings providing vehicles for communication and production of an agenda for action.

Every possible opportunity to educate communities about the role of libraries must be seized. The necessity for *expert* deciphering, collection, and preservation of complex amounts of information to be freely and equitably dispensed must be understood, and helping communities to comprehend and support these roles may require reviewing effective, past methods of outreach. Applying technological tools to those basic methodologies could create new strategies and services.

When considering the future of black librarians in academia, library education, and special libraries, BCALA has provided many years of political and social support. It becomes expedient to reach out to other organizations concerned with similar matters, especially those entities representing educators. Stronger alliances seem imperative in the near and distant future.

America has moved beyond the era when black librarians were subject to public humiliation supported by law. Statistics, however, show substantial deficits in the overall progress of blacks. Change was noted with the election of an African American president, but subtle and hidden prejudices are still rampant, and recent increases in hate groups are problematic. The future in a world of global communication promises much more complex interaction between people of color to effect positive change. In the final essay of *The Black Librarian Revisited*, E. J. Josey stated, "It appears that democratic, pragmatic and cultural concerns will outweigh exclusively ideological issues" (1994b, p. 360). Matters of survival such as global warming and the depletion of resources will require international attention and cooperation and therefore can become unifying forces for all peoples of the world to become effectively *human.*

REFERENCES

Alford, T. (1970). Dream into reality—In the seventies? In E. J. Josey (Ed.), *The Black Librarian in America.* Metuchen, NJ: Scarecrow Press.

Allen Shockley, A. (1970). A soul cry for reading. In E. J. Josey (Ed.), *The Black Librarian in America.* Metuchen, NJ: Scarecrow Press.

Baker, A. (1970). My years as a children's librarian. In E. J. Josey (Ed.), *The Black Librarian in America.* Metuchen, NJ: Scarecrow Press.

Cunningham, W. D. (1970). Rock Chalk, Jayhawk: Oh, Excuse me, Rock Chalk Blackhawk. In E. J. Josey (Ed.), *The Black Librarian in America.* Metuchen, NJ: Scarecrow Press.

Davidson Hewitt, V. (1970). A special librarian by design. In E. J. Josey (Ed.), *The Black Librarian in America.* Metuchen, NJ: Scarecrow Press.

Josey, E. J. (1970). A dreamer—With a tiny spark. In E. J. Josey (Ed.), *The Black Librarian in America.* Metuchen, NJ: Scarecrow Press.

Josey, E. J. (1994a). Introduction. In E. J. Josey (Ed.), *The Black Librarian in America Revisited.* Metuchen, NJ: Scarecrow Press.

Josey, E. J. (1994b). More than two decades later. In E. J. Josey (Ed.), *The Black Librarian in America Revisited.* Metuchen, NJ: Scarecrow Press.

Mapp, E. (1970). From my perspective: A social responsibility. In E. J. Josey (Ed.), *The Black Librarian in America.* Metuchen, NJ: Scarecrow Press.

Marshall, A. P. (1970). The search for identity. In E. J. Josey (Ed.), *The Black Librarian in America.* Metuchen, NJ: Scarecrow Press.

Moses, L. J. (1970). The black librarian: Untapped resource. In E. J. Josey (Ed.), *The Black Librarian in America.* Metuchen, NJ: Scarecrow Press.

Owens, M. R. (1994). The specter of racism in an age of cultural diversity. In E. J. Josey (Ed.), *The Black Librarian in America Revisited.* Metuchen, NJ: Scarecrow Press.

Robinson, C. C. (1970). First by circumstance. In E. J. Josey (Ed.), *The Black Librarian in America.* Metuchen, NJ: Scarecrow Press.

Smith, J. C. (1970). The four cultures. In E. J. Josey (Ed.), *The Black Librarian in America.* Metuchen NJ: Scarecrow Press.

Tate, B. (1970). Traffic on the drawbridge. In E. J. Josey (Ed.), *The Black Librarian in America.* Metuchen, NJ: Scarecrow Press.

Williams, II, J. F. (1994). A black dean of an ARL library. In E. J. Josey (Ed.), *The Black Librarian in America Revisited* (pp. 152–161). Metuchen, NJ: Scarecrow Press.

45

E. J. Josey: The Internationalist

Mary Biblo and Herb Biblo

Many of E. J. Josey's accomplishments are known to us. His many publications have been cited. His many struggles for equality have inspired us. Many of our colleagues have never experienced segregated state library association chapters. E. J. led the fight to integrate these chapters and was a leader in the establishment of the Black Caucus of the American Library Association (BCALA), which has made significant changes in our professional organization.

But often overlooked is E. J., the internationalist. At the ALA he served as a member and later as the chair of the International Relations Committee. His interest in international librarianship never abated; of course his interests were reflected in African libraries, librarians, and librarianship.

In 1984, coincidental with his presidency of ALA, the International Federation of Library Associations (IFLA) had scheduled its first annual conference on the African continent, in Nairobi, Kenya. This was an opportunity to exhibit and expand his interests. E. J. planned and developed a preconference program and agenda jointly with the Kenya Library Association. This was a unique program and opportunity, which was well received by all the participants. After many successes within our profession, E. J. led the struggle to support the cultural boycott of the apartheid regime in South Africa. In ALA and IFLA, he was a leader and organizer of all the efforts to support the cultural boycott of the South African apartheid regime.

In 1985, the IFLA met in Chicago. The IFLA was, and still is, a rather staid organization. IFLA leadership generally comes from national and international figures. It did not and does not expect any disruption from its orderly agenda. However, in 1985, E. J. rose from the audience at the first plenary session to denounce the IFLA leadership for allowing libraries and library associations that enforced the policy of apartheid to retain membership in IFLA, and particularly the apartheid South African Library Association. This may well have been the first open denunciation of apartheid within international librarianship.

At the Stockholm IFLA meeting, E. J. and other U.S. colleagues joined with the Swedish anti-apartheid movement to leaflet the IFLA conferences, asking delegates to support the cultural boycott movement.

At ALA, E. J. was a tower of strength. On July 5, 1990, he sent the following memo to his colleagues:

University of Pittsburgh
Department of Library Science
TO: Colleagues who Spoke at the IRC hearings on the AAP Report and South Africa
FROM: E. J. Josey
DATE: July 5, 1990
RE: Thanks and Appreciation

I wish to take this opportunity to express my deepest appreciation and thanks for your presentation at the International Relations Committee's Hearing on the AAP Report and South Africa. Your forthright position set the tone for what followed. Those of you who were able to attend Council III are aware of the fact that the Council adopted Council Document 97 which reaffirmed ALA's position on South Africa and did not approve the AAP's position of breaking the cultural boycott. You helped ALA maintain its integrity!

A copy of the resolution is enclosed. Once again my thanks. Continuing the struggle!

Library and information science building, Pittsburgh, PA 15260

The resolution that he refers to follows:

Revised CD #97
Resolution on The Starvation of Young Black Minds:
The Effects of Book Boycotts in South Africa

WHEREAS, the American Association of Publishers (AAP) has requested that the American Library Association endorse *The Starvation of Young Black Minds: The Effects of Book Boycotts in South Africa*.

WHEREAS, an endorsement of this report would be in conflict with ALA Policy 9.4 regarding racist institutions; ALA Policy 9.3 regarding affiliation with organizations which violate human rights and social justice; ALA Policy 57.3, the abridgement of the rights of freedom of foreign nationals; ALA Policy 53.4, government intimidation policy; Council Resolution 1986; and

WHEREAS, the ending of the ban on the ANC and other organizations, the lifting of the National Emergency Powers, the freeing of some political prisoners including Nelson Mandela and Walter Sisulu, the partial lifting of the Separate Amenities Act have not ended the vicious system of apartheid, since elementary human, economic, and political rights have not been granted to the black majority population; and

WHEREAS, the foregoing changes are only the beginning of the process to abolish apartheid, Nelson Mandela has urged the nations of the world to continue the sanctions, and Walter Sisulu advised "until there are clear, visible signs that there is an end of apartheid, the pressure must continue," and

WHEREAS, at a hearing on the AAP Report, the overwhelming majority of ALA members applauded the recent changes initiated by President F. W. deKlerk but went on record strongly supporting the continuation of the boycott against South Africa until apartheid is completely dismantled; and

WHEREAS, South African librarian colleagues in the forefront of the anti-Apartheid and anti-censorship struggle have called upon us to uphold the boycott, urging that we actively support all those committed to democracy in South Africa while continuing to frustrate those involved in the perpetuation of apartheid through military, commercial, financial and other means; and

THEREFORE BE IT RESOLVED that the ALA reaffirm its current policies and not endorse the AAP Report.

Endorsed by
The ALA International Relations Committee
The ALA Executive Board
ALA Policies: 9.3; 9.4; 9.5; 53/4; 57.3; 1986 ALA Council Resolution

Surprisingly, many of E. J.'s friends in the publishing world did not support this resolution, but he did not permit personal relationships to deter him. It is noteworthy that E. J. fought on many fronts, domestic and international. He never accepted that when a battle was won, the struggle was over. There was still another issue to be pursued. To stand still would be to slide back.

You will note E. J.'s final words on the memo, "Continuing the struggle!"

We think that in all our endeavors, this is the message that E. J. passed on to us.

Resist complacency! The battles are not over! What you received from the last generation, pass more on to the next one.

46

A Soldier in Dr. Josey's Army

Linda Saylor-Marchant

I can do all things through Christ who strengthens me.

—Philippians 4:13

This scripture brings to mind the continuous struggles of black people all over the diaspora. We are tireless soldiers who are strengthened and uplifted by the achievements of our brothers and sisters. The black librarian is also a soldier, a soldier who fights with information to free the minds of the people and encourage them to be:

- The president of the United States, or other local, state, or national elected official
- The librarian of Congress
- The president of the American Library Association
- Library director
- Mentor
- Educator
- A contributor or leader in skill trades and all academic fields
- Anything that they desire and work for
- An athlete
- An entertainer, and much more

POLITICAL SOLDIERS

We have yet to witness the appointment of the first African American librarian of Congress; however, the people of our nation now have Barack Hussein Obama, the first recognized African American president of the United States. Barack Obama is also an advocate for libraries and information. In his speech to librarians in 2005, while he was still a U.S. senator, he referred to libraries as: "More than a building that houses books and data, the library represents a window to a larger world, the place where we've always come to discover big ideas and profound concepts that help move the American story forward and the human story forward."

Other African American library advocates who served as elected officials include Major Owens, Democrat, Brooklyn, New York; and the late assemblywoman Cynthia Jenkins, Democrat, from Southeast Queens, New York.

Congressman Major Owens held office for 20 years (1987–2007) or 12 consecutive terms. Before winning the congressional seat that Shirley Chisholm retired from, Major Owens served as a state representative. From 1958 to 1966, he worked as a librarian at the Brooklyn Public Library. The late Cynthia Jenkins, Democrat from Southeast Queens and library activist, co-founded the Black Caucus of the American Library Association (Queens, New York, chapter). Jenkins provided numerous jobs for Queens' residents through her employment agency. It was she who introduced me to Dr. E. J. Josey, a phenomenal librarian, a soldier who fought racism to the very end.

SAVANNAH, GEORGIA

Today, approximately 25 years after receiving my master's degree in library and information science, I am working in Savannah, Georgia, one of Dr. Josey's old stomping grounds. It was here that Josey fought for civil rights and economic empowerment. In Savannah, Josey met Dr. Martin Luther King, Jr. The two men spoke not just about school segregation but also about separation in public libraries. Josey worked alongside other Savannah civil rights activists, including W. W. Law, Hosea Williams, and Reverend Jessie Blackshear. When you visit Savannah, stop by the main branch (Bull Street) of the Live Oak Public Libraries, formerly known as the Savannah Public Library. You will see Dr. Josey's name on a bronze plaque next to other board members. He was the second black person to serve on the board of directors at the Savannah Public Library. At this same location I worked tirelessly to provide informational services and programs to people of all races and ages. I can recall my first Black History Month book display. Josey's biography, books, and photos were front and center beside books and pictures of other African American achievers. The pictures appeared to have been taken during the late 1950s or early 1960s. Mary Jo Fayoyin, who is now the director of the Savannah State University Library, was very gracious to loan them to me for this historic display. It was really and truly a blessing to enlighten the community about Dr. Josey and his struggle to end segregation in libraries and library associations.

Currently, I am employed part time at the Asa Gordon Library, Savannah State University Library, under the leadership of Mary Jo Fayoyin. Dr. Josey served as director of this library from 1959 to 1966. He was the brain behind the library's 360-degree architectural design. He also established a rich African American collection, which is currently housed on the second floor of Asa Gordon Library.

SUPPORT—PAST AND PRESENT

As soldiers, we have numerous jobs to do, including providing support to black independent authors and publishers. We support them by purchasing not one, but many copies of their books for our library collections. They work endlessly creating and bringing to market some of the best positive resources for our readers. Black resources were not always so positive. Dr. Nancy Tolson, professor at Grinnell College and the University of Iowa, reflects on black librarians, authors, and resources of the early 1930s. Her article, "Making Books Available: The Role of Early Libraries, Librarians, and Booksellers in the Promotion of African American Children's Literature" (1998), is quite interesting. Here are some quotes from this article:

> The positive African American images that Baker [1975] wanted the children to encounter was not possible because few children's books portrayed African Americans respectfully. White writers were basically the only creators of children's titles and they tended to perceive African Americans as submissive. (p. 79)
>
> During the 1930s it was almost unheard of for publishers to give African American writers the opportunity to write for children. Author Carole A. Parks [1972] has pointed out that "white publishers were not interested in accepting works by black authors. They thought there was no market for such materials and were not interested in points of views held by those authors." (p. 67)
>
> Publishers did not believe that most African Americans could read, and they assumed that those who could were financially incapable of purchasing books. E. J. Josey [1972] contends that, because "publishers of the past, like authors, had little or no contact with [black people] and knew absolutely nothing about their way of life," those publishers "desired materials (stories) that reflected the majority thought patterns of the day."
>
> Thus, the responsibility for changing the images of African Americans for children's literature fell upon African Americans who had the power to make a difference in the publishing market. Two of the main supporters of the children's collections, Arthur Schomburg and James Weldon Johnson, died in June of 1938, several months prior to the Collection's completion. In 1939, it became the James Weldon Johnson Memorial Collection for Children. The Collection came very close in meeting all the criteria established earlier for children's books, even though very few could fully meet those three requirements in the late 1930s, or even the early 1940s. Subsequently, New York Public Library's Negro Division, located on the third floor of the 135th Street Branch Library was renamed The Schomburg Center for Research in Black Culture. (p. 278)

ARE YOU A TRUE SOLDIER?

If you are a librarian who supports equal access to library resources, you are a soldier in Dr. Josey's army. If you are a librarian who purchases resources written, published, and distributed by African Americans and other minorities on a regular basis, you are a soldier in the army of Dr. Josey. Let's just say that a soldier in the army of the late Dr. Josey makes sure that materials, employees, and services that the library provides mirrors the community it serves. As a soldier in this army, you may not be the most popular person on staff; you may be passed over, or even ignored when applying for a promotion; you may even be falsely accused by your superiors of poor work performance.

Without strong soldiers, high illiteracy rates in the black and minority communities will continue to soar; children may never meet a local black librarian, author, publisher, or book distributor. Left-over and limited information will be resources for the day.

Without your voices, dreams of teens who seek library employment would be deferred; without your voices, funds allocated for the underserved would go to the served; without your voices, library programs designed for children and youth of color would not include how to invent, design, manufacture, and sell your goods and services worldwide or even how to build and sustain the second black Wall Street.

With your voices, youth of color will receive scholarships and fellowships to colleges and universities around the world. With your voices, the unemployed become employed, the homeless have a home, and the voiceless now have a voice. We need you soldiers, to continue fighting till the battle is won.

SPECIAL THANKS

I would like to thank my parents Violet and Waymond Saylor, and my brothers, Wayne, Larry, and Waymond, for making my writing a reality (Waymond Saylor, Jr. is also a librarian). I would also like to thank my children (Garth, Aziza, and Eleanor), my grandson (Omarr), and other family members, friends, and librarians who purchased books I have published. Georgia and Charles Buggs, Hezekiah and Lillian Smith, strong family supporters; Elaine Landau, a prolific young adult author who helped to supplement my income by becoming a content reader and writer for a major book publisher. Andrew Jackson (Sekou), my classmate from York College (CUNY) and of course a soldier in Dr. Josey's army. Sekou continues to support black authors and publishers. Thanks go to Wendell Nolan of thesentinelnews.org, a newspaper publisher and webcast producer who highlights achievements of people worldwide. Thanks also to the editors of this publication: Akilah S. Nosakhere, Julius C. Jefferson, and Andrew P. Jackson (Sekou Molefi Baako) for giving me and others the opportunity to share our experiences as 21st-century black librarians.

RECOMMENDED BLACK AUTHORS

Check your collections for their books and if they are not present please order: Charles Campbell, Andrew Jackson, Valeda Dent, John Brown, Maurice Glenn, Linda Saylor-Marchant, Vince Sanders, Arthur Sanders.

REFERENCES

Baker, A. (1975). The changing image of the black in children's literature. *Horn Book*, *51* (February), 79–88.

Josey, E. J. (1972). *What black librarians are saying*. Metuchen, NJ: Scarecrow Press.

Park, C. A. (1972). Goodbye black Sambo: Black writers forge new images in children's literature. *Ebony* (November), 60–70.

Tolson, N. (1998). Making books available: The role of early libraries, librarians, and booksellers in the promotion of African American children's literature. *African American Review*, *32*.1 (Spring), 9–16.

47

Pay It Forward for Effie Lee Morris: A Tribute

Satia Marshall Orange

The many obituaries that were disseminated about Effie Lee Morris read like ones of so many from her generation, the "first," the "creator," the "visionary," the "founder." So my tribute to her reflects on how she impacted *my* life, something I didn't seriously consider until near the end of hers.

Soon after I moved to American Library Association (ALA) in 1997, Effie Lee called and read me the riot act on what was not happening with the profession, with my office (the ALA's Office for Literacy and Outreach Services [OLOS]), and specifically with the Coretta Scott King Book Awards Committee. In that first very long conversation I learned that:

Effie Lee Morris was a part of the conversation leading to the founding of Black Caucus of the ALA (BCALA).

Effie Lee Morris was selected by Dr. E. J. Josey to be the first chair of the Coretta Scott King Book Awards Committee, when it became a part of ALA, through the Social Responsibilities Round Table (SRRT), in the mid-1980s.

Effie Lee Morris is the only person to date who has served as chair of the Caldecott, Newbery, and Coretta Scott King Awards committees. (She chaired the Caldecott and Newbery committees when they were one, and then separately, when they became two committees. She accepted the leadership of the King committee when it became a part of ALA.)

Effie Lee Morris was the second president of the Public Library Association (PLA) in 1971–1972.

In her questioning the direction of my office *and* the Coretta Scott King Awards Committee, I realized that I would learn a lot about ALA from Effie Lee, as well as about BCALA and the Coretta Scott King Book Award's illustrious histories! At the end of that first conversation Effie Lee let me know she would be checking on me, a promise she earnestly kept for my next 12 years at ALA. I would schedule our telephone conversations late in the afternoon, when I could take the time to listen to her prepared list of discussion topics. Her institutional memory was invaluable to the liaison responsibilities of my office, although it often made decisions that were not to her liking.

My father, A. P. Marshall, talked about Effie Lee as "that little girl" with the big voice, not in volume, but in effort, contribution, and focus. An active ALA member at the time himself, he told me about her adept participation in closed door meetings, held by selected attendees in ALA conference hotel rooms during the 1960s to address such issues as unlimited access to onsite conference resources and benefits to conferees of color, segregated library organizations in Southern states, and the selection of librarians of color to strategic association positions. Effie Lee and those others, skilled and talented, and mostly African Americans, developed an informal foundation that garnered association-wide support for important resolutions that impacted communities of color and the profession at large. She also participated in the historic meetings that led to the founding of BCALA.

I remember reminiscing about attending some of those ALA annual conferences as a child with my parents, and being put to bed in one of those rooms during some of those meetings. She was quiet for a moment, looked me in the eye, and responded, "I don't remember your being there. I do remember those heated discussions that usually resulted in positive outcomes. There were lots of them." I stopped laughing, stopped talking, and went back to listening.

Effie Lee was a mover and shaker, as were many in that era. Although not meaning to, she sometimes ruffled feathers of many who confused her targeted focus in conversation and action for narrowness and unwillingness to accept the newer generations' ideas. Those who worked with her closely came to respect her dedicated and informed perspectives.

She even ruffled my feathers a few times, reminding me of a historical event or policy that paved the way for whatever current situation had arisen. "You should have known that," she'd say, and I knew she was right. "I just wanted you to know," she added, which was her way of informing me that she was not in agreement, but felt better for having shared her thoughts with someone who cared to listen and learn. And I did listen, and learned a lot.

Along each step of my ALA path, with new efforts considered and accomplished, Effie Lee was either accepting my calls, or calling me, still supportive of the later generations of librarians dedicated to realizing quality of effort for noble causes, and understanding her concern for presenting quality literature to children and youth. Many of her calls to me were in response to something she had read on the BCALA discussion list, to get clarification and give suggestions. Often she shared her thoughts on that list herself.

Very early in her career, she broadened her efforts toward issues for youth of gender, ethnicity, language, poverty, and incarceration, and other underserved concerns, taking giant steps toward challenges that wrongly addressed stereotypes. She often shared her experiences in traveling around the world, speaking, leading, collaborating, and advocating for the purest form of dedication to her noble perception of library services to young people.

Such librarians as E. J. Josey, Virginia Lacy Jones, Clara Stanton Jones, and other African American library leaders of that era, including my father, A. P. Marshall, Effie Lee's generation believed in making important things happen to heed an inherent call to action. Their names would not always be well known in today's local or even professional communities, but their contributions, most often fighting racism in librarianship, would continue to stand tall and stand out. They not only attended and participated in major professional issue discussions, they also initiated, motivated, mentored, and collaborated on implementation!

Effie Lee did not want to be forgotten, and she wasn't! At ALA conferences she dined with winning authors and illustrators and their editors, ALA past and current leadership, and lots of old friends who loved her and with whom she had worked throughout her career. She was always delighted to attend the conference award celebrations, whether it was Coretta Scott King, Pura Belpre, Newbery/ Caldecott, PLA, or BCALA. She was especially ecstatic about receiving ALA's honorary membership in 2008!

She valued the literature experience for children, youth, and their families, and championed all efforts to support their teachers, librarians, caregivers, and others. She was steadfast in her advocacy for librarians, teachers, authors and illustrators, educational institutions, publishing houses, publications, and resources that were sensitive to the needs and reading interests of youth, and her life's journey exemplifies that commitment.

Effie Lee Morris enjoyed celebrating and supporting the works of others, and genuinely relished others celebrating her contributions. She mentored, taught, supported, and was loved by many of us. From her early employment, she demonstrated her loyalty to what became her journey of productivity, advocacy, and contribution.

Attending the private memorial service in California soon after Effie Lee's death, I became privy to the global respect and admiration of friends and colleagues for her hard work, hearing glorious and loving stories of her impact in her home communities, across the country, and around the world. It was there that I learned that beyond her ALA and Children's Defense Fund's Langston Hughes Library (in Clinton, Tennessee) involvement, over the years she was a central figure with a significant number of other organizations and initiatives.

Effie Lee was 88 years old when she died. Most recently remembered for her active presence at the previous 2009 ALA conference in Chicago. This woman, small in stature, always elegantly attired, and mighty in presence and perspective, accepted no excuses for poor behavior, inactivity, or lack of purpose or direction in career or personal life! She expected more of herself and everyone she met!

I hope that she and those early comrades would be proud to know that many whom they touched are still heeding their calls to action and carrying the torch they've been passed in this 21st-century environment. I'd like to think that over the years Effie Lee became comfortable with the new directions taken and the achievements that followed.

I imagine that Effie Lee Morris's message to all of us today would include the following guidance, which she advised over the time that I knew her:

- If your voice is not heard, don't talk louder; talk more strategically!
- If your actions are not recognized and welcomed, review them, garner more support, and present them better!
- Don't wait for others to make things happen! Work to make change yourself!
- Remember to advocate on behalf of those who have less power than you!
- Legacies are built as you work, whether celebrated or not. So concentrate on doing the work, not on building a legacy.

Effie Lee Morris's life is a tribute to those who continue to blaze trails of distinction for those who follow. And we are called to blaze those trails. Effie Lee would expect no less!

Epilogue

Searching for Spring

Julius C. Jefferson, Jr.

It's winter
Winter in America
And ain't nobody fighting
Cause nobody knows what to say
Save your soul, Lord knows
From Winter in America[1]

In 2011, we said goodbye to poet and self-proclaimed bluesologist Gil Scott-Heron. Gil was one of America's most prolific, insightful social critics. Scott-Heron's metaphorical analysis of the state of black America was, in 1975, timely and now 37 years later, prophetic. In 2012, in the minds of many black librarians, it is still *Winter in America*.

This essay is a brief review of the themes first identified by Dr. E. J. Josey and his black librarian colleagues in the seminal volume *The Black Librarian in America,* and its 1994 update *The Black Librarian Revisited.* Collectively, these volumes documented the issues and experiences of black librarians in America from the 1950s to the 1990s. This current edition is the latest collection of essays to capture the black librarian experience.

In the first two volumes of *Black Librarians in America* the dominant issue was race. The 25 essays in volume one, referred to in this epilogue as *Genesis*,[2] revolved around themes of racial pride, identity, and social and professional activism, juxtaposed against efforts to confront, cope with, and overcome obstacles of racism, discrimination, and exclusion. As Josey noted, he

. . . became a better librarian not by working only in the library and classroom, but more importantly, by being part and parcel of the swiftly moving social currents that were going on around me in my community. I believed that in this way I obtained a more informed, disciplined and stringent understanding of what libraries could do for people.[3]

Josey was referring to being politically active for social change in America. He directly confronted racism and understood that the issues of inequality that affected black Americans were just as prevalent in the library profession. Unequal and disparate treatment could and has adversely affected the health, psyche, and economic stability of black librarians.

The essence of *Genesis* is an examination of black Americans struggle to be accepted and respected as professional librarians, despite a climate of entrenched white privilege in America. Josey and his contributors were librarians of the "Greatest Generation,"[4] a generation of professionals who pushed for inclusion and acceptance at the dawn of the modern civil rights movement and who made significant strides in the progress against racial and social injustice during the 20th century. Josey emphatically and clearly notes that his involvement in civil rights became a catalyst for his fight for equality in the library profession. In turn, many barriers were broken. *Genesis* was also about "finding our place as black librarians." In another commentary about the state of blacks, Dr. Robert Wedgworth documented the state of black professional inequality by examining black participation in and appointment to the American Library Association (ALA) leadership ranks. Dr. Wedgworth noted,

There were 405 members of the Association who served on the various standing committees between July 1960 and January 1970. Of the 405 members serving, 374 represent appointments made during the decade. Only five of the 374 went to Black librarians.[5]

Not only did black librarians feel discrimination on the jobs but in the professional association, which presented other impediments to professional advancement.

Shortly before the publication of *Genesis*, Josey wrote about "terrorism of blacks in the workplace,"[6] and the lack of blacks in leadership positions in the profession. Blacks became targets of professional defamation whose ramifications included economic and reputational impacts. Josey states:

No black librarian holds the directorship of a major library in this country. There are a number of very able black librarians who have the qualifications and the experience who should have been chosen library directors long ago. To illustrate the point of racism which prevents the employment of black librarians: two and a half years ago, this writer received a letter from an administrator of a major university library asking for suggestions of names of black librarians that he might employ, because the university was faced with an accusation that it had not complied with Title VII

> of the Civil Rights Act. A letter was sent containing the names of several librarians who headed predominantly Negro college libraries, three of whom had doctorates. My correspondent replied that he was anxious to employ recent library school graduates and not persons with considerable experience. In short, he wanted to employ the black librarian as the assistant to the third assistant. There was no concern or interest in employing the black bibliophile even in a middle management position.[7]

At that time, the climate for promoting qualified black librarians at best may be described as cold as winter in America.

The next volume, *The Black Librarian Revisited,* documented the experiences of black librarians from 1970–1990. *Revisited* included 30 essays and 19 new contributors; the themes of this volume echoed the sentiments of the first volume. *Revisited* documented the black librarians struggle to be recognized as professionals and their efforts to deal with subtle and covert racism.

During this period, on the heels of the 1950s and 1960s civil rights victories, there was evidence of both advancement and retrenchment in the struggle against racism, and the fight for full enfranchisement across all institutions and professions. Through persistence and preparation and amid the setbacks during the 1970s and the Reagan era, black librarians continued to break down barriers in the profession. In 1976, the ALA elected its first black president, Clara Stanton Jones. Eight years later, Dr. E. J. Josey became the first black male to be elected president of the ALA.

In spite of his personal accomplishments, Josey pointed out, "there are only four blacks who direct Association of Research Libraries (ARL) in this country and only six who direct major public libraries."[8] These stark statistics revealed a truth as cold and obvious as the sentiments captured in Scott-Heron's metaphorical ode to, *Winter in America.* Josey affirmed that black librarians were being marginalized and the strides and gains that had been made were achieved not by acquiescence of the status quo but by the grit, determination, and tenacity of black librarians.

The 21st Century Black Librarian in America introduced a new generation of voices concerned about the future of black librarianship. In this volume, "Generation Xers" and "Millennials," our newest generation of librarians, are letting their voices be heard. The 47 essays echo the same issues of racism in librarianship that confronted past generations. Though less prevalent today, even these barriers are more complex and difficult to define and combat. Recent gains in the profession have been achieved and must be acknowledged.

The 1990s saw the election of Dr. Franklin Hardy as president of the ALA. The 2000s saw Carla Hayden elected as the fourth black president of the ALA in the 135-year history of the association. Diversity programs championed by Dr. Hayden in *Black Librarian Revisited*[9] resulted in many black librarians gaining access to the profession. In his essay, *A Charge to Keep I Have*, Steven Booth noted that new black librarians have opportunities to participate in diversity programs, such as the ALA Spectrum Initiative, Mellon Librarian Recruitment

Program, and REACH 21. Other recruitment programs include Academic Residency programs and Association of Research Librarians (ARL) Diversity programs that include mid-career librarians. But do these programs live up to their promise of diversifying librarianship? Do they provide enough support and opportunity for black librarians to be successfully retained and prosper? These questions, as best answered by Margaret Gibson in her essay, *Dismiss the Stereotype! Combating Racism and Continuing Our Progress*, show that a black male librarian at a professional reception can still be mistaken by a white librarian for hired help.

Although the policies and programs are now in place, is the power structure in America's libraries willing to demand a climate of equality? Library Director Theresa Byrd disclosed that black librarians continue to battle exclusion and established cliques in the profession. Syntychia Kendrick-Samuel in her essay cited the Jena 6 incident as an example of America's double standard of justice based on race and the disconcerting view that black Americans are savages.

Maurice Wheeler confirmed in his essay *African American Faculty in Library and Information Science: Unresolved Issues in a New Era*, the presence of black library faculty is a major ingredient in the recruitment of black librarians. We are also reminded of how important black librarians are when trying to navigate the current 21st-century economic crisis. Linda Bannerman-Martin and Sandra Michele Echols informed us in *What Does Black Librarianship Look Like in the Proverbial Information Age?* that with America in financial woes, black public librarians are more relevant now than ever to provide an array of services.

School librarians debuted in this memorial edition establishing the importance of their role in the development of an informed nation. The editors of this volume agree that school librarians are important in shaping the intellectual futures of black students. The disparity of resources affect the service librarians provide and contribute to an uneven playing field. Their contributions illuminate the crucial role of school librarians in making culture relevant and reading a pleasurable and transformative experience. As noted, the fight to save school libraries represents one of the most challenging issues facing this new century.

One topic not given much attention in this volume[10] was the current and future role of the Black Caucus of the American Library Association (BCALA)[11]. BCALA was founded to provide for black activist librarians a united front to address the issue of black librarianship and ensure that black people would receive first-class access to library services and resources. BCALA became the conscience of ALA, the collective voice for black librarians, and the black populations they serve. Does BCALA today have the same will to lead constituent communities closer to full and equal participation in the "information age?"

In this new century, BCALA must strengthen its roots in social responsibility and become the catalyst for change leading the way for black librarians to excel in the profession. The organization must maintain an ongoing collaborative relationship with ALA ensuring that the leaders cultivated by BCALA share in opportunities and a voice in ALA governance. We envision a new generation of activist librarians at the helm of BCALA in the near future. Our hope is that this volume will be the spark that ignites the engine of a new generation of activists committed to social responsibility.

Black librarians are in search of spring—a climate of fair and equal treatment. This volume introduces a new generation of black librarians who give voice to the issues that confront them at the infancy of the 21st century. It is the expectation of contributors to this volume that it will serve as a reminder of our past struggles and as a marker of our passion and commitment to advancing the conditions of black librarians and the communities they serve.

> We were born at midnight in the darkest time but surely the first minute of a new day brings new strength.[12]
>
> —Gil Scott-Heron

NOTES

1. Gil Scott-Heron, From "Winter in America" on the album *The First Minute of A New Day*, 1975.
2. This volume was the first documentation of the collective experience of black librarianship in America.
3. E. J. Josey, *The Black Librarian in America* (New Jersey: Scarecrow Press, 1970), 323
4. The ages of the contributors range from two persons having received their first library degree in 1933 to a librarian who received his degree in 1969. In popular vernacular, "the greatest generation" refers to those persons coming of age during the Depression and WWII.
5. Robert Wedgeworth, "ALA and the Black Librarian: Strategies for the 70's," *The Black Librarian in America*, ed. E. J. Josey. (New Jersey: Scarecrow Press, 1970), 70.
6. The state in which black professionals are continually harassed and are in fear of not being promoted because of the racist views of decision makers within their workplace
7. E. J. Josey " Black Aspirations, White Racism, and Libraries," *Wilson Library Bulletin* 44 (1969): 97–98
8. E. J. Josey, *The Black Librarian in America Revisited* (New Jersey: Scarecrow Press, 1994), 360.
9. Carla Hayden, "New Approaches to Black Recruitment," in E. J. Josey, ed., *The Black Librarian in America* (Metuchen, NJ: Scarecrow Press, 1994), 55.
10. Taneya Gathers briefly mentions the early history of BCALA in chapter 41 of *The 21st-Century Black Librarian: Renewing Our Commitment to Liberation and Cultural Activism.*
11. Lisa Biblo covered this topic in "Black Caucus of the American Library Association: An organization of Empowerment," in E. J. Josey, ed., *The Black Librarian in America* (Metuchen, NJ: Scarecrow Press, 1994), 324.
12. Gil Scott-Heron, From "Morning Thoughts" on the album *Reflections*, 1981.

Contributors

Linda Bannerman-Martin
Assistant community library manager, Queens Library's Langston Hughes Community Library and Cultural Center

Jennifer W. Baxmeyer
Electronic resources cataloging coordinator, Princeton University Library; part-time lecturer, Rutgers University School of Communication and Information

Herb Biblo
Director, Long Island Library Resources Council

Mary Biblo
Retired, head librarian University of Chicago Laboratory Schools

Cheryl L. Branche, M.D.
Graduate student, Graduate School of Library and Information Studies, Queens College (CUNY)

Steven D. Booth
Archivist, United States National Archives; former project archivist for the Martin Luther King, Jr. Papers housed at Boston University

RaShauna Brannon
Electronic resource librarian, University of Memphis

Pauletta Brown Bracy
Director, Office of University Accreditation, North Carolina Central University; professor, School of Library and Information Sciences

Rhea Brown Lawson, Ph.D.
Library director, Houston Public Library, Texas

Ellie Bushhousen
Assistant university librarian, Health Science Center Libraries, University of Florida

Theresa S. Byrd
University librarian, Helen K. and James S. Copley Library, University of San Diego

Johnnie O. Dent
Community library manager, Queens Library, East Elmhurst Community Library

Sandra Michele Echols
Case manager, Adult Education Literacy Zone, Queens Library

LaVentra E. Danquah
Team leader, Education Services, Liaison Services, Shiffman Medical Library, Wayne State University

Valeda Dent Goodman
Dean and chief operating officer, University Libraries, Long Island University

Lisa A. Ellis
Associate professor, Information Services Librarian, William and Anita Newman Library, Baruch College (CUNY); visiting professor, Pratt Institute's School of Information and Library Science

Michele Fenton
Catalog librarian, Indiana University

Taneya D. Gethers
Librarian, Macon Library and African American Heritage Center, Brooklyn Public Library

Margaret J. Gibson
Assistant community library manager, Queens Library's East Elmhurst Community Library

Emily R. Guss
Assistant professor, access and technical services librarian, University of Illinois at Chicago

Tracie D. Hall
Founder, GoodSeed Consulting; strategy analyst, Global Corporate Citizenship Division, The Boeing Company

Allene Farmer Hayes
Coordinator, Digital Projects, Acquisitions and Bibliographic Access Directorate; acting chief of the U.S./Anglo Division (USAN), Library of Congress

Phyllis Hodges
Assistant director, Prospect Research and Management, University of Texas Medical Branch

DeLoice Holliday
Multicultural outreach librarian, Indiana University

Jos N. Holman
County librarian, Tippecanoe County Public Library, Indiana, BCALA President (2010–2012)

Andrew P. Jackson (Sekou Molefi Baako)
Executive director, Queens Library's Langston Hughes Community Library and Cultural Center; adjunct professor, Graduate School of Library and Information Studies, Queens College (CUNY), BCALA past president (2004–2006)

Ruth M. Jackson, Ph.D.
University librarian, University of California Riverside

Julius C. Jefferson, Jr.
Information research librarian, Congressional Research Service, Library of Congress

Syntychia Kendrick-Samuel
Young adult librarian, Uniondale Public Library, New York

Em Claire Knowles
Assistant dean, Simmons College Graduate School of Library and Information Science, Massachusetts Black Librarians Network, Massachusetts Board of Library Commissioners

Karen Lemmons
Library media specialist, Detroit School of Arts

Silvia Lloyd
Doctoral candidate, St. John Fisher College; former director of libraries in Buffalo and Rochester, New York

Effie Lee Morris (deceased)
Grand dame of children's librarianship; founding member of Black Caucus of the American Library Association (BCALA)

Satia Marshall Orange
Retired director, Office for Library and Outreach Services, American Library Association; ALA Spectrum Doctoral Fellowship

Barbara Lynn Johnson Montgomery
Doctoral candidate, School of Library and Information Science, University of South Carolina; retired school library media specialist

Joyce F. Ndiaye
Middle school library media specialist, Virginia, honors graduate, Howard University, studied French at the University of Senegal Dakar, M.A. in English from University of Illinois

Akilah Shukura Nosakhere
Director of library services/assistant professor, New Mexico State University–Carlsbad

Carol Nurse
Reference librarian/assistant professor, Sprague Library, Montclair State University

Ayodele Ojumu
School librarian, Lafayette High School, Buffalo, New York

Gloria J. Reaves
Retired library media specialist with three decades of varied public school and university library administrative and instruction experience

Ira Revels
Programming and education director, Hartford Public Library

Linda Saylor-Marchant
Librarian, Savannah State University, Colleague of Dr. E. J. Josey

Jahala Simuel
Reference librarian, adjunct professor, Department of Computer and Information Science, Shaw University

Gladys Smiley Bell
Peabody librarian, William R. and Norma B. Harvey Library, Hampton University, BCALA Past President (2000–2002)

Deirdre D. Spencer
Head of Fine Arts Library, University of Michigan

Tamara Stewart
Recipient of New York Black Librarians Caucus and E. J. Josey Scholarship Awards; member, Beta Phi Mu the International Library Science Honor Society; certified archivist and records manager

Harvey J. Stokes, Ph.D.
Professor of music, Department of Music, Hampton University; founder and director, Computer Music Laboratory

Binnie Tate Wilkin
Retired librarian, author, storyteller

Andre Taylor
School library media specialist, Charles Hamilton Houston Elementary School, District of Columbia Public Schools

Brendan Thompson
Information specialist, Gnarus Advisors, LLC, an environmental consulting firm, former an academic librarian

Lucille Cole Thomas, Ed.D.
Member, board of trustees, Brooklyn Public Library

Fantasia A. Thorne
Learning commons librarian, Bird Library Learning Commons, Syracuse University

Rose Timmons Dawson
Director, Alexandria Public Library, Virginia

Felix Eme Unaeze
Director of library services, Grambling State University

Angela Washington-Blair
Library media specialist, Dallas School District

Angela K. Washington Durr
Graduate student, Graduate School of Library and Information Science, University of North Texas

Michele Welsing
Communications director, The Southern California Library, Los Angeles

Maurice B. Wheeler, Ph.D.
Associate professor, Department of Library and Information Sciences, University of North Texas

Index

CPSIA information can be obtained at www.ICGtesting.com
Printed in the USA
BVOW071312080412

287090BV00003B/1/P

9 780810 882454